NEW *ILLUSTRATED* ENCYCLOPEDIA OF GARDENING

UNABRIDGED

[0]

Summer Garden with Roses and Perennials

[1]

Summer Garden of Annuals

NEW *ILLUSTRATED* ENCYCLOPEDIA OF GARDENING

UNABRIDGED

EDITED BY T. H. Everett

Assistant Director (Horticulture) and Curator of Education
The New York Botanical Garden

WITH CONTRIBUTIONS FROM

TWENTY HORTICULTURISTS AND AUTHORITIES IN THE UNITED STATES AND CANADA

Growers, Breeders, Exhibitors, Plantsmen, Writers, Lecturers, Professors, Editors and Superintendents of Famous Estates, who are Experts in all Fields of Horticulture, including Pests and Their Control.

VOLUME ONE—Garden Calendar, A-Art

GREYSTONE PRESS/NEW YORK · TORONTO · LONDON

EDITOR'S ACKNOWLEDGMENT

The editor wishes to acknowledge a debt of gratitude to the following persons, all of whom aided in the vast undertaking of producing the *New Illustrated Encyclopedia of Gardening—Unabridged:*

Mr. Frederick Drimmer, M.A., for his editorial counsel on the selection of material and preparation of the manuscript; Dr. Caroline K. Allen for her careful reading and correction of the text to assure its botanical accuracy; to Mrs. Lillian Weber for the great task she accomplished as assistant to the editor in keeping all the many details of a complex production in order; to Mr. Howard S. Swift for assistance in locating photographs; to Miss Nancy Callaghan for so carefully typing much of the manuscript; to Miss Elizabeth C. Hall, Librarian of The New York Botanical Garden, for much patient assistance and library research; to Dr. H.W. Rickett, Bibliographer of The New York Botanical Garden, for his expert assistance on especially difficult botanical matters and to Miss Hannelore Leissner of The Greystone Press for her expert handling of the many details connected with the organization of the text and illustrations in readiness for the printer.

PICTURE CREDITS

Air-Wrap Company; American Cyanamid Company; J. F. Anderson; Armstrong Nurseries; Associated Bulb Growers of Holland; George J. Ball, Inc.; Bartlett Tree Research Laboratories; John Black and Associates; Bobbink and Atkins; Buntings' Nurseries Inc.; W. Atlee Burpee Company; D. V. Burrell Seed Growers Company; California Agricultural Experiment Station; Carbide and Carbon Chemicals Company; Cornell University; English Encyclopedia; T. H. Everett; Ferry-Morse Seed Company; Germain's, Inc.; Fred C. Gloeckner and Company; Gravely Tractors, Inc.; Joseph Harris Company, Inc.; Henderson's Seedsmen; A. C. Hornberger; Huntington Botanical Gardens; Johnson Cactus Gardens; Irving Kaufman Studio; Jackson & Perkins Company; Lawn Grass Development Company; Lord and Burnham Company; Ernest E. Martin, Logee Greenhouses; Monsanto Chemical Company; The Morris Arboretum; The Morton Arboretum; New York State Agricultural Experiment Station; The New York Botanical Garden; New York Zoological Society; Oregon State College; Panogen Company; P. P. Pirone; Plasti-Plant Hood Company; Premier Peat Moss Corp.; Roses and Home Flower Arranging; Max Schling; O. M. Scott & Sons Co.; Shaw Color Studio; Shell Chemical Corporation; The Siebenthaler Company; Stark Bro's. Nurseries; State College of Washington; Sutton & Sons; Swift & Company; Texas Lawn Sprinkler Company, Inc.; United States Department of Agriculture; University of Minnesota; U. S. National Arboretum; University of California, Agricultural Experiment Station; M. Van Waveren & Sons, Inc.; Whitney Seed Co., Inc.; Roy F. Wilcox & Co.; New Jersey State Experimental Station; T. H. Everett.

CONTENTS

COLOR PHOTOGRAPHS INDEX AND CREDITS

(First number is the volume; name in parenthesis is the source)

ABOUT THIS BOOK

The *New* **Illustrated** *Encyclopedia of Gardening* provides the reader with a complete, up-to-date, and practical illustrated guide to the cultivation of the trees, shrubs, flowering plants, bulbs, fruits and vegetables which are, or may be, cultivated in gardens in the United States and Canada, both out of doors and in the greenhouse. Clearly and simply it explains the meaning of gardening and botanical terms, and describes in detail all gardening operations—garden planning, construction, planting, digging, the various methods of plant propagation, lawn making and management, crop harvesting, etc.—and the important subject of pest and disease control.

This encyclopedia is for the beginner and the advanced gardener alike. If you want to improve your home grounds, to provide flowers and plants to decorate your home and vegetables and fruits for your table—or if you want to extend your knowledge of the best modern gardening practices or grow prize-winning flowers—you will find in these pages all the information you need, and much, much more.

WRITTEN BY EXPERTS

The *New* **Illustrated** *Encyclopedia of Gardening* has been written by a group of garden experts famed for both their knowledge of practical horticulture and their skill as popular writers. The Editor, T. H. Everett, Assistant Director (Horticulture) and Curator of Education of the New York Botanical Garden, is well known to the public as the author of innumerable articles and books, and enjoys a nationwide reputation as a gardening expert. So, too, do the distinguished contributing writers whose qualifications are set forth later in this work.

Incorporated in the text are the writings of other distinguished authorities, drawn from *The Woman's Home Companion Garden Book*, edited by Dr. John C. Wister. Thus the *New* **Illustrated** *Encyclopedia* represents a distillation of the experience and best judgment of a great number of skillful and successful gardeners ranked among the most eminent in America today.

HOW TO GROW THOUSANDS OF DIFFERENT PLANTS

This encyclopedia has been planned to be a lifetime library of gardening, containing all the information necessary for the novice to become an expert. Thousands upon thousands of different kinds of plants are described, and their recommended varieties, propagation, culture, and other matters of significance are discussed in step-by-step detail. No one person has grown all of these plants or even most of them; no one person could. But somewhere in North America all, or nearly all, of the plants mentioned are growing, and it is easily possible that any one of them will be of some interest to you.

When you want to learn more about virtually any plant, you can rely upon this encyclopedia to tell you what you wish to know; the book has been built on the principle that it is better to give information about more plants than you will ever see or desire to know about than to omit any about which you may possibly wish to learn.

A WEALTH OF HELPFUL ILLUSTRATIONS

Illustrations add greatly to the attractiveness of a book of gardening. However, that is not the only reason why you will find such a wealth of photographs, diagrams and drawings in this work. Because the *New* **Illustrated** *Encyclopedia of Gardening* presents information about an extraordinary variety of plants, many of which may be unfamiliar to you, hundreds of illustrations, with over 600 in color, have been included with a view to showing the typical appearance of these plants, as well as special aspects of their growth likely to prove of interest or importance to you. Striking lawn and flowerbed arrangements are frequently suggested in the illustrations.

By and large, this is a library that tells you how to do things. Words cannot always convey instruction so well as pictures, and so an exceptionally large number of illustrations have been provided to show you exactly how to perform an indicated task. Often, a complete procedure such as taking cuttings, digging, planting, or pruning is pictured step by step. If you pay close attention to the illustrations, you will find that they will make your gardening not only easier, but more enjoyable and successful, too.

AN ENORMOUS RANGE OF SUBJECTS

As you read through these pages, you will discover that the *New* **Illustrated** *Encyclopedia of Gardening* is a guide to *every* branch of gardening and to every subject of interest to the gardener. The range of material included is enormous. If, for example, you are especially interested in hydroponics or soilless gardening, soil testing, or hormones, you will find enlightening discussions of these subjects. If you want to know how to build garden seats, arbors or arches—if you wish to provide a bath for birds, or a feeding station for them in the winter, or if you wish to protect your garden from them in the summer, you will find direct, specific guidance in this book.

Although practical information is emphasized in this encyclopedia, there is a great variety of fascinating garden lore and general reading as well, on such topics as the medicinal uses of plants today and yesterday, the curious symbolism of plants, monastic gardens, the quaint garden practices and literature of bygone years, the naming of plants, great botanists of the past and hundreds of other subjects that will intrigue and inform the gardener, both beginner and expert.

GUIDE TO HARDINESS

The gardener is particularly concerned whether plants he has never tried before, but now wants to grow, will flourish in his section of the country. It should be borne in mind that the geographical limitations of a particular plant's ability to survive are rarely exactly definable, and even among individual kinds of plants the degree of hardiness may vary; nevertheless, so far as practicable, guidance is offered on this score in the *New* **Illustrated** *Encyclopedia of Gardening*.

The term "hardy," as used in the various articles, indicates that a plant may be expected to survive winters such as are experienced in most parts of the northern United States and those parts of Canada with similar temperatures, but not necessarily the winters of the coldest·parts of the two countries. The word "tender" indicates that the plant is not generally hardy in the northern United States and equivalent parts of Canada. Variations of these terms are frequently employed, and you will find such phrases as "hardy as far north as southern New England," "hardy in sheltered locations in the vicinity of New York City," and "tender except in the far South" applied to various plants where their range of hardiness is known to be distinctly limited. For general guidance the reader should also consult the helpful article on Regional Gardening.

In the notes dealing with greenhouse plants the temperatures which must be maintained are in degrees Fahrenheit, freezing point being 32 degrees.

UNIQUE GARDEN CALENDAR

The amateur gardener will also want to know when he should do certain things in the garden. Gardening is an art as well as a science, and many variables enter into the picture: the kind of soil, elevation above sea level, seasonal differences, and other factors. However, a general average has been struck, and dates are suggested for seed sowing, planting, taking cuttings, and performing many other garden tasks.

In this connection, a special feature of this encyclopedia which should prove of immediate value to every gardener is the unique Garden Calendar prepared by the Editor. This is not the traditional meager list of a few flowers and vegetables and their planting dates, but an illustrated work of 35,000 words presenting detailed instructions, region by region and month by month, concerning the special care that should be given the flowers, shrubs, trees, vines and other plants commonly grown in the United States and Canada, both outdoors and indoors. By telling you just what to do and when to do it, Editor Everett's Garden Calendar will enable you to avoid troublesome or costly errors and grow plants that are healthier and more attractive.

VARIETY OF METHODS EXPLAINED

Many gardeners with limited experience suppose that there is only one way to go about a particular task. The truth is that, although the basic principles of gardening cannot be violated with impunity, details of their application can often be varied with beneficial results. In different sections of the *New* **Illustrated** *Encyclopedia of Gardening* you will occasionally find different procedures recommended for accomplishing the same purpose. Where such varying methods exist, you may take it for granted that each procedure is practical; not only will all give good results, but a knowledge of alternative methods will increase your versatility and skill in gardening.

PESTS AND DISEASES

Inevitably, the gardener is concerned with various pests and diseases that harm, or may harm, his garden. To give him all the advice he needs, a special substantial entry almost of book length, has been provided, complete with information about the latest control measures devised by science. If you are seeking guidance on these subjects, turn to Pests and Diseases, read the helpful general information given there and, in the listing that follows, consult the name of the plant in which you are particularly interested for the control of special pests and diseases that are likely to be bothersome.

ALPHABETICAL ARRANGEMENT WITH CROSS-REFERENCES

Considerable thought has been given as to how to make the vast amount of information in the *New* **Illustrated** *Encyclopedia of Gardening* as readily usable as possible. All entries are arranged in alphabetical order, including the common and botanical names of trees, shrubs, and other plants, and there are numerous cross-references. If, for example, you want to learn about a plant known to you as Goat's Beard, you will be led to the information you need just as certainly by looking under that name as if you were familiar with its botanical name, Aruncus.

If you are interested in the origins of the plants, you will find that their native countries and the families to which they belong are given; so, too, are the derivations, often quite meaningful, of the names of important plants. The pronunciation of the plant name is indicated in parentheses immediately following the botanical and popular name. The syllable which is stressed is marked by an accent; thus, **Abu'tilon** indicates that the accent is on the letter u.

In recent years, owing to the advancement of botanical knowledge, the names of many plants have undergone considerable changes. When a new and now correct name is used, the superseded one is given in parentheses.

FOR AMATEURS AND PROFESSIONALS ALIKE

Those who are without a technical knowledge of horticulture or botany will in particular appreciate the thoroughness and clarity with which every procedure and gardening detail is explained in the *New* **Illustrated** *Encyclopedia of Gardening*. It has been prepared with special concern for the needs and interests of the more than thirty million amateur gardeners who live in the United States and Canada, a vast army of tillers of the soil that is constantly increasing in numbers and enthusiasm. At the same time, the enormous amount of accurate, carefully presented information it contains cannot help but be of value to professional gardeners, florists, nurserymen, landscape architects, park department employees and others whose profession or business it is to grow plants and to design and maintain gardens.

THE PUBLISHERS

CONTRIBUTORS AND AUTHORITIES

EDWIN BECKETT

Horticultural Director (Retired), Berkshire Garden Center, Inc., Stockbridge, Massachusetts. Outstanding horticulturist, grower of fine plants, International Flower Show exhibitor, flower show judge, writer, and lecturer on gardening. Former superintendent of some of the finest private estates in America.

ERNEST CHABOT

Distinguished writer on horticulture and authority on the cultivation of greenhouse plants. Author of *Greenhouse Gardening for Everyone* and *How to Grow Rare Greenhouse Plants,* and contributor to National horticultural magazines and *The New York Times* Gardening Section.

LOCKWOOD DE FOREST

Landscape architect and editor specializing in California gardening.

HENRY E. DOWNER

Horticulturist (Retired), Vassar College, Poughkeepsie, New York. Former instructor in horticulture and in charge of the Botanic Garden, Smith College, Northampton, Massachusetts. Graduate of the Royal Botanic Gardens, Kew, England. Well-known writer on horticulture. Specialist in private estate, nursery, landscape and florist work.

JAMES G. ESSON

Consulting Horticulturist, Former Editor, *Gardeners Chronicle of America* and Instructor in Gardening, The New York Botanical Garden, New York City, and Consulting Horticulturist for the Horticultural Society of New York. Well-known grower, exhibitor, and judge of plants and gardens, and estate manager. Twice winner of the Holland Gold Shield at the International Flower Show in New York, winner of the George D. Pratt Medal of Achievement for Professional Gardeners (Horticultural Society of New York), etc., etc.

T. H. EVERETT

Assistant Director (Horticulture) and Curator of Education, The New York Botanical Garden. New York City, Member of the Editorial Board, *Flower Grower* Magazine, and Conductor of the Gardeners' Forum Column of the *New York Herald Tribune.* Author of *Gardening Handbook, Flower Garden Guide, How to Grow Beautiful House Plants, American Gardeners' Book of Bulbs, Lawns and Landscaping,* etc. Winner of the George D. Pratt Medal of Achievement for Professional Gardeners (Horticultural Society of New York) and the Thomas Rowland Medal for Skill in Horticulture (Massachusetts Agricultural Society). Graduate of the Royal Botanic Gardens, Kew,

England. Outstanding garden writer, lecturer, plantsman, and teacher.

PAUL F. FREESE

Staff Member, the Brooklyn Botanic Garden, Brooklyn, New York. Distinguished writer and lecturer on gardening and judge of flower shows. Former Editor, *Flower Grower* and *Popular Gardening* Magazines and staff member of *Horticulture* Magazine and *House Beautiful.* Authority on roses and bulbous plants.

JOHN A. GRANT

Landscape architect, lecturer, and writer. Authority on the trees and shrubs of the Pacific Northwest.

H. HAROLD HUME

Dean Emeritus of the Florida College of Agriculture and Provost (Retired), the University of Florida. Winner of the Governor-General's Medal of Ontario Agricultural College, the Jackson Dawson Memorial Medal of the Massachusetts Horticultural Society, the Florida Academy of Science Achievement Medal, the Arthur Hoyt Scott Garden and Horticultural Award, and the Norman J. Coleman Award for Services to Horticulture. Author of *Gardening in the Lower South, Citrus Fruits and Their Culture, Azaleas—Kinds and Culture, The Pecan and Its Culture,* etc., etc.

MILTON J. KEEGAN

Specialist in plants of the Rocky Mountain States. Author of many articles on gardening.

W. R. LESLIE

Head, Dominion Experiment Station of Morden, Manitoba, Canada. Author and expert on plant hardiness.

P. J. McKENNA

Late Staff Horticulturist, *Flower Grower* Magazine. Former instructor in Landscaping and Horticulture, Hunter College, New York City, Assistant Horticulturist, The New York Botanical Garden, New York City, and Associate Editor, *Home Garden* Magazine. Well-known lecturer and writer on gardening.

B. Y. MORRISON

Distinguished horticulturist, landscape architect, lecturer, and writer. Past Director, United States National Arboretum, Washington, D.C., and Principal Horticulturist in charge of the Division of Plant Exploration and Introduction of the United States Department of Agriculture (Retired). Editor, *The National Horticultural Magazine.* Honorary Vice President, the Royal Horticultural Society of England, and recipient of the Arthur Hoyt Scott Garden and Horticultural Award and many other honors.

HARRIET K. MORSE

Noted authority, lecturer, and writer on gardening. Author of *Gardening in the Shade* and *Gardening Easily,* and contributor to gardening magazines and the garden sections of *The New York Times* and other prominent newspapers.

P. P. PIRONE

Distinguished gardening writer, lecturer, and consultant. Plant Pathologist, The New York Botanical Garden, New York City. Former Professor, Cornell University, Ithaca, New York, and Rutgers University, New Brunswick, New Jersey. Author of Maintenance of Shade and Ornamental Trees, etc., etc. Authority on plant pests and diseases.

GEORGE L. SLATE

Professor of Pomology, New York State Agricultural Experiment Station, Cornell University, Geneva, New York. Noted breeder of small fruits and originator of many varieties. Associate Editor, *The Rural New Yorker,* and Editor of the Yearbooks of the North American Lily Society and the proceedings of the Northern Nut Growers' Association. Distinguished writer on horticulture.

R. S. STURTEVANT

Past Editor, American Iris Society.

EDNA RUTHERFORD WHITSITT

Distinguished lecturer, teacher and flower show judge. Author of *Roses and Home Flower Arranging* and articles for garden magazines and *The New York Times.* Creator of arrangements for Jackson & Perkins at the Rose Festival at Newark, New York, and at the International Flower Show, the Boston Flower Show, and the Philadelphia Flower Show. Director of the Silver Bowl Tournament at Newark, New York. Past President, Scarsdale Garden Club, etc.

JOHN C. WISTER

Landscape Architect. Director of the Arthur Hoyt Scott Horticultural Foundation at Swarthmore College, Swarthmore, Pennsylvania, and of the John J. Tyler Arboretum at Lima, Pennsylvania. For many years Secretary of the Pennsylvania Horticultural Society. Author of *The Iris, Lilac Culture, Bulbs for American Gardens, Four Seasons in Your Garden,* and of numerous technical papers and popular magazine articles. Editor, *The Woman's Home Companion Garden Book.*

JOHN J. WURDACK

Associate Curator, The New York Botanical Garden, New York City. Specialist in the study of tropical plants. Noted botanist and collector of South American plants.

A. F. YEAGER

Head, the Department of Horticulture, University of New Hampshire, Durham, New Hampshire. Former Professor of Horticulture, North Dakota Agricultural College, Fargo, North Dakota.

NEW *ILLUSTRATED* ENCYCLOPEDIA OF GARDENING – UNABRIDGED

❋

This Garden Calendar tells you, month by month, what you should do as a gardener, both indoors and out. Its advice is presented by regions, under the headings "In the North," "In the South," and "On the West Coast." Gardeners in Canada who live in the eastern and central provinces should refer particularly to the monthly section "In the North." Those who live in western Canada should consult the monthly section titled "On the West Coast."

WHAT TO DO IN JANUARY

The Month to Plan Your Garden on Paper

What miracle of weird transforming
Is this wild work of frost and light,
This glimpse of glory infinite?
 —John Greenleaf Whittier

If you have not yet sent away for the new catalogues of favorite seedsmen, do so without delay. Seedsmen's catalogues are fascinating publications and are well worth close study.

Lose no time in making out your seed orders and sending them in; the seedsman can give more detailed attention to early-placed orders than to those received in the rush of the shipping season.

Notebooks in which you have recorded the behavior of flowers and vegetables you have grown in previous years, as well as observations of varieties that have appealed to you as you have seen them growing in other gardens, will be of great help in deciding what kinds to order.

When making out your seed orders, keep chiefly to varieties of known performance—kinds that have done well for you before, or that are known to thrive in your locality. But be venturesome enough to try a few of the new kinds of flowers and vegetables offered in the catalogues, the varieties the seedsmen term "novelties." By growing some of the season's novelties you will add zest and fun to your gardening.

Seed catalogues need first attention, but send, too, for the catalogues of nurserymen, if this spring you intend to plant any trees, shrubs, evergreens, fruit trees or bushes, roses, perennials or other plants, that you will buy as plants rather than as seeds.

Early ordering is as essential here as it is with seeds. It is of the utmost importance to set out plants at the right times for their kinds; too-late planting is a frequent cause of distress or failure. Only by placing your orders early can you be sure that the nurserymen will be able to deliver at the most favorable times for planting.

Buy only from reliable dealers and expect to pay fair prices. Plants offered in sensationally worded advertisements, especially when apparently low-priced, are very apt to be inferior and disappointing.

Cold Frames

Cold frames should be watched carefully and ventilated with discretion. Biennials and young perennials that are in them are dormant now. Do not let the temperature inside the frames become too high on sunny days. Ventilate gradually as soon as the frost starts to melt on the glass. If snow falls and lies on the frames, do not brush it off; it forms a good natural protection. On cold nights, when the frames are without a snow covering, cover them with mats to give added protection if they contain somewhat tender plants.

In the South and other mild regions, sowings of early annuals and vegetables may be made in cold frames about a month before it is safe to plant the same kinds outdoors. Plantings of Gladioli bulbs may also be made in frames a

Reed mats or similar types of insulation may be placed over cold frames on very cold nights to protect tender plants.

After Poinsettias are through blooming, their stems are shortened somewhat and the plants are stored in a dry, cool place to rest.

month ahead of the earliest outdoor planting date, to provide a supply of early blossoms.

In the Greenhouse

In the greenhouse, improved growth will be noticed on most plants shortly after the New Year. Longer days and better light conditions are responsible for this. Great care must be taken not to overwater; this is especially true in cool greenhouses, in dull weather, and of plants that are not in very active growth or have not yet

To help produce fine Cinerarias such as these, apply fertilizer at regular intervals from the time the pots are well filled with roots until the first flowers open.

filled their available soil with active roots.

Watch temperatures carefully, especially night temperatures. So far as possible, these should not vary more than two degrees either way from the established night temperature for a particular greenhouse, except that on unusually cold nights it is more advisable to let the temperature sink another few degrees rather than to use so much fire heat that the pipes or other heating elements become excessively hot and the atmosphere very dry.

As plants grow and need more room they should be spaced out as much as possible; crowding can only result in weak, leggy growth.

Primroses, such as Primula malacoides, P. obconica and P. kewensis, raised from seeds sown last spring, will now be in 6-in. pots, and the more temperamental P. sinensis in 5-in. pots. Begin feeding them weekly with dilute liquid fertilizer as soon as their pots are filled with healthy roots.

Cinerarias that are now showing buds will respond to the same feeding schedule.

Keep "on the dry side" stock plants (Chrysanthemums, Buddleias and other kinds that have flowered and yet retain some leaves) which are being kept to furnish cuttings later. Stir their surface soil occasionally. Pick off all dead leaves and spray the plants with insecticide to make sure that they are free of aphids and other pests.

Poinsettias that have finished flowering should

[1–2]
Narcissi may be forced into early bloom in greenhouses

[1–2a]
Young seedlings need full sun in winter

[1–2b]
Propagation benches may be cleaned and filled with fresh sand

[1–2c]
Many kinds of plants may be propagated by cuttings in a greenhouse in winter

[1-3]

African Violets and other flowering house plants need full sun in winter

[1-3a]

Foliage house plants need good light in winter, not necessarily full sun

Delphiniums raised from seeds sown in a greenhouse in January are seen here blooming outdoors in July.

be dried completely and laid on their sides under a bench or in a cellar where the temperature is 55-60 degrees. Cut them back only lightly at this time.

Cuttings of Carnations should be inserted in a well-firmed bed of sand this month.

Hyacinths and other hardy bulbs for forcing, which have been buried under sand or ashes in a cool location, may be brought indoors as soon as they are well rooted. Inverted pots are being placed over these Hyacinths to shade the young shoots and induce them to lengthen.

Examine Hippeastrum (Amaryllis) bulbs that are in storage and, as soon as the first sign of new growth appears, top-dress or repot them, and encourage them to make new growth by placing them in a warm temperature and keeping them watered.

Bulbs for forcing into bloom early that have been buried outdoors or kept in a cool cellar should be brought indoors in successive batches. These bulbs include Hyacinths, Narcissi, and Tulips as well as such lesser bulbs as Crocuses, Snowdrops and Scillas. Place them in a cool temperature at first. It is very important that they be well rooted before they are brought indoors.

South African bulbs such as Freesias, Lachenalias, and Tritonias must be kept growing steadily under cool, frost-free conditions in full sun.

Seeds of many annuals sown this month and grown on in a greenhouse having a 45-50 degree night temperature will make fine plants for spring flowering in the greenhouse. Among useful kinds for this purpose are Baby's Breath, Clarkia, Godetia, annual Chrysanthemum, Leptosyne (Coreopsis), Salpiglossis, Larkspur, Stock, and Nemesia.

Annuals that were sown in the fall and are now in small pots may need transferring to larger containers or planting out in beds or benches.

In a 65-70-degree night temperature, sow seeds of Gloxinias and tuberous-rooted Begonias; the seeds are fine, so do not cover them with soil.

It is yet generally too early to make sowings of plants that are needed for summer display outdoors, although sowings of some kinds that need a very long season of growth, such as Lobelias, Verbenas, Vinca rosea and annual Carnations may be made towards the end of the month.

Pansies and Sweet Peas, sown now in a cool house, will make satisfactory plants for setting in the outdoor garden in early spring and will bloom there over a long period.

A number of perennials, chief of which are the hybrid Delphiniums, bloom splendidly the first year from seeds sown in January in a cool greenhouse.

Prepare for Busy Days. Soon, activity in the greenhouse will increase tremendously. In preparation for busy days make sure that you have

on hand the "makings" for the soil mixtures you will need—topsoil, coarse sand, humus, leaf mold or peat moss—and have these under cover where they will be reasonably dry and not frozen when you need them.

Make sure, too, that you have ready pots, pans, flats, labels, tying materials, bone meal and other fertilizers, and other paraphernalia that you need for your spring work.

Cleanliness is of supreme importance in the greenhouse. Before the spring rush begins put your greenhouse in order. Slugs, sow bugs and other unpleasant creatures thrive among moist, decaying plant remains which are bound to accumulate under benches and even on benches unless great care is taken.

Now is a good time to wash the gravel on benches or replace it with new, to clean out under the benches, to replace sand or other rooting media in propagating benches, to wash pots that are green with moss or in other ways dirty, to sponge the leaves of permanent plants with insecticide, and to spray and use approved

In January growers of indoor plants should remember that pots, soil and other supplies will soon be needed in quantity. Arrangements to have these on hand should be made early.

smokes or vapors to make sure that the plants in the greenhouse are free of pests.

House Plants

House plants face rather difficult conditions during January. Where winters are cold the air indoors is likely to be excessively dry due to use of much artificial heat. Make every effort to counteract this by keeping your plants standing on shallow trays filled with moss, sand, cinders or some similar material that is kept constantly moist. Spray the foliage of kinds that are not very hairy with clear water from an atomizer syringe once or twice a day.

Daytime temperatures indoors are likely to be too high for many house plants. Keep kinds that prefer low temperatures in cool locations. Never put plants over radiators.

Night temperatures near windows may be too low. On very cold nights pull down the shades and place sheets of paper between the plants and the window. Alternatively, move the plants away from the window at night.

Lack of sufficient light is one of the difficulties that house plants must survive in deep winter. Even shade-loving house plants such as African Violets, Begonias and Ferns appreciate full exposure to sunshine at this time.

During the short days of winter all house plants respond favorably to exposure to maximum sunlight.

Branches of Pussy Willow and other early-spring-flowering shrubs, cut and placed in water indoors, soon come into bloom in a warm room.

Insufficient light, especially if coupled with excessively high temperatures, encourages long, leggy, weak growth.

Avoid overwatering, but take care that no plants suffer from lack of water. In warm rooms, plants often need more frequent watering than they do in a moist greenhouse; in nearly all cases the object is to keep the soil evenly moist but not constantly saturated. Very few plants will need fertilizing during this season of short, dull days.

For suggestions for Hippeastrum (Amaryllis) and other bulbs, see recommendations for the greenhouse, above. Read that section, too, for advice regarding preparations to be made for seed sowing, potting and other work to be done later.

Branches of Pussy Willow, Forsythia, Spiraea prunifolia and some other early-blooming shrubs may be brought indoors now and stood in containers of water in a warm, light room. In no time at all, it seems, they will be in full bloom, providing a foretaste of spring.

In the North

In the North, outdoor tasks are few during January. Do all that you can to prevent heavy

Heavy accumulations of snow should not be allowed to remain on evergreens or the branches may break.

accumulations of snow from breaking evergreens. Shake or brush off the snow before it becomes wet and heavy and before it freezes into solid masses. A wooden rake and a broom are useful tools for this work.

Beware of damage to evergreens and, to a lesser extent, to other plants set under the eaves of the house, by snowslides from the roof. When the weather is cold and the branches brittle, such shrubs as Yew, Boxwood, Rhododendron and Mountain Laurel are easily split apart by heavy snowslides.

Keep a mulch of leaves, salt hay, or some similar material on the ground around plants that are on the borderline of hardiness but that will renew themselves from the roots if the tops are killed but the roots preserved. Among such plants, in some localities, are Abelia, Amorpha (False Indigo), Buddleia Davidii (Butterfly Bush), Callicarpa (Beauty-Berry), Cytisus (Broom), Elsholtzia, Hydrangea, Indigofera (Indigo), Lespedeza Kirilkowii (Bush Clover),

Spiraea Bumalda and its varieties, Spiraea japonica, Tamarix gallica, Tamarix pentandra, Tamarix odessana, Vitex Agnus-castus (Chaste Tree) and Vitex Negundo.

Damage caused by sun may occur towards the end of the month and later. Yellowing (scalding) of evergreens and the cracking or splitting of the bark of trees, particularly young and newly transplanted specimens, on their south sides are common manifestations of sun damage. The bark-splitting, which may extend for considerable distances up the trunks, is the result of hard freezing, often at nights, alternating with periods of bright sunshine.

Shade from strong sunshine is the only really satisfactory preventative of sunscald. The trunks of newly planted trees and of young trees may be wrapped with burlap or with a special paper made for the purpose. Evergreens that have been recently transplanted, as well as those in especially exposed positions, such as any planted on the east or west side of the house, may be

Discarded Christmas trees can be put to good use as a winter protection for herbaceous perennials, rock-garden plants, low evergreens and bulbs.

shielded by screening with burlap.

The branches of Christmas trees make good winter protection for low evergreens and for perennials that retain their foliage throughout the winter. Use those from your own tree for this purpose as well as any others you are able to obtain.

In the South

In the South the amount of outdoor gardening that demands attention during January depends upon where you are located. In the upper South not a great deal more can be accomplished than in northern gardens, except that soil preparation may be undertaken whenever the ground is in suitable condition to work.

Few practices promote good gardening more than having beds and borders spaded and manured well in advance of planting time. Any new construction work or cleaning up of the garden that can be accomplished at this time is all to

the good; it saves precious time later.

In the middle and lower South the planting of woody plants, both evergreen and leaf-losing kinds, should be started without delay. Trees, shrubs, evergreens and roses are all included in this category.

Dormant spraying of fruit trees as well as ornamental trees and shrubs that are infested with scale insects, or other pests that may be controlled by this kind of spraying, should be done before new growth begins and at a time when the temperature at night is not expected to go lower than 35 degrees.

Finish pruning Grape vines, if this has not already been done, and attend to the pruning of other fruits well in advance of new growth beginning.

Sowings of the hardier kinds of vegetables such as Lettuce, Carrots, Spinach, Radishes and early round-seeded Peas may be made. Set out Onion plants and sets and early Cabbage plants. Plant Asparagus, Rhubarb, and Horse-radish.

Dormant spraying of fruit trees and ornamentals should be completed before their leaf buds open.

Sowings of annuals may now be made in the lower South and plants raised from fall sowings may now require thinning out. Kinds suitable for seeding now include Sweet Alyssum, Arctotis, Baby's Breath, Calendula, Candytuft, Clarkia, Cornflower, Coreopsis, Dimorphotheca, Gaillardia, Godetia, Larkspur, Nemophila, Nicotiana, Phlox, Poppy, Salpiglossis, Scabious, Sweet Pea, and Verbena.

In the middle and upper South, sow the hardiest kinds of annuals, such as Sweet Pea, Larkspur, Cornflower, Scabious, and Poppy as soon as the soil is in suitable condition.

Irrigation will be needed at least once during the month in gardens in the dry Southwest.

On the West Coast

On the West Coast, complete the pruning of all fruits that lose their leaves in winter before the middle of February.

Prune ornamental trees and shrubs that need this attention. Roses may be pruned this month in California, but in the Northwest it is better to wait until later.

In southern California, following rains, there will be much planting to be done. Fruit trees and bushes, Grape vines, Roses and ornamental leaf-losing trees and shrubs may all be set out.

In southern areas set out plants of perennials and annuals. Seeds of quick-growing annuals such as Sweet Peas, Gaillardias and Poppies may be sown, in beds protected from heavy rains, to bloom this spring.

Make first planting of Achimenes, tuberous Begonias, Cannas, Calla Lilies, Gladioli, Gloxinias, and Tigridias after the middle of the month in California.

Dormant spraying should be done now. In regions where low temperatures occur, do not apply these sprays when the temperature is likely to approach freezing.

Carrots and other hardy vegetables and flowers may be sown in the South as soon as the ground can be made ready.

WHAT TO DO IN FEBRUARY

The Month of Preparation for Outdoor Planting

The February sunshine steeps your boughs
And tints the buds and swells the leaves within.
—William Cullen Bryant

Don't delay longer those tasks that could have been done in January and that *must* be done now if your garden is not to suffer. Just to remind yourself of them, read over again "What to Do in January."

Make an inventory of tools and implements. Repair any that are broken and put all into first-class condition. Before the end of the month carefully examine all lawn mowers; send out for repairs any that need them, and send all to be sharpened. Choose experienced and reliable people to do this for you. By avoiding the last-minute rush you are likely to get better work done.

Look over garden furniture and ornaments in storage, clean them and, where desirable, give them a fresh coat of paint, varnish or other appropriate finish.

The conditioning of lawn mowers and other equipment and tools needs attention before the season is far advanced.

Continue to check regularly all bulbs that are being stored. Remove any that show signs of rot promptly, or cut out the decayed part and dust the cut surfaces with sulphur.

Cold Frames

Cold frames require very careful attention now. In the North, plants such as English Daisies, Wallflowers, Pansies, and others that are being kept essentially dormant, must be kept as cool and well ventilated as possible on all days when the temperature is above freezing, and some ventilation should be provided whenever the temperature inside the frame is sufficiently high to melt the frost off the glass.

Avoid ventilating in such a way that cold, sweeping winds enter the frame; make sure that the sash are closed and the plants are adequately protected against excessively low night temperatures.

Cold frames and hotbeds in the South and other mild-climate areas can be put to good use now for raising plants of vegetables and flowers that will be needed for setting in the open ground later. Among kinds responsive to this treatment are Tomatoes, Peppers, Eggplants, and Onions, as well as Dahlias, Verbenas, Salvias, Zinnias, Petunias, Snapdragons, Asters and Calendulas. There are many others.

Special Attention. In managing cold frames in which young, actively growing plants are accommodated, try to maintain conditions that duplicate the kind of good spring growing weather that may be expected outdoors later. Ventilate freely in mild weather. Protect with glass sash at night. Water whenever needed on mild sunny days, and do this sufficiently early in the day so that the water will be certain to dry off the foliage before nightfall.

Thin plants out to prevent undue crowding. Watch carefully for bugs and blights and take prompt remedial measures if either appear. Keep the surface soil between young, growing plants stirred to a depth of half an inch and pull all weeds promptly.

In the Greenhouse

Greenhouse work becomes really interesting in February. A strong urge to grow is apparent in many plants that have been more or less quiescent until now. This means more work to do and makes many tasks imperative.

The repotting of permanent plants such as Ferns, Palms, Aspidistras, Dracaenas, Anthuriums, Asparagus, Dieffenbachias, Crotons, and others that require this attention may be done now or during the following month. For the most part, tropical plants should receive attention first, coolhouse plants such as Grevillea, Plumbago, and Agapanthus somewhat later.

Don't Neglect Them. Greenhouses in which Orchids, Ferns, and many other tropical foliage plants are grown will need shading lightly some time after the middle of the month.

Plants of fall-sown annuals that are to bloom indoors during April should be transferred to their final pots now, if this was not done last month. Those that have filled their containers

At this season, watch bulbs of Hippeastrum (Amaryllis) carefully for signs of new growth. When this occurs top-dress or repot them, water them and bring them into a sunny, warm location.

with healthy roots and are not to be potted should be fed regularly with weak liquid fertilizer.

Freesias and other bulbous plants that are pushing up flower spikes should be fed regularly until the flowers begin to show color.

Encourage Hippeastrums (Amaryllis) that have started to grow vigorously by keeping them in a 65-70-degree night temperature and maintaining a moist atmosphere. When leaf growth is well started, feed those that have been

Asparagus Ferns (which are really not Ferns at all) and other greenhouse foliage plants may be repotted in February and March.

Miniature Roses, such as this one grown in tree form, and other Roses may be potted in February for forcing into bloom in greenhouses.

established in their pots for at least a year, but not newly potted ones.

Lilies for Easter will now have filled their pots with roots and should be making nice top growth. Careful control of temperatures is necessary to "time" the flowers so that they will open when wanted.

Dormant Roses, particularly Rambler and Baby Rambler or Dwarf Polyantha types, make excellent indoor flowering plants if potted in rather heavy soil and brought into a 45-50-degree greenhouse in February. Higher temperatures may be given after growth is well started.

Potted Spireas (Astilbes) soon develop into magnificent flowering specimens if taken into the greenhouse now. Once they start to grow they need plenty of water.

Continue to bring batches of such hardy bulbs as Tulips, Hyacinths and Narcissi, that were planted in pots and flats in the fall, into the greenhouse to ensure continuous bloom.

Start tubers of Gloxinias, Caladiums, Achimenes and tuberous Begonias.

Seed sowing in the greenhouse calls for attention this month. Additional sowings may be made of the kinds that could be seeded in January. Seeds of many plants intended for greenhouse decoration may now be sown, including Asparagus, Grevillea, Coleus and Celosia.

The beginner is often in too great a hurry to sow seeds of plants that are needed for transplanting outdoors later, with the result that when planting-out time comes the plants are leggy, partly starved, woody and hard. Such plants do not take hold out of doors nearly so well as plants from somewhat later seed sowings that are growing vigorously and have not suffered any check of their growth.

Avoid sowing too early. This applies to both flowers and vegetables. Towards the end of the month a sowing of Cauliflower, early Cabbage, and Lettuce may be made indoors. Sowings of all the annuals recommended for January seeding may also be made, as well as some others, including Snapdragons, Stocks and Mexican Tulip Poppies.

Cuttings of Geraniums, Heliotropes, Fuchsias, Lantanas, Begonias, Verbenas, and Coleus will root readily now in a 60-degree night temperature.

Many tropical foliage plants such as Dracaenas, Dieffenbachias, Philodendrons, and Crotons root easily from cuttings set in a close propagating case where a 70-degree temperature is maintained.

Flowering plants for the greenhouse include many kinds that are truly perennials but that are usually raised afresh from cuttings each year. February and the following month are good times to insert cuttings of these. Examples are Aphelandras, Shrimp Plants (Beloperone), Eranthemums, Begonias and Manettias.

Achimenes which have been stored dry in a cool place may now be removed from their pots and the tubers taken and planted in new soil and started into growth again.

Cuttings of Chrysanthemums made and insterted in the greenhouse now will soon root and be ready for potting individually or for setting out in flats of soil.

Chrysanthemum cuttings and the cuttings of Stevia (Piqueria), Salvia leucantha and Buddleia asiatica should be inserted now to provide plants for blooming in the greenhouse next fall and winter.

House Plants

House plants require the same general care as detailed for January. None is likely to require any protection from even the strongest sun yet.

Preparations may be made to repot any permanent plants that need such attention this spring, but it is usually better to wait and do this work a little later than is customary in greenhouses.

Air-layering is a sure-fire method of propagating such house plants as Dracaena, Dieffenbachia, Fatsia, Fatshedera and Rubber Plants, particularly specimens that have grown tall and leggy. This is a good time to do it.

Geraniums, Lantanas and Hibiscus may be pruned back quite severely now in preparation for repotting next month. After cutting them back, keep their soil on the dry side.

Trees and Shrubs. Branches of many spring-flowering trees and shrubs open their flowers beautifully indoors if stood in water in a moderately warm room. Try Flowering Quince, Apple, Cherry, Almond and Peach as well as Dogwood (from cultivated trees only; respect con-

servation measures and do not cut from wild trees). Force, in the same way, branches of Birch, Horse Chestnut and other trees. Even though they do not flower, they soon develop delightful greenery that is a real foretaste of spring.

In the North

In the North, watch perennials carefully. Rains and thaws may form puddles that damage plants by excluding air and by freezing solidly about their crowns. Such damage can often be prevented by making miniature ditches with a hoe to drain superfluous water away from the plants.

If you notice young perennials partly heaved out of the ground by frost action, take the opportunity afforded by spells of mild weather to push them back into place.

Salt hay and some other types of winter covering are apt to be blown off plants by winter storms. If this occurs, replace them in position without delay.

Make sure that winter covering put on plants in late fall or early winter is still in place, but take care that it does not pack down and exclude air from rock plants and other perennials that retain their leaves during the winter.

The earliest bulbs, such as Snowdrops, will be well above ground, and a few of the earliest may have been in bloom for some time. Other bulbs

Air layering is a simple and sure method of propagating many kinds of greenhouse and house plants.

These neatly pruned and tide Grape vines serve as a reminder that all pruning of Grapes should be completed as soon as possible.

may show above ground prematurely during mild spells of weather through having been planted too shallowly. When this happens and it is feared that cold weather will later harm them, cover them with a two- or three-inch layer of peat moss, or peat moss and sand, as soon as the tips of the bulbs appear above the surface

The pruning of Gooseberries, Currants and most other fruits may be done at any time before the buds begin to swell in spring.

and before the leaves begin to separate.

Pruning selected subjects may receive attention this month although most of it may be left until March if you so wish. However, if a spell of fair weather gives opportunity to get some of this work done without discomfort, why not take advantage of it and steal a start on spring work?

One type of pruning should be completed without delay, the pruning of Grape vines. If this is left too late, "bleeding" from the cut ends occurs.

Other fruit trees may be pruned to whatever extent is necessary between now and the middle of March.

The pruning of some flowering shrubs may receive attention now, particularly old, tangled, overgrown specimens, and kinds that bloom in summer on shoots that begin to develop this spring. Here belong Peegee Hydrangea (but not the blue-flowered, pink-flowered and white-flowered H. macrophylla varieties), Rose of Sharon, Vitex, Spiraea Bumalda and its varieties, and Butterfly Bush (Buddleia).

Spring-flowering shrubs and trees which bear their flowers on shoots produced last year should not be pruned now if they are in good condition, but if they are really overgrown it may well be worth while to sacrifice some or even most of the spring display to get them back in good condition. There is more time to thin out tangled shrubbery now than later, and it is easier to see what you are doing before the leaves are on the bushes. Furthermore, if the bushes are infested with scale insects or other pests, a good thinning will give opportunity to apply a dormant strength spray effectively and economically.

Trees, shrubs and vines that are espaliered against walls may be pruned now if they are kinds that flower on new shoots; if they produce their blossoms on last year's shoots, delay pruning until after they have flowered.

Dormant spraying of trees, shrubs and vines that need this treatment may be done late in the month or any time before the buds begin to open. Be careful to apply oil sprays only when the temperature is above 45 degrees and when there is no chance of it dropping below freezing the night following application.

In the South

Pruning. In the South pruning is an important task that requires attention during February, beginning early in the month in the lower South and proportionately later northwards. In the upper South the latter part of the month is a suitable time for this work.

None of the early-flowering trees and shrubs should be pruned now unless, as explained above in the notes for gardens in the North, a rehabilitation job is being done on overgrown specimens.

Summer-blooming kinds that are pruned at this time include Crape Myrtle, Oleander, and Poinciana, as well as those mentioned above under "In the North." Attend now to the pruning of the kinds of Roses that require this attention in spring.

The pruning or shearing of evergreens that call for such treatment should be done just before new growth begins. The cut ends are quickly hidden by new growth.

The Crape Myrtle, favorite tree of the South, in full bloom. This tree may be pruned in early spring.

Lose no time in completing the planting of trees, shrubs and Roses.

The dividing and replanting of perennials that are to be given this treatment should be done before new growth has made much headway.

Applying Fertilizer. Perennials, including bulbs, that have been planted a year or more, will benefit from fertilizing as soon as new growth above ground becomes active. Scatter the fertilizer evenly and, except in grassed areas, cultivate it shallowly into the surface. Apply fertilizer, too, to Roses, shrubs, and evergreens, but

A spring application of a complete fertilizer is beneficial to most garden plants.

For the best results Peas should be sown as early as it is possible to get the ground in condition. Here, sowing is being done in a wide drill.

delay fertilizing Azaleas and Camellias until they are through blooming.

Recondition the lawn by raking off old dead grass, fertilizing, and making over bare spots. Rolling, when the soil is in just the right condition, neither too wet nor too dry, will be of benefit.

Vegetables. Activity in the vegetable garden really gets under way this month. In the extreme lower South some of the hardier vegetables will have been sown outdoors last month, but in the middle and upper sections February is the time for doing this.

Kinds to sow include Carrots, Lettuce, Beets, Mustard, Turnips, Swiss Chard, Chinese Cabbage, Parsley, English Peas and Spinach. Plants of Cabbage, Cauliflower, Broccoli and Onions as well as Onion sets may also be set out.

Seeds of all but very tender annuals should be sown directly outdoors as soon as the soil can be gotten into a nice, crumbly condition for sowing.

On the West Coast

On the West Coast, delay no longer the pruning of such summer-blooming shrubs as Tamarix (not the spring-blooming kinds), Ceanothus, Buddleia and Hypericum. Spring-bloom-

ing shrubs that benefit from pruning should be attended to after they are through flowering.

In the Northwest, spring is just around the corner. Prepare trenches for Sweet Peas. Make a sowing of garden Peas towards the end of the month. Get land in condition for spring sowing and planting.

This is a good time to propagate Chrysanthemums by tip cuttings.

The planting of trees and shrubs of all kinds may be proceeded with and, in the milder parts of the Pacific Coast region, flowering plants in great variety may now be set out. Stocks, Calendulas, Pansies, Primroses, Cinerarias and Snapdragons are among kinds to plant now.

Spring bulb beds and many other plantings will benefit from a dressing of fertilizer applied to the ground and gently scratched in, just as the tips of the bulbs show above ground and as perennials begin to grow.

Seeds of the hardier kinds of vegetables such as Carrots, Cabbage, Spinach and Turnips, as well as hardy types of annual flowers, may be sown in many sections.

The remaking of perennial borders should be

Narrow drills, such as this, are prepared for the sowing of most vegetable seeds. In many parts of the West Coast all the hardier vegetables may now be sown.

given attention before new growth gets under way. This is a task that should be undertaken every 3-5 years.

In southern California, Citrus trees and Avocados may be planted this month.

Start tubers of fancy-leaved Caladiums and tuberous Begonias, Achimenes, Gloxinias and Cannas if you did not do so in January. Yellow Calla Lilies may now be started into growth indoors or out.

This month or next is the time to prune, repot and start Fuchsias into new growth.

Caladium tubers started into growth in a warm, moist greenhouse or in a terrarium grow rapidly and soon form attractive specimens.

WHAT TO DO IN MARCH

The Strategic Time for Laying the Foundations for Your Summer Garden

With rushing winds and gloomy skies
The dark and stubborn Winter dies:
Far-off, unseen, Spring faintly cries,
Bidding her earliest child arise:
March!

—Bayard Taylor

This is an active month in the outdoor garden in all but the very coldest sections of North America. Everywhere the greenhouse gardener is busy.

To keep abreast of spring work it is necessary to plan carefully and, above all, to take advantage of every favorable opportunity the weather affords.

In March are laid some of the very foundations for summer gardens. Weeks, days and even hours frittered away at this time can never be regained; indeed, the results of such procrastination will be increasingly evident as the season progresses.

Cold Frames and Hotbeds

Cold frames and hotbeds are mighty useful whether you have a greenhouse or not. In the North this is the month when hotbeds are started to raise young vegetable and flower garden plants for setting out later.

Locate your hotbed in a sheltered place where it will not be subjected to cold winds and where

it will receive all possible sunshine. On cold nights, cover it with mats or boards to conserve heat but do not put these into position until darkness comes, for every half hour of daylight is valuable.

Hardy plants in cold frames should be grown

Cold frames need much attention now. Weeds that appear among the plants grown in them may be pulled out on a warm day when removing the sash will not harm the plants.

as cool as practicable now, in preparation for their transfer to the open garden. Keep the glass sash off the frames on all favorable occasions and give a little ventilation at nights, except when it is expected that the temperature will drop below 30 degrees.

Plants moved from the greenhouse to cold frames, as some will be towards the end of the month, should be kept a little warmer and the air inside the frame a little "closer" than is customary for plants that have been wintered in the frames. This is done by ventilating less freely and by spraying the plants lightly with water (but not soaking them) once or twice on sunny days. Make sure that the last spraying is done early enough so that the foliage will dry before nightfall.

Plants in hotbeds should be given treatment similar to that of tender plants newly moved from the greenhouse to cold frames. The idea is to simulate about the plants the conditions that occur outside on a warm spring day . . . on what the gardener considers a good growing day.

Although hotbeds and cold frames that contain tender plants must not be overventilated, it is important that a little ventilation be provided early on sunny days, otherwise the inside temperature may soon rise to 80-90 degrees or even more, which is harmful.

In the Greenhouse

In the greenhouse, March is a month of great activity. Now a great variety of seeds are sown, cuttings of many kinds must be inserted, and young plants coming along from earlier propagations need attention in the matter of transplanting and repotting. Growth is phenomenal. Good planning and an orderly attack on the jobs to be done are necessary to keep ahead of the work.

Seeds of annuals that grow fairly quickly, intended to provide plants to set in the garden in six to eight weeks time, will in many parts of the country be sown during March. It is a mistake to sow too early. Better by far to have at planting time specimens that could have stayed another week or two in the flats or pots without

When more than one variety of seeds are planted in the same flat, short pieces of bamboo cane may be used to separate them.

A little shade is often beneficial to germinating seeds. A layer of cheesecloth may be used to provide this in the greenhouse.

A flat containing germinating seeds of Carnations. The seeds were sown in rows rather than broadcast.

harm, than to set out plants that have been growing too long in cramped quarters and have suffered because of this.

Annuals to sow include Petunias, Verbenas, Calendulas, annual Phlox, Strawflowers, Globe Amaranths, Marigolds, Asters, Stocks, Zinnias, and many others.

Vegetables. Make sowings of early vegetables indoors—Cabbage, Cauliflower, Broccoli, Lettuce, Celery, Tomatoes, Peppers, etc.

Tubers. Start into growth tubers of Cannas, Caladiums, and tuberous Begonias in order to have good, strong plants to set out when the weather becomes really warm and settled.

Watering will need more attention now. Plants that are well rooted are likely to dry out quickly on sunny, windy days. They must be prevented from wilting by watering before the earth becomes excessively dry, and by damping down (wetting) floors, paths, and the benches on which plants in flats and pots stand.

Syringing (spraying lightly with clear water) is of benefit to many plants and will be needed more frequently from now on. Never syringe in dull weather or so late in the day that the foliage will not dry off before nightfall.

Potting. Permanent plants in pots and tubs

Leaf cutting of Peperomias and sectional stem cutting of Dieffenbachias root readily in pans of sand in a humid, shaded greenhouse.

that did not receive this attention last month should be now examined to determine whether they are in need of potting. If they are, the task should be completed before new growth is much advanced.

If it is decided that they are to go another year without repotting, they will surely benefit from top-dressing. This consists of removing some of the surface soil without disturbing the upper roots too violently, and of replacing it with new, rich earth mixed with fertilizer.

Among plants that will need these attentions are Clivias, Hibiscus, Agapanthus, old Geraniums, old Fuchsias, Acacias, Amazon Lilies, Ixoras, Plumbagos, and large specimen Begonias, as well as Dracaenas, Crotons, Ficus, and other foliage plants.

Apply Fertilizer Regularly. Plants in the greenhouse that are in active growth and are well rooted should be fertilized regularly as long as active growth continues. At least once a week, and usually oftener, they should be given dilute liquid fertilizer. Calla Lilies, Primroses, Cinerarias, Hydrangeas, Roses, Sweet Peas and all other annuals that are to flower indoors, will benefit from this attention.

Cuttings. Continue to insert cuttings of such fast-growing plants as Coleus, Ageratum and

Many greenhouse plants are growing rapidly at this season and with longer days and more intense light, need more frequent watering.

Lily of the Valley pips planted in flower pots or in fancy containers may be forced into bloom in three to four weeks.

Cuttings may be rooted readily in an adequately drained box filled with sand or vermiculite and covered with polyethylene plastic film.

Begonia to give small plants to use later in the outdoor garden. Insert, too, cuttings of many plants that will be grown for greenhouse and house decoration in late summer, fall and winter. Among these latter are Chrysanthemums, Stevias, Salvia leucantha, Ibozas, Ruellias, Begonias, Geraniums, Fuchsias, Acalyphas, Abutilons (Flowering Maple), Aphelandras, Jacobinias, Dieffenbachias, Philodendrons, and Dracaenas.

Astilbes (Spireas) potted now and grown in a warm greenhouse will take about nine weeks to bloom. Be sure that they at no time suffer from lack of moisture.

Lily of the Valley may be flowered in 21-25 days from the time the "pips" (roots) are potted. Easter Lilies take about six weeks in a 60-degree night temperature (65-75 by day) from the time they show their flower buds until they are at their best—something to keep in mind when forcing plants for Easter.

House Plants

House plants should now be making good growth. If you air-layered any a month or so ago, the roots may now be showing on the outsides of the moss balls. When this happens, the rooted tops may be severed from the lower stems and be potted separately. There is still plenty of time to make new air layers.

Cuttings. March is a good month in the house to make cuttings of a great many plants. With the exception of Cacti and other succulents, all root much more readily in a terrarium, a glass-covered or a polyethelene-covered propagating box or under a bell jar.

Leaf cuttings of African Violets, Peperomias, Rex Begonias, Pickaback Plants and others that can be propagated in this way, if inserted now, will give young plants that can be grown into nice, sizable specimens by fall.

Stronger sunshine now makes it desirable to move African Violets, Ferns, Pickaback Plants, and others that are known to prefer subdued lighting, to positions where they do not receive full, middle-of-the-day sun; or, alternatively, to shade them lightly during that period.

Repotting is an important task during the present month. Examine all plants to determine their needs for this treatment. Some kinds need repotting every spring, others more than once a year, and some at intervals of several years only. Old specimens in large containers are likely to belong in the latter class. Many bulbs and semi-bulbous plants such as Clivias, Agapanthus, Urgineas and Hippeastrums (Amaryllis) also belong there.

Plants that are not to be repotted will benefit from top-dressing with fresh, rich soil after as much as possible of the old surface soil has been removed as can be without doing too much damage to the roots.

Make sure that the drainage in all pots is in

Azaleas and many other potted flowering plants remain in good condition longer if they are kept in a cool room.

good condition and is not stopped up. Wash the pots, if they are dirty, in plain water without soap or detergent.

Gift Plants. Keep gift plants such as Azaleas, Genistas (Cytisus), Hydrangeas, Cyclamens, Cinerarias, Primulas and the like in a cool room. A temperature of 40-50 degrees at night is ideal for prolonging their blooming season. Make sure that they do not suffer from lack of water.

Plants for Outdoors. If the Azaleas are hardy kinds, they may later be planted out of doors, and so may Hydrangeas in localities where they are hardy. Other indoor plants that are useful for transferring to the garden later are most hardy bulbs that have been forced into bloom early—Daffodils, hardy Narcissi, Hyacinths, Crocuses, Squills, Grape Hyacinths and the like. Tulips forced indoors are rarely satisfactory for outdoor planting. Easter Lilies, even in the North, if planted outdoors after being forced, will often give a crop of rather short-stemmed flowers in August or September.

The trick with all plants forced early indoors that are later to be planted outdoors is to keep them growing without drying them off, and to gradually harden them to outdoor conditions. They should not be planted out until the weather is warm and settled. Until then keep them watered and growing in a cool room in a sunny window. A sunroom usually affords suitable conditions.

Narcissus bulbs that have been forced indoors may later be planted outside for blooming in future years.

In the North

In the North the amount of outdoor work that can be accomplished this month depends largely upon geographical location. Where the ground remains frozen or in a wet, muddy condition until late in the month, not a great deal more can be done than in February; but where it dries sufficiently to be worked and walked upon without sticking unpleasantly to tools and shoes, planting and sowing may be begun, and soil preparation for later plantings completed.

Take advantage of every break the weather provides to push on with these tasks. Spring usually blesses the gardener with a few days when the soil is in perfect condition for seed sowing and planting, followed by wet weather that renders such work impossible or, at least, inadvisable. If you "miss the boat" and fail to get your Peas and Sweet Peas sown, your Onion sets planted, and your new lawn seeded at this time, the results are likely to be less than the best.

The planting of deciduous trees and shrubs should be completed before they leaf out in spring.

Sowing Seeds. Sow seeds of the following at the very first opportunity: Peas, Radishes, Sweet Peas, Larkspurs, Cornflowers and Poppies. Plant Onion sets at the same time.

The planting of leaf-losing trees and shrubs may be proceeded with whenever the soil is in a suitable condition. With evergreens it is generally advisable to wait until they are just ready to start into new growth before transplanting them. In most parts of the North this will be in April rather than March.

If the digging of beds and borders in preparation for planting was not completed in the fall, get busy as soon as the ground is workable. Areas that were sown with Winter Rye will be ready for digging before bare patches of ground are.

Removing Winter Protection. Do not be in too great a hurry to remove winter protection from perennials and biennials. An early spell of mild weather may easily lure one into a false sense of security . . . but spring weather can be treacherous; and early warm days may be followed by bitter nights and cold, windy, sunny days, a combination that is hard on newly uncovered plants. See that winds do not blow away winter covering and expose plants too soon.

If the covering is at all thick, take it off gradually; don't remove it too early, but do take it away before the new shoots have made much growth. If possible, choose dull, moist weather for uncovering.

Complete all spring pruning, including that of

The pruning of Roses and other deciduous plants should be completed now.

Now is the time to complete any pruning and tying of Red Raspberry canes that need this attention.

Hybrid Tea, Floribunda, Dwarf Polyantha, Hybrid Perpetual and other types of Roses that need this attention in spring.

Fruits of various kinds need attention this month. If you did not cut the old fruiting canes from Red Raspberries after the crop was gathered, do so without delay. Thin out the weaker of the new canes that grew last year and have not yet fruited, and remove the upper 12 in. or so of those allowed to remain.

Complete the pruning of any fruit trees that need this attention before new growth begins. Follow faithfully the spray schedules recommended by your State Agricultural Experiment Station for various fruits. Only by doing this can you expect to get good, clean crops.

Hedges that are overgrown or unshapely may be pruned or sheared severely now in order to improve their outline, reduce their size and thicken their growth. An advantage of doing this work now is that the stub ends will soon be hidden by new growth.

Lilacs, Rhododendrons, Yews, and other plants known to be capable of renewing themselves from their bases, that are straggly and overgrown, may be cut back now to within a foot of the ground. Follow this severe treatment by mulching with old manure or rich compost and by watering freely in dry weather. The new shoots that spring from the stumps will soon form shapely plants.

The ground beneath shrubs may be forked over shallowly and compost or other organic matter turned under. Do not fork or otherwise disturb the earth beneath Rhododendrons, Azaleas, Mountain Laurels and other shallow-rooting kinds. A surface mulch over the ground beneath these is of great benefit.

Care of Perennials. As soon as most of the perennials in the border are a couple of inches tall, spread a dressing of fertilizer over the soil and fork it in shallowly. Take great care not to disturb kinds that do not show above ground until late, such as Balloon Flower and common Rose Mallow.

The stub ends of the branches of this severely cut-back Privet hedge will soon be hidden by new growth.

Spring transplanting and dividing of perennials should be finished before the new shoots have grown much.

If the perennial border is crowded, some thinning out of surplus and overgrown plants is in order. The lifting, dividing and replanting of many perennials may be done with facility in spring; and, in the really cold sections, this, for many kinds, may be a better time than early fall. Exceptions to this are spring-blooming kinds which are always better divided in fall than in spring.

When dividing old perennials, the outer younger and more vigorous parts of the clumps should be retained, and the older inner worn-out central portions discarded.

Don't delay longer than necessary in setting out in their flowering quarters such biennials as English Daisies, Polyanthus Primroses, Pansies, Violas, Canterbury Bells, Foxgloves, Wallflowers, and Forget-me-nots that have been wintered in cold frames or nursery beds and that will be treated as biennials and discarded after blooming.

Plant out, too, as early as is reasonably possible, young perennials. This is particularly necessary with early-flowering ones if a fair spring show is to be had. Included in this group are Arabis, Basket-of-gold (Alyssum saxatile), Blue Phlox (Phlox canadensis), Polemonium and many others.

Delphiniums, Coreopsis, Pansies, and other perennials raised from seed sown early indoors with the idea of having the plants bloom the first year, should not be planted out until the ground is somewhat warm and the weather settled—about the time the major shade trees are pushing forth their young leaves. Two or three weeks before this (which may be this month or in April, depending upon locality) they should be removed to a cold frame to harden off in

Transfer biennials from nursery beds and cold frames to their flowering locations at the first good opportunity.

Bare spots in the lawn may be repaired as soon as the ground is dry enough to work. Fork them over, fertilize them, rake them level and then sow grass seed over them. After the seed is sown, firm the soil by tamping it with a rake.

preparation for their transfer to the open ground.

The hardier annuals such as Stocks, Snapdragons, Carnations and Scabious, raised from seeds sown inside early, should be handled in the same way; and so should Chrysanthemums, for planting in the outdoor garden, that have been raised from cuttings in the greenhouse.

If Lily bulbs are to be planted this spring, get them into the ground at the earliest possible date.

Lawns will benefit greatly from sweeping, topdressing with a mixture of humus, leaf mold or peat moss, and soil with which some fertilizer is mixed; or, if this can not be done, from fertilizing. If bare spots exist, they may be renovated by fertilizing them and forking them over, firming the soil, raking it fine and level, sowing grass seed and raking it into the surface and then, finally, rolling or patting the surface firm.

Roll the lawn with a medium-weight roller when it is moist but not wet. As soon as practicable, give attention to patching or repairing lawn areas that need attention, for grass seed succeeds best when sown early.

If new lawns are to be seeded this spring, do not delay sowing longer than necessary. It is essential to have a fertile soil and a well-prepared

Where soils are very acid a spring dressing of lime may be applied as a corrective.

seedbed for good results. If you do not have time to fix the soil properly, and yet want a green lawn this summer, sow a temporary lawn of Italian Rye Grass now, turn it under in early fall, prepare the seedbed thoroughly and sow your permanent lawn then. Turning under the Rye Grass will add humus to the soil and improve it. If a test indicates that the soil of a lawn is too acid this is a good time to correct the condition by applying lime.

In the South

In the South, fertilize Azaleas and Camellias as soon as they are through blooming. Use acid-type fertilizers especially compounded for these shrubs. Both Camellias and Azaleas respond well to a mulch of rotted manure or rich compost.

Begin spraying or dusting Roses as soon as new growth begins, and repeat these treatments at weekly intervals throughout the growing season.

Annuals. In the far South, annuals that are blooming may be induced to keep up a long season of display by keeping the faded flowers regularly picked. Frost-tender annuals may now be sown outdoors in the lower South and in cold frames in the middle and upper South. Late sowings of most annuals may be made outdoors.

A top-dressing of decayed manure or other organic matter is of great benefit to lawns.

To secure early bloom, clumps of Dahlia tubers may be divided now and the divisions planted in the garden.

Perennials. It is not yet too late in the middle and upper South to divide and set out many perennials, but this should be done before new growth is very far advanced. Divide and replant Dahlia tubers for early blooming; if late flowers are required, do not do this until April or May. Later plantings give the best results.

Care of Lawns. Various lawn grasses, such as Centipede, St. Augustine, Zoysia and Bermuda, that are grown from sprigs or plugs, may be planted any time from now until midsummer.

Do not neglect to cut lawns regularly that were overplanted with Rye Grass. Set the mower to cut at a height of 1 in. so that sufficient light will reach the permanent lawn grasses beneath to encourage new growth. Rye Grass grows quickly now and twice-a-week mowings will be needed.

Sowing Vegetables. Many vegetables may be planted this month. In the upper South, make sowings of the kinds listed under "What to Do in February"; and, in addition, plant Potatoes, Horse-radish, Asparagus, and Rhubarb. In the middle South, early plantings of Sweet Corn may be made.

In the lower South, plant Beans, Beets, Cantaloupes, Carrots, Corn, Cowpeas, Cucumbers, Eggplants, Okra, Peppers, Pumpkins, Spinach, Squash, Tomatoes and Watermelons.

Bulbs for summer blooming that may be planted outdoors in March are: Calla Lilies, Gloriosas, Crinums, Cannas, Tuberoses, Caladiums, Elephant Ears, Gladioli, Hymenocallis, (Spider Lily, Ismene) Montbretias, Oxalis and Tigridias. Make successional plantings of Gladioli at two-week intervals to ensure a long season

Removing plugs of Zoysia Grass for planting to form a new lawn.

The scuffle hoe is one of the most useful tools for shallow cultivating.

At planting time the roots of dormant Roses are spread out carefully.

Good soil is then worked among the roots and packed with a stick.

More soil is added and trodden firm until grade level is reached.

of bloom. In the upper South the planting of the more tender of these bulbs may be delayed until April.

Keep the cultivator busy between growing crops. It is so much easier to destroy weeds when they are small than later. Quite apart from destroying weeds, shallow surface cultivation promotes the growth of all plants except those like Azaleas and Camellias which are surface-rooting.

On the West Coast

Trees and Shrubs. On the West Coast, in the southern sections, complete the planting of deciduous trees and shrubs, including Roses, by the middle of the month; and, in the northern parts, by the end of the month or the first week in April. Subtropical kinds such as Avocados, Citrus and Guavas may be planted this month and next.

Other subtropical trees and shrubs may be planted in March and April in southern California—Gardenias and Hibiscus for example. This is a good time to plant Camellias.

Perennials. If you have not completed the planting of perennials, do so. Plants from pots, cans and flats, in many varieties are available from dealers and will produce a display this season if planted now.

Annuals. Seeds of all kinds of annuals may be sown except in the colder sections where it is better to delay for a while the outdoor sowing of the more heat-loving kinds such as Verbenas and Zinnias.

Keep These Chores in Mind. Sow hardy kinds of vegetables when the weather permits.

Old clumps of Cannas may be lifted and divided. Plant them back in deep, rich soil.

In all but the coldest sections Gladioli may now be planted and successional plantings made every 10-14 days until June.

Keep up with the spraying and dusting program. In this way only can you be sure to have healthy plants. Baits for snails and slugs must be used at the first indication that these creatures are becoming troublesome.

Spring-blooming shrubs that need pruning should receive this attention as soon as they have finished flowering.

WHAT TO DO IN APRIL

A Busy Month Both Indoors and Out Will Make Your Garden a Success

A gush of bird-song, a patter of dew,
A cloud, and a rainbow's warning,
Suddenly sunshine and perfect blue—
An April day in the morning.
—Harriet Prescott Spofford

April brings no letup in garden work. Indeed, there is more to do now, at least in northern gardens, than in any previous month. Both in the greenhouse and outdoors, eternal vigilance and constant application to the tasks at hand are the price of later success.

Cold Frames

Cold frames are now chockablock full of plants that were raised in the greenhouse or in hotbeds and are to be planted out after danger from frost has passed. Both vegetables and flowers are included here.

Except for plants recently moved from the greenhouse or hotbed, which must be kept warm and close for a few days, all plants in frames must be aired freely whenever the weather is at all favorable. Short-jointed sturdy growth must be encouraged; too high temperatures, too much shade, and crowding can result only in weakly, drawn specimens.

Hardy plants—biennials and perennials—that occupied cold frames all winter will be planted out where they are to flower sometime in April, if this was not done earlier. Keep the covering

glass sash off them for a week or so before transplanting them.

Gladioli, to provide early flowers, may be planted in cold frames 3-4 weeks before it is practicable to plant them outdoors. The same procedure may be followed with Montbretias.

Proper Ventilation. Hotbeds protecting tender plants will need more careful attention in the matter of ventilating than will cold frames. The objective is to encourage sturdy growth rather than to prepare the occupants for imminent transfer to the outdoors.

Excessively high temperatures within the frame are to be avoided as harmful, but, by the same token, cold drafts and too-low night temperatures must not be tolerated.

If days are windy and the sun is bright, be sure to open the hotbed sash, if ventilation is needed, on the side opposite to the direction from which the wind is coming. Close the sash sufficiently early in the afternoon so that the temperature inside rises to 80 degrees or so. A very light misting of the occupants with tepid water before the frame is closed is of benefit in sunny weather.

A little ventilation will be needed on dull,

moist days if moisture collects in droplets on the inside of the glass. An atmosphere saturated with moisture for long periods tends to encourage disease.

In the Greenhouse

In the greenhouse it is now time to sow seeds of Cinerarias if large specimens are wanted in bloom next February and March. Primulas for winter blooming indoors may be sown now, too. Kinds to sow are Primula malacoides, Primula obconica, Primula sinensis and Primula kewensis.

Seeds of good strains of Celosia sown now will make fine pot plants to be in full bloom in late summer and early fall.

Continue to insert cuttings of Chrysanthemums and other cool greenhouse plants that will flower indoors in pots in fall and early winter. The names of some of these were listed in "What to Do in March."

Dahlias may be readily increased by means of cuttings inserted in a warm propagating case this month. The cuttings are taken from tubers started into growth 3-4 weeks earlier in a temperature of about 60 degrees.

Tropical Plants. Cuttings of the various tropical plants mentioned in last month's calendar may also still be inserted. In particular, many Begonias are very satisfactory when raised from April cuttings.

Start Calanthe orchids into growth early in

the month. Water them sparingly at first. They need warm, moist growing conditions.

Start young plants of Violets, for blooming in a cool greenhouse or frame next winter, by taking strong, rooted crowns or "cuttings" from the old plants and setting them in rich, woodsy soil in a cool location outdoors. This should be done at the end of the month.

Potted Azaleas. Do not permit potted Azaleas that have flowered to form seeds. Pick off all faded blossoms. Immediately after flowering, attend to the repotting or top-dressing of any that

Pot-grown Azaleas make a fine display in spring. As soon as their flowers have faded, pick them off to prevent the formation of seeds, which exhausts them.

need this treatment. Begin a regular schedule of feeding for Azaleas that are not repotted now. Applications of dilute liquid fertilizer three times weekly will not be too much.

Rooted Cuttings. Give attention to potting rooted cuttings and other propagations before the roots get too long and the young plants starved for lack of nutrients in the rooting medium. Most cuttings should be removed from the cutting bed and be transferred to soil when their roots are 1-1½ in. long.

The Right Shading. As the sun increases in power it will be necessary to give additional shading to many plants in the greenhouse.

Primula obconica. Seeds of this and of many other Primroses may be sown in April.

Wooden lath roller shades that can be raised and lowered as light intensities change are ideal for Orchids and many tropical plants grown in greenhouses.

Ferns, Orchids and most tropical foliage plants will need fairly heavy shade; tropical flowering plants mostly somewhat less. But even many coolhouse sun-loving plants will need a little shade now. This particularly applies to annuals and other kinds that are in bloom. The flowers of Clarkias, Godetias, Sweet Peas, annual Chrysanthemums, Carnations and many other plants will be of better color and will last longer, if a very light shade is provided to make harmless the fierce rays of the April sun when they strike through clear glass.

The Right Pots. Cyclamens and early propagated Chrysanthemums will soon need larger pots. Don't let them get pot-bound and hard before shifting them to bigger containers.

Greenhouse Carnations that are to be planted in outdoor nursery beds ("in the field," as gardeners say) for the summer, or that are to be planted in benches in the greenhouse in June, should now be in 4-in. pots or be well spaced and well established in flats. Continue to pinch a few shoots each week to ensure continuous bloom next winter. If pinching is not done for

A young Carnation plant ready for repotting in a 4-in. pot.

two or three weeks, the flowers will tend to come in gluts rather than in a fairly even succession.

House Plants

House plants require essentially the same care as during last month. Cuttings of most kinds may still be inserted, and those propagated earlier that have roots 1-2 in. long should be planted in small pots without delay.

Many home gardeners seem to prefer rooting cuttings in water to using sand, sand and peat moss, vermiculite or other media that are more commonly favored by professional growers. With few exceptions cuttings rooted in water are more difficult to establish in soil than are those rooted in other media.

Baby Plants. It is important to use a very sandy soil for the first potting, not to pack it too firmly about the roots and, if possible, to keep the newly potted baby plants in a terrarium or under a bell jar until they are well established in their new pots.

This treatment assures that the atmosphere

Wash the foliage of smooth-leaved house plants periodically to remove dust and grime, reduce the likelihood of damage by insect pests and promote the health of the plants.

around the plants is moist and that the plants will not dry excessively during their struggle to adapt themselves to the new conditions. Watering the soil alone does not take the place of keeping the atmosphere moist. One other point to remember is to shade newly potted plants from strong sunshine.

Spraying the Foliage. A weekly trip to the bath tub or kitchen sink for a forceful spraying of the foliage, both on the upper and lower surfaces, with water will benefit all plants except those in bloom or those that have very hairy leaves.

Begin a regular fertilizing program for all plants in active growth that have filled their containers with roots. Dilute liquid fertilizer of a kind especially prepared for house plants may be given with advantage once a week to all plants that meet the above conditions, except perhaps when they are in full bloom. Even twice-a-week feeding will not be too much for most plants. The trick is to use the fertilizer well diluted, even weaker than the manufacturer recommends, and to use it regularly and frequently.

Water all growing plants often enough to keep the soil moist but not constantly saturated. Newly potted specimens may be allowed to get a little drier than usual before watering, until their

Cuttings of many kinds of house plants root readily in water.

roots have taken possession of the whole body of soil in the pot, but even these must not be allowed to get really dry.

Plants that have been severely pruned back should also be kept a little drier than normal until a good quantity of new growth is in evidence.

Don't dry off Hippeastrums (Amaryllis) or other bulbous plants immediately after they have finished flowering; wait until the foliage obviously begins to turn yellow and die naturally; then gradually increase the periods between waterings and finally withhold moisture entirely. In the case of Hippeastrums this treatment will not be needed until late summer or early fall.

Tubers. Tubers of Gloxinias, tuberous Begonias and Caladiums may be started into growth now in a terrarium or in a glass-covered box containing in its bottom a layer of moist sand, peat moss or leaves. Set the tubers in leaf mold or sand and peat moss to start them; transfer them to soil when the new shoots are a couple of inches tall. A temperature of 65-75 degrees is suitable to promote growth.

Dormant, bare-root Roses should be planted before they begin to leaf out. After that time, only container-grown Roses, such as the one pictured here, should be set out.

In the North

In the North, outdoor work really begins to demand attention this month. Check over the suggestions made in "What to Do in March." If you have not yet attended to the lawn, set out early-flowering biennials, or done other work there detailed, delay no longer than weather conditions make necessary.

April is the great spring planting month. Complete the setting out of nearly all deciduous (leaf-losing) trees and shrubs before the new leaf buds expand. Exceptions to this general rule are Magnolias, which are better transplanted in May.

Evergreens may be planted later than leaf-losing trees and shrubs, but even they should be installed in their new positions before their new growth is much advanced.

Roses. In many sections early April affords the last chance to plant dormant Roses. If you miss this opportunity and still want Roses in your garden this year, rely upon setting out plants already started in containers. Many nurserymen offer these and they can be safely transplanted even when in bloom. This is true, too, of other container-grown plants which are obtainable in considerable variety.

Perennials. Check perennial borders to see if any plants have been winterkilled and arrange to replace these. Complete the planting of perennials this month.

Before growth is far advanced, plants of perennial Phlox, perennial Asters (Michaelmas Daisies), Boltonias, Physostegias, Chrysanthemums, Heleniums, and other late summer- and fall-flowering perennials which form readily divided clumps may be split up and replanted. The strong outer portions of the clumps, which consist of young growths, are to be preferred for replanting to worn-out, older, inner parts.

Do not divide now such early-flowering subjects as Bleeding Heart, Oriental Poppy, Columbine, Heuchera, Iris or Pyrethrum. If you must transplant these now move them in large clumps; however, it is better to delay transplanting them until later in the season.

Christmas Roses and other kinds of Helleborus may be divided, after they are through flowering and just as new leaf growth begins, if increase is desired; but, unless absolutely necessary, it is a mistake to disturb these plants if they are doing well, for they resent interference with their roots.

New perennial plantings may now be made if basic soil preparation has been well done. Often the rush of spring work does not permit the time and effort to be spent on this that should be; it is then better to plant annuals to provide a display of color for the first year and to take advantage of the longer fall season to get the ground into really good condition for planting perennials.

The first planting of Gladioli may be made a week or ten days before the expected date of the last frost and Montbretias and Galtonias may also be planted then.

The Rock Garden. After the winter covering has been removed from the rock garden, attention must be given to pushing back into place plants that have been heaved out of the ground during the winter.

Top-dressing of the rock garden should proceed as soon as practicable and before growth is much advanced. For top-dressing use soil of a character known to suit the various plants—a humus-rich soil for woodland kinds, a peaty soil for acid-soil plants, a soil containing limestone chips for kinds that enjoy a limey diet. This work is facilitated if plants of similar needs are grouped together, a good point to remember when planting.

Young rock garden plants that have been wintered in frames or nursery beds may be set out now. The lifting and dividing of later-blooming kinds that require this treatment may be given attention. Leave the division of spring-blooming kinds that are to be split until after they have bloomed.

Sowing Annuals Outdoors. About the time the major forest trees come into leaf is excellent to sow directly outdoors seeds of all but the very tenderest annuals. Both in the cutting garden and in decorative beds and borders this may be done. Among the kinds that may be sown are Sweet Alyssum, Coreopsis (Calliopsis), Gaillardias, Asters, Cornflowers, Larkspurs, Poppies, Gypsophilas, Calendulas, annual Chrysanthemums, California Poppies, Clarkias, Godetias,

Brushwood stakes pushed into the ground to form temporary "hedges" are excellent supports for garden Peas. Chicken wire stretched between vertical posts may be used as an alternative.

Dimorphothecas, Arctotis, and Love-in-a-mist.

In the vegetable garden, make sowings of all the hardier vegetables, but do not attempt, outdoors, the tender ones such as String Beans, Lima Beans, Corn, Cucumbers, Tomatoes, Peppers, or Okra, yet. It is still too early to plant Melons outdoors.

Cultivate regularly between the rows of early sown vegetables from the time they show clearly above ground.

Continue to make ready plots that are to accommodate later sowings. Succession sowings, in comparatively small quantities, with many vegetables, provide the secret of having succulent, young crops to harvest over a long period.

Fruit Trees. Follow approved fruit-tree spray schedules with care. Recommendations for the fruits you grow, suitable for your particular locality, may be had from your State Agricultural Experiment Station.

In the South

In the South continue to dust or spray Roses regularly as a preventative of Black Spot and other troubles. If you wish to obtain fine, long-stemmed blossoms of exhibition quality disbud Hybrid Teas and Teas to one bud to each stem.

Heat-resistant Annuals. Sow seeds now of such heat-resistant annuals as Cosmos, Marigolds,

By disbudding Roses — removing all buds other than the terminal one on each shoot — large, long-stemmed blooms are produced.

Sunflowers, Petunias, Morning Glories, Tithonias, Salvias and Zinnias. It is too late to sow cool-weather kinds such as Larkspurs, Clarkias, Sweet Peas and Cornflowers.

Early-blooming shrubs such as spring-flowering Spiraeas, Flowering Almonds, Flowering Quince, Jasmines, and Forsythias need pruning after flowering; as soon as they are through blooming, attend to them. Cut out the oldest flowering shoots and encourage strong new shoots that will provide most of next year's bloom.

Gladioli. In the middle South and lower South, continue to plant Gladioli at two-week intervals; in the lower South make the last planting of these. If you have not planted the other bulbs mentioned in "What to Do in March," do so this month.

Frost-tender annuals and bedding plants may be set directly in the garden now even in the

Periods during which the ground is fairly dry and can be worked into a fine, crumbly condition should be chosen for sowing seeds outdoors.

Young annuals of many kinds that have been raised indoors may be planted in the garden as soon as all danger of frost has passed and the ground has warmed up a little.

upper South. Among the many plants that belong here are Amaranthus, Asters, Balsam, Castor Oil Plant, Celosias, annual Chrysanthemums, Coleus, Cosmos, Dahlias, Four o'clocks, Geraniums, Globe Amaranths, Marigolds, Moonflowers, Morning Glories, Petunias, Salvias, Tithonias, Thunbergias, Verbenas, Vinca rosea, and Zinnias.

Care of Lawns. If you did not do the lawn work mentioned in last month's calendar, attend to what needs doing now. Don't neglect to mow Rye Grass lawns twice a week. In the upper South there is yet time, but not much, to seed down grass seed mixtures that contain Kentucky Blue Grass or Merion Blue Grass. In the lower and middle South seed of Bermuda Grass may now be sown.

This is a good time to fertilize established lawns if it has not been done earlier. Use a special lawn fertilizer or a fertilizer that is high in nitrogen.

When mowing lawns, take care not to cut the foliage of Narcissi or other bulbs until it has turned brown naturally.

Water Lilies of tropical kinds may be planted this month, in the upper South towards the end of April, in the middle South earlier.

Mulching trees and shrubs, especially those recently planted, is very helpful. It conserves ground moisture, checks weed growth and, with some types of mulches, provides the roots with nutrients.

Straw, salt hay, pine needles or other suitable material laid between rows of Strawberries and tucked well under the foliage keeps the berries clean.

Mulching. Mulching leaf-losing trees and shrubs as well as evergreens with a 3-4 in. layer of peat moss, ground corncobs, bagasse, buckwheat hulls, leaves, Pine needles, compost or other suitable material will aid tremendously in conserving moisture, keeping down weeds and protecting the roots from excessive heat.

Roses, Dahlias and other widely spaced plants also benefit greatly from mulching. Have the mulch in place before really hot weather comes.

The Vegetable Garden. Continue to make succession sowings in the vegetable garden and to set out plants of tender crops. All kinds of tender vegetables may be planted and sown after danger of frost has passed.

Give careful attention to pest and disease control, following carefully recommendations made by your State Agricultural Experiment Station and other authorities.

Before the berries begin to form, mulch Strawberries with straw, Pine needles, or other suitable material to keep the berries off the ground and prevent them from being splashed with mud. Mulching also makes for more even ripening.

On the West Coast

Rock gardens in the northern parts will now be at their best. After the plants flower, check any rampant-growing kinds from spreading to the detriment of less vigorous neighbors. Check name labels.

As soon as the blooms of winter and early spring-flowering shrubs are finished, kinds that need pruning should receive this attention.

In northern areas, fill in perennial borders with additional plants where these are needed, and fertilize any perennial plantings that have not received this attention earlier.

Dahlias may now be set out in most sections. Planting may be done any time between March and June. Early planting produces early blooms but the best Dahlia blooms result from late planting.

Annuals of all kinds may now be sown directly in the garden in most sections. Started plants of annuals that you have raised at home or obtained from nurseries may be planted in the garden. Cool-weather annuals such as Snapdragons, Calendulas, Larkspurs, Clarkias and Godetias may be sown in the Northwest.

In vegetable gardens in the Northwest, it is time to sow all the hardier vegetables such as Spinach, Peas, Carrots, Lettuce, Radishes, Onions, Swiss Chard and Parsnips. As soon as danger of frost is past, the first Sweet Corn and Beans may be sown.

As soon as the weather has settled and the ground has warmed a little, tomatoes may be set out. They should not be planted while cold nights prevail.

In warmer sections tender vegetables such as Squash, Beans, Corn, Cucumbers and Melons may be sown outdoors; Tomatoes, Eggplants and Peppers set out as young plants from flats or pots.

WHAT TO DO IN MAY
The Season When Spring Flowers Are at Their Best

The Maple puts her corals on in May,
While loitering frosts about the lowlands cling, . . .
—James Russell Lowell

Frost and cold spring weather are fairly long past in the southern sections of the United States and are over in most of its northern parts and in Canada. May brings weather that makes it possible to put outdoors the majority of tender plants.

In this month many of the characteristic flowers of spring attain the height of their glory; indeed, May sees the last of them, for in popular acceptance June flowers are summer flowers.

The spring rush of work subsides and the more steady pull of summer chores takes its place. The rewards of earlier planning and planting become apparent and mistakes and errors of judgment are revealed.

Keep a Notebook. The wise gardener keeps an up-to-date notebook at all seasons. Now is the time to make sure that you have entered in it your evaluations of the garden results attained this spring, with notes on changes or improvements which you believe would be advantageous. When you visit other gardens and nurseries make careful and lucid notes of plants and combinations of plants that interest you.

Cold Frames

Cold frames will be used chiefly this month for hardening tender plants raised in greenhouses and in hotbeds, preparatory to planting them in the garden and in window, porch and terrace boxes.

The care of plants being so handled does not differ materially from that suggested for last month, except that more attention will probably have to be given to watering.

In the Greenhouse

Greenhouse work slackens in May. Flower and vegetable plants grown for the outdoor gardens will mostly be planted there before the end of the month; some few will be in cold frames awaiting transfer to the garden. Most flower crops grown indoors in pots or benches for winter and spring bloom will be out of the way or very definitely on the wane; the end of the indoor flowering season is in sight.

From now until fall, cool greenhouse plants being grown for fall and winter bloom, such as Chrysanthemums, Calceolarias, Cinerarias, Cyclamens, Primulas and the like, should be given as much ventilation as possible; a free circulation of air, night and day, after the weather becomes warm, is essential.

Calceolarias and the others mentioned above, except Chrysanthemums, must be shaded from strong sunshine and a moist atmosphere maintained by wetting down floors, benches and other surfaces and by syringing the plants lightly on bright days.

Chrysanthemums need full sun, but the greenhouse in which they are grown should be damped down in hot, dry weather and the plants syringed judiciously on sunny days.

Chrysanthemums need plenty of room from now on. Space the plants so that each gets a good circulation of air around it and good light. Spray regularly with insecticide to keep pests in check.

Seeds of Primulas of kinds recommended for sowing last month, Calceolarias, and Cinerarias may be sown, and, if the plants are allowed to grow without check, they will be really big

Modern strains of hybrid Calceolarias are among the most splendid of winter-blooming cool greenhouse plants. Seeds may be sown in May.

plants by flowering time.

Young plants of these cool-climate subjects need skillful care to bring them through the heat of the summer; if you cannot give them this, it will be better to defer sowing until August. Results are surer though plants are smaller from late sowings.

Now is the time to thoroughly clean the Carnation greenhouse if plants are to be set in benches next month. Remove the old soil from benches, scrub down the glass and woodwork, clean beneath the benches, whitewash walls, and bring in new soil. If new roses are to be planted

Calla Lilies that were growing and blooming through the winter and spring should now be dried off and the pots stored on their sides in a cold frame or cellar.

[1–4]
Turning over the soil in preparation for planting is an important spring task

[1–4a]
Seeds of hardy crops such as Peas are sown as early as the ground can be made ready

[1–4b]
Plants wintered in cold frames are hardened by leaving the glass off for a time before planting them in the garden

[1–4c]
Biennials and perennials are planted in early spring before they have made much new growth

[1–5]
Seed heads should not be allowed to form on Tulips

[1–5a]
Tulips removed from beds to make room for summer annuals should be carefully heeled in elsewhere

[1–5b]
After the foliage has died, heeled in Tulip bulbs should be cleaned and stored

[1–5c]
Narcissus foliage should not be removed until it is quite brown. To preserve neatness the leaves may be knotted together

in benches next month make similar preparations.

If you are growing Gerberas in benches, begin withholding water this month but do not dry them off entirely. Around the middle of May, let up on watering Calla Lilies and finally keep them completely dry after the end of the month.

Pruning. In early May, prune Acacias, Ericas and Cytisus. Thin out weak, spindly stems, cut out any dead branches and, if compact plants are desired, cut last season's wood back to within an inch or so of the base except in the case of small plants that are to be grown larger, in which case the shortening back should not be so severe.

After pruning, do not overwater but syringe freely. When new growth is half an inch long

Hydrangeas for blooming next spring in 4-in. or 5-in. pots can be raised from cuttings made at this time.

Hydrangeas grown from cuttings rooted in May will make nice plants, each with a single flower head, for blooming next spring. Cuttings of Erlangea tomentosa rooted now and later planted in a greenhouse bench will provide good cut flowers in winter.

Pansies. If you would like to have Pansies flowering indoors at Christmas, now is the time to sow the seeds. The plants must be grown as

Cuttings of Paris Daisies or Marguerites rooted now provide good winter-blooming pot plants.

repot or top-dress according to the individual needs of the plants.

Flowers for Christmas. Cuttings of Marguerites (Paris Daisies) inserted now, potted when rooted, and grown in a cool house, or plunged outdoors during the summer, will make nice 5-6-in. pot plants for flowering at Christmas time. Old specimens of these, planted about the end of the month in a sunny spot in the garden with plenty of room left around them, and pinched two or three times during the summer, will make fine plants if lifted and potted before frost, for winter flowering in the greenhouse.

For blooming at Christmas the beautiful blue-flowered Coleus thyrsoideus is a choice greenhouse plant. It may be propagated in May.

cool as possible and under light shade through the summer.

Blue flowers are rare at Christmas. A most interesting plant for greenhouse decoration that has flowers of this color is Coleus thrysoideus. It requires the same cultivation as the tenderer kinds of Begonias. Seeds may be sown now, or cuttings taken from old stock plants may be inserted.

Propagate Plumbago rosea this month. It is well worth growing for winter bloom.

Bring out the Poinsettia plants that have been stored dry since they finished blooming, cut them back to a height of 6-12 in., according to their strength (the weaker ones are cut back more severely than strong-shooted specimens), shake away most of the old soil and repot in new soil in as small pots as will comfortably contain the roots, or plant in benches.

In a warm, moist atmosphere in full sun they will soon produce suitable cuttings for insertion next month. Keep the plants lightly and frequently syringed to encourage sturdy "breaks" but do not overwater the soil; simply keep it moderately moist.

Geranium cuttings taken in May give rise to plants that, if allowed to grow steadily, occasionally pinched and kept picked free of all flower buds during the summer, will bloom freely in a sunny 50-55-degree greenhouse in winter.

House Plants

House plants of nearly all kinds should be showing considerable improvement now. As the need for artificial heating subsides, the atmosphere indoors more nearly approaches the natural humidity of the outdoor air. Plants are no longer called upon to endure a degree of aridity that is reminiscent of desert conditions.

Longer days and improved light, too, play their parts in bringing about a better appearance of house plants.

Watering. Because less heat is now used, you may well find that less frequent watering is needed at times than but a few weeks ago; but so much depends upon a number of variables that exact recommendations about this cannot be given.

In sunny, windy weather—on what the laundress calls good drying days—pot-bound specimens will still need frequent watering to keep their soil as evenly moist as it should be. But in dull, cloudy, or moist weather the demands for water will be less.

Naturally the soil of newly potted plants that have not yet filled their containers with roots will need less frequent wetting than that of well-rooted specimens. Plants with ample foliage will need to be watered oftener than sparse-leaved samples or specimens that have been pruned back.

Continue using dilute liquid fertilizer at regular intervals on all well-established plants that are healthy and in active growth. This includes Hippeastrums (Amaryllis), Oranges, Lemons, Camellias, Fuchsias, Palms, as well as a host of others.

By potting three small plants together in one fairly large pan or pot, fine, sizable specimens of many kinds of house plants are soon obtained. Here Rex Begonias are being treated in this way.

Small plants raised from seeds or cuttings earlier should be potted and repotted as their growth makes necessary. Cuttings of most kinds of house plants that can be propagated by that means may still be inserted and, if your conditions for rooting are not too good, may do better now than earlier when the indoor atmosphere was drier.

This is a good time to purchase young house plants from dealers. Plants obtained now and potted as needed will have an opportunity of growing into nice specimens during the most favorable part of the year, and will be well acclimated to your conditions by the time the more unfavorable winter months have arrived.

In the North

In the North, gardens are a wealth of color. Flowering trees and shrubs in great variety contribute to the truly gorgeous display. Bulbs, biennials and perennials of many kinds give of their best. He (or she) is a poor gardener who can not have a gay garden at this season.

Even while the feast of bloom is being enjoyed, tasks need doing to ensure the continuance of a show during the summer and fall; as plants pass out of bloom, many of them need some attention to encourage them to give of their best next season.

Pruning. Not all spring-flowering shrubs and trees need regular pruning. Many do not—Magnolias, Azaleas, Crab Apples and Flowering Cherries, for example—but others do benefit from some attention in the matter of pruning every year and some every two or three years.

Immediately after they have finished flowering, look over such kinds as Forsythias, Spiraeas, Corylopsis, Fothergillas, Deutzias, Weigelas, and Cornelian Cherries; cut out weak and ill-placed branches and whichever old branches can with advantage be spared. Retain young, vigorous growths that are appearing now; these will flower well next year.

Evergreens. There is still time to plant evergreens. It is important to get this done before the new shoots have made appreciable growth. Thorough watering after planting, mulching with peat moss, compost or other appropriate

Complete the planting of evergreens before they have made any conspicuous amount of new growth.

material, and regular soakings during dry weather throughout summer and fall are the care needed to promote success.

Magnolias and Tulip Trees. Late spring is the best time to transplant Magnolias and Tulip Trees. The latter are notoriously difficult to move. It is important to preserve as many of their roots as possible.

Spring-flowering bulbs of many kinds are now in lush foliage. Do not make the mistake of removing leaves of any of them until they have browned and died naturally. As long as they are green the leaves are busy manufacturing food

Bulb foliage should not be removed until it is quite dead. For the sake of neatness the leaves of Narcissi growing in beds and borders may be tied in bundles and left that way during the ripening-off period.

and storing it in the bulbs; this is needed to ensure next year's blooming.

Narcissi. As explained, even though the grass grow tall among naturalized Narcissi, do not mow it until the Narcissus leaves die. Resolve to endure the slightly untidy look that fading bulb foliage may give to flower borders, firm in the knowledge that the bulbs are benefiting. If the dying leaves sprawl, their unsightliness may be alleviated by tying them together in neat bundles while they are yet attached to their underground parts, and permitting them to ripen completely while so tied.

Removing Tulips from Flower Beds. If it is necessary to remove Tulips from flower beds to make room for summer occupants before their leaves have died, dig them carefully with as much soil attached to their roots as possible, and heel them in (plant them temporarily closely together) in a place where they are shaded from strong sun and water them well. There let them complete their ripening before cleaning and storing them.

If May is dry, early-flowering plants that are rapidly progressing towards bloom will benefit from copious watering at weekly intervals. Among plants that so benefit are Tulips, Peonies and Roses.

Do not worry about ants that are found on Peony buds; they do no harm, they are merely feeding on a sweet liquid the buds secrete.

Make plantings of Gladioli and Montbretia bulbs every two weeks or so to ensure a succession of cut flowers later.

Other bulbs that may be planted this month are Galtonias, Ismene, Zephyranthes, Tigridias, and Lycoris.

Dahlia tubers may be set out about the time it is safe to plant Tomatoes; green plants of Dahlias some two weeks later.

Early May is a good time to plant hardy Water Lilies and other hardy aquatic plants.

Staking of plants that need this attention should not be delayed too long. Delphiniums, Lilies and other kinds that have tall stems are easily damaged by wind and rain storms. Adequate staking before damage occurs is necessary. Set stakes for Pole Beans in advance of sowing and for Dahlias before planting.

Peas and Sweet Peas will now be making vigorous growth. Do not let them suffer at any time

The tips of the shoots of young Chrysanthemums should be pinched or cut out periodically to induce branching.

from lack of moisture. Apply a side dressing of fertilizer to encourage continued growth, and water this well in. Keep the surface soil around them shallowly stirred with the cultivator or hoe. Make sure that before the plants begin to sprawl they are furnished with adequate supports to which they may cling.

Growing Crops. Cultivate freely but shallowly between growing crops. This promotes healthy growth, reduces the need for watering and induces roots to strike deeply in search of moisture and food. Early in the season surface cultivation is, for many plants, better than mulching

Young leafy green plants grown for cuttings or seeds may be planted outdoors about the time it is safe to plant Tomatoes.

To have Cucumbers like these later in the season, sow seeds in May.

because it does not delay the warming of the ground.

Pinch the tips out of Chrysanthemums when the plants are 6 in. high and again when the side branches are about 6 in. long.

Keep pulling up unwanted sucker growths that appear around Raspberries. Do this when the shoots are about a foot high. If they are merely cut off, several new suckers appear from each cut end.

In the vegetable garden the first sowings of Sweet Corn, Snap Beans and Lima Beans will be made this month as well as seedings of Cucumbers, Squash and Melons. Continue with successional sowings of Beets, Carrots, Lettuce, and other vegetables that are best grown from repeated sowings. Sow seeds in early May to produce a late crop of Celery. When Beans have made sufficient growth some soil should be hilled up around the lower parts of their stems.

Sowing Annuals. In the early part of the month sow seeds of the hardier annuals. As soon as the weather is settled and reasonably warm (about the time it is safe to plant Corn and Snap Beans) seeds of tender annuals may be sown directly outdoors.

Certain annuals, such as Portulacas, Phlox Drummondii, Sweet Alyssum, and Nasturtiums, are best sown where they are to bloom; others, such as Calendulas, Zinnias, Marigolds, and Asters, may be sown where the plants are to bloom or may be sown in a seedbed and transplanted to their flowering locations as soon as they are large enough to handle.

Tender Plants. When the weather is settled and fairly warm it is time, too, to plant outside

Soil hilled up around the bases of young Beans affords support and promotes the growth of additional feeding roots from the stems.

Heliotropes and many many other tender summer bedding plants should be planted in gardens and window boxes after the likelihood of cold nights has passed.

Seedling vegetables and annuals that are in need of thinning out should receive this attention before they harm each other by crowding.

many annuals that have been brought along from early sowings indoors. In the case of really tender plants that have been raised indoors, such as Begonias, Heliotropes, Lantanas, Geraniums and Coleus it is better to wait 3-4 weeks longer; and in many parts of the North these should not be planted outdoors until June.

Everbearing Strawberries bear better crops later if all blooms that appear in May are picked off promptly. It is wise, too, to pick all flowers off Strawberry plants that were set out this spring. They will make sturdier plants and will bear better next year if this is done.

Thin Them Out. Remember to thin out early sown annuals as well as vegetables that become crowded. Do this in two or three operations rather than pulling the excess out all at one time.

Pests and Diseases. Watch continually for the very first evidences of trouble and take prompt measures against pests and diseases. A cutworm, a few slugs, borers in fruit trees, or beetles or caterpillars chewing foliage can do an immense amount of damage in a very short time.

It is far easier to control such diseases as Black Spot on Roses, Rust on Hollyhocks, and Botrytis Blight on Peonies before they become well established than afterwards. Your State Agricul-

tural Experiment Station is one of the best sources of up-to-date information on the control of pests and diseases in your locality.

Perennials. The latter part of the month is a good time to sow outdoors, in a carefully prepared seedbed or in a cold frame, the seeds of perennial plants of kinds that can be satisfactorily raised in this way. Delphiniums, Coreopsis, Gaillardias, Liatris, Geums, Pyrethrums, are among those that do well from seeds at this time.

Biennials and short-lived perennials of many kinds that are treated in gardens as biennials give good results when sown in late May or early June. Sow the seed in drills, a few inches apart, in a cold frame or in a nicely prepared outdoor bed. When the seedlings' second pair of leaves are well developed, transplant to nursery rows to be grown in readiness for transfer in fall or spring to their flowering quarters.

Plants that may be handled in this way include Foxgloves, Honesty, Siberian Wallflowers, Verbascums, Forget-me-nots, Hollyhocks, Columbines, Aubretias, and English Daisies.

In the South

In the South, spring is rapidly passing; in the lower parts early summer has already arrived. Maintenance chores now require more attention, planting less, although there is still some to do

Hollyhocks like these will bloom next summer from seeds sown now.

and some seeds that should be sown.

Started plants of tender annuals may yet be set out. These come in mighty handy for filling gaps and bare spaces left by the passing of early-flowering bulbs.

Petunias are useful, for example, for planting over Tulips that are to be left in the ground rather than lifted and stored for summer.

Succession sowings of annuals made now and later will provide bloom all season. Zinnias may be seeded until July, Marigolds well into June. Dwarf Dahlia seeds sown directly outdoors early this month will provide a splendid display of bloom later; the plants will be gay over a long season.

The Vegetable Garden. Proceed with the planting and sowing of tender vegetables. Set out Tomatoes, Eggplants, Peppers, Collards and slips of Sweet Potatoes. Sow Sweet Corn, New Zealand Spinach, Beans, Okra, Squash and Cucumbers. Cantaloupes and Watermelons may be sown now.

Dahlias planted in late May or early June give better results than earlier-set-out plants or tubers. They will produce their finest blooms in September and October.

Other tuberous and bulbous plants that may be set out this month are Elephants Ears, Fancy-leaved Caladiums, Cannas, Lycoris radiata, Tigridias, Tuberoses, Gloriosas, Hedychiums, Crinums, and Gladioli. Make plantings of the latter every two weeks.

Tender Water Lilies and other tender aquatics may be planted as soon as the water is warm enough.

Care of Lawns. Lawns of Bermuda Grass may be seeded this month in the middle and upper South. Thorough soil preparation before sowing is important to success. Established lawns of Bermuda Grass will benefit from fertilizing at this time.

Crab Grass now begins to grow rapidly. The time to destroy it, either by the use of a selective weed killer or by hand-picking, is before it begins to seed. May is a good month to give attention to this.

Do not cut lawns too closely now. Set the mower blades to cut at a height of 1½-2 in.

Weeds will make rapid headway unless prompt

Spraying a lawn with a selective weed killer to eliminate Crab Grass.

steps are taken to control them while they are young. Employ the hoe and cultivator vigorously and use selective weed killers and mulches, where appropriate, to keep these pests in check.

Chlorosis (insufficient green coloring in leaves resulting in a yellowish appearance) is likely to become apparent in Azaleas, Roses, lawn Grasses and some other plants in parts of the middle and lower South. It may be combatted by treating the soil or foliage with iron chelates or by spraying the foliage with iron sulphate at the rate of one half of a teaspoonful to a gallon of water.

The shearing of narrow-leaved evergreens such as Junipers and Arborvitaes, that are clipped to formal shapes, should receive attention when the new growth is completed.

On the West Coast

Camellias, Rhododendrons and Azaleas will be improved if they are fertilized just as they begin their new season's growth.

As spring-flowering shrubs pass out of bloom, continue to prune those kinds that need pruning.

With the coming of warm summer weather it is well to pay attention to mulching. This practice reduces weeding, keeps the roots cooler and moister and, in the case of some mulches such as compost and leaf mold, provides nourishment.

Ranunculus that have finished blooming and have foliage that is naturally starting to turn yellow should be dried and lifted and stored for the summer.

Plant succession sowings of vegetables and flowering annuals. Pinch back annuals planted earlier that need this treatment to make them bushy.

WHAT TO DO IN JUNE

The Time to Keep the Garden Growing and Free from Pests and Diseases

A noise like of a hidden brook
In the leafy month of June,
That to the sleeping woods all night
Singeth a quiet tune.
—Samuel Taylor Coleridge

Now that June is here, it is important to keep crops growing without check. In the vegetable garden, the cut-flower garden, and in flower beds and borders, frequent shallow cultivation of the soil is of great aid in doing this. Only where a mulch has been applied, where plants are growing among grass or other ground covers, or in the cases of plants known to have a large number of roots near the surface, as do Rhododendrons, Azaleas, Blueberries and Dogwoods, should the stirring of the surface soil be omitted.

Watering is an important aid in keeping crops growing when the weather is decidedly dry. The rule to water thoroughly and then to give no more until the plants are about to show signs of dryness again is still the best. Surface sprinklings at frequent intervals are ineffectual.

Those crops that need the aid of a little fertilizer to keep them healthy and growing satisfactorily should not be neglected. Here, "little and often" is the rule to follow rather than heavy applications at infrequent intervals.

Watch for Infection. Wage constant, well-planned warfare against pests and diseases. Rout the enemy, if possible, before he is well established. Be observant at all times for signs of infection by disease and invasion by insects. Take pains to get a correct diagnosis and apply appropriate remedies. It is no use working in the dark here. Your State Agricultural Experiment Station will make diagnoses and recommend treatments if you send them good samples of your affected plants.

Cold Frames

Cold frames are nearly as useful to the provident gardener now as early in the year. They give excellent protection to newly sown seeds of perennials and biennials; true, such seeds can be sown outdoors but a bed in a cold frame is easier to shade until the seedlings are up, and afterwards, if this is needed; moreover, it is easier to protect from torrential rains than an outdoor bed.

A great many kinds of cuttings, particularly of shrubs and herbaceous perennials (including many rock garden plants) root well in a cold frame set on the north side of a wall or building. But little ventilation should be given until the cuttings are rooted.

Many greenhouse plants benefit from being grown in a cold frame during the hot weather; this is especially true of cool greenhouse plants.

In all cases, some shade must be provided for plants growing in cold frames if the glass is kept on them and often shade is needed to mitigate the reflected heat of the sides of the frame even if the sash are left off. Shade may be supplied by whitewashing the glass. But removable wooden slat shades are better. The slats should be so spaced that the distance between them is about one half the width of the slats. As an alternative to a shaded cold frame a specially constructed lath house is amirable for sheltering plants set outdoors for the summer. Lath houses are made of wood or of aluminum slats.

Cymbidium Orchids prosper in a lath house in summer.

In the Greenhouse

The potting of Chrysanthemums in the pots in which they are to bloom should receive attention this month. Water with moderation after potting until new roots begin to fill the new containers.

Carnations from 4-in. pots should be planted in soil-filled benches if they are to be grown throughout in the greenhouse rather than planted outdoors for the summer.

New Roses may be planted in greenhouse benches and old ones rested by partially drying them and pruning them back.

Foliage plants of many kinds are likely to need potting this month. Take care that kinds that do not thrive with their roots crowded are not permitted to get pot-bound before potting receives attention. There are, of course, many foliage plants that thrive well when their roots are crowded; these should be sustained through the summer by feeding them with dilute liquid fertilizer two or three times a week.

Gloxinias and Achimenes may be grown in more airy conditions when really warm weather arrives. They need shade from strong sunshine.

Seeds and Cuttings. Seeds of tuberous Anemones sown indoors now will give young plants that, if carefully grown, will provide most excellent bloom next spring.

Young Chrysanthemums that have filled their pots with roots need to be transferred to larger pots.

Now is the time to attend to the repotting of many kinds of foliage plants.

Snapdragons for winter blooming in the greenhouse should be sown this month.

Seeds of Stocks sown now will give fine 6-in. pot plants for blooming in a cool greenhouse early in the New Year.

Iboza riparium rooted now from cuttings and allowed to grow without pinching will be handsome in bloom in 6-in. pots in December and January.

Cuttings of Poinsettias should be inserted in successive batches in June and July to ensure having plants of varied size for use at the Christmas season.

Primulas sown earlier will now be ready for pricking off (transplanting) to flats filled with light, humus-rich soil. At all stages these plants need cool growing conditions as also do Cinerarias, Calceolarias and Cyclamen. In hot summer weather these plants may be handled in a shaded cold frame on the north side of a building.

Nursery Rows. Plant young plants of Christmas Cherries and Christmas Peppers in nursery rows outdoors in full sun to make their summer growth preparatory to being lifted and potted before frost.

Give attention to all plants set out in nursery rows in the garden that are to be lifted later for use in the greenhouse; it is important that they be kept cultivated, watered and fed and free of pests and diseases. Included here are such plants as Carnations, Campanulas, Foxgloves, Rambler Roses, Baby Rambler Roses, Christmas Peppers, Christmas Cherries and Hydrangeas.

Greenhouses that are empty give an oppor-

tunity for thorough cleaning. This is a great aid in growing clean crops. Clear all debris from beneath the benches. Remove old soil and old ashes or gravel from the benches. Wash glass and woodwork and apply a coat of paint to painted surfaces if needed. Whitewash all walls. Before plants are returned to the house, make sure they are free of insects and disease and that their pots are scrubbed clean. Fumigate the houses before returning plants to them.

House Plants

House plants in June thrive with minimum attention. Conditions are generally favorable to their growth. The time when heating made the atmosphere too dry for their well-being is past. Light is now good.

Into Larger Containers. Those that grow fairly fast should be potted into larger containers. Such attention is especially likely to be needed by young specimens of such subjects as Begonias, Geraniums and Fuchsias in small pots.

It is not too late to repot large house plants that grow comparatively slowly, but the time is passing when this may be done and yet gain advantage of the summer growing season for them to re-establish themselves. Delay no longer if you intend to repot such plants as Ficus, Dracaena, Fatshedera, Pandanus, Palm, Aspidistra, Fern and Philodendron.

Spraying. Make sure that house plants, except

Fuchsias are among the many kinds of house plants that are likely to need potting into larger containers this month.

those very few that are known to react poorly to having their leaves wet, are forcibly sprayed with water at least once a week through the summer. See that the water reaches the undersides of the leaves as well as the upper. This will do much to keep down insect pests.

Cuttings of many kinds root readily now and produce strong young plants before winter. When the weather has become settled and summery such cuttings may be rooted in a shaded place outdoors, either in a cold frame or under an inverted mason jar or similar contrivance.

Bulbs that rest in summer should now be kept dry but do not make the mistake of drying Hippeastrums (Amaryllis) yet or any others that grow at this season. It is after they have finished blooming that the green leaves of Amaryllis work to store in the bulbs food to ensure next year's bloom.

Setting House Plants Outdoors. After the weather is warm most house plants benefit from being placed outdoors. Before they are put out, attend to their potting or top-dressing needs, prune them to shape, clean off dead foliage and, if needed, stake them securely.

Choose locations shady or sunny according to the needs of particular kinds. Bury the pots to their rims in a bed of sand or ashes or, if this can not be done, in soil. If you sink the pots in soil, place a piece of slate, crock or a flat stone beneath each pot so that earthworms will not crawl into the pots and to prevent the roots from growing through the drainage hole.

Choose moist, dull weather for setting house plants outdoors. Their foliage may scorch if they are put out when the weather is hot and dry.

In the North

June brings really settled warm weather. Before the middle of the month even the tenderest plants may be set outdoors. These include tropical Water Lilies and other tender aquatics.

Plant out early in June such bedding plants as Geraniums, Fuchsias, Lantanas, Heliotropes, Cannas, tuberous Begonias and other Begonias, Abutilons, Acalyphas, Iresines.

Plants of warm-weather annuals grown in flats, pots and cold frames, or raised in outdoor seedbeds for later transplanting, may be planted in their flowering quarters.

Sow in the garden seeds of fast-growing annuals for later blooming. Zinnias, Marigolds, Globe Amararanths, Cosmos, Sweet Alyssum and Sunflowers give good results from seeds sown now.

In the vegetable garden, replant without delay areas from which early crops have been removed. Fertilize and turn over the soil thoroughly before sowing such crops as Beans, Beets, Carrots, Lettuce, and New Zealand Spinach. Cabbage, Cauliflower and Broccoli may be sown in seedbeds now to give plants for setting out later.

Start runners of Strawberries in small pots filled with soil and buried to their rims in the ground. Pin the Strawberry runners to the soil in the pots so that they will root into them. Young plants rooted in this way and planted in a bed in August will fruit next year.

Spring-flowering bulbs sometimes retain their foliage longer than the gardener would wish, had he only the tidiness of his garden or the convenience of making summer plantings in mind. This is especially likely to be the case if the spring is wet, for then the foliage of many bulbs remains green longer than usual. However, the gardener may be comforted by the thought that the longer the leaves remain green

Narcissi and other hardy bulbs that are to be transplanted may be dug up as soon as their foliage has completely withered.

the more time they have to manufacture food to store in the bulbs for next season's flowers.

When the foliage of early-flowering bulbs that are to be lifted has browned, lose no time in digging them up, cleaning them and placing them in storage.

This is a good time to transplant Daffodils and other Narcissi that are to be moved from one part of the garden to another and to lift, grade and replant in enriched and deeply prepared soil, bulbs of these that are overcrowded and are blooming sparsely.

Tender summer-flowering bulbs such as Ismenes, Caladiums, Tigridias, and Begonias may be planted now. Continue making plantings of Gladioli at two-week intervals up to the end of the month.

Early June is an excellent time to set out Dahlias. Cultivate the soil about them freely until they are well established and are growing thriftily. Later, when the soil has warmed up and the weather becomes really hot, a mulch placed on the soil about them is highly beneficial.

In the rock garden and perennial garden many flowering plants, Arabis, creeping Phlox, Aubretia, Snow-in-summer, Arenaria, and evergreen Candytuft for instance, will benefit from clipping back to make them more bushy.

Cuttings of many rock garden plants will now root readily if planted in a well-firmed bed of sand or vermiculite in a frame shaded from strong sun and kept close to ensure a humid atmosphere about the cuttings.

Hedges of most kinds that are kept clipped will need shearing this month. Remember to trim so that the base of the hedge is slightly broader than the top. This ensures more even light reaching the lower portion, and helps to prevent it from becoming bare.

Keep the garden tidy by picking faded blossoms promptly from perennials and annuals. Stake and tie plants that need this before the stems grow out of shape and before the plants suffer storm damage.

Check to see that plants that need mulching have received this attention. Surface-rooting kinds such as Azaleas, Rhododendrons and Pieris are especially benefitted by this care. To cul-

Faded blooms of Iris and other garden flowers should be removed promptly.

tivate the soil around such plants is harmful because it destroys roots.

Sowing Perennials. June is a good month in which to plant in a well-prepared outdoor bed, or in a bed made up in a cold frame, seeds of any perennials that are to be propagated in this way. Remember that named horticultural varieties of perennials such as those of Peonies, Day Lilies, Phlox, and Irises, do not come true from seeds. There are many perennials, however, that do breed true from seeds, and even those that don't will often produce a proportion of fine plants when so raised. Among kinds to raise from seeds are Columbines, Delphiniums, Flax, Campanulas, Lychnis, Stokesias, Anchusas, Geums, Alyssum saxatile, evergreen Candytuft and Sidalceas.

Delphiniums a year or more old will bloom this month. Keep old flower stems cut off as fast as the blossoms wither, but do not remove more foliage than necessary in this process. After the plants are through blooming, apply a dressing of fertilizer, spray them thoroughly two or three times with an insecticide, and water well if the weather is dry. All this will encourage a good second crop of flowers.

Peas and Sweet Peas should be kept well watered and all spent blossoms should be picked off the latter before they have a chance to set seed. Pick garden Peas for eating before they get

Peas will continue to crop longer if the soil is watered regularly in dry weather.

the lawn mower blades ½ in. during really hot weather so that the grass is not cut too close.

In the South

Take immediate steps to eliminate Crab Grass if you have not already done so. Lawns of Bermuda Grass will now be thickening up and making good growth. Winter Rye will begin to die out as the summer grasses take over.

There is still time to plant sprigs and plugs of vegetatively reproduced lawn grasses such as Centipede, St. Augustine, Bermuda and Zoysia.

Spring bulbs that are to be dug and stored over summer in a cool, dry place may be lifted after the foliage has died naturally.

Shrubs and Trees. June is the month in which to insert cuttings of shrubs to be propagated from what is known as half-ripe wood—shoots that are neither very soft nor fully hardened. Many Azaleas are easily increased in this way.

Air-layering by making use of polyethylene plastic film to wrap around the moss balls to conserve moisture is a practical way of increasing Azaleas, Camellias, Magnolias, Hollies and many other outdoor trees and shrubs. It may be done this month.

Sow succession crops of warm-weather annuals and vegetables such as those mentioned in "What to Do in May."

Until the middle of the month you may still plant Dahlias, Gladioli and Cannas. Plant also Sternbergias and Irises.

June is a good time to set out tender water plants in the upper South. Late Chrysanthemum plants may also be planted now.

In the upper South, tender bedding plants such as Geraniums, Begonias, Heliotropes, Lantanas and Fuchsias, should be set out before the month has far advanced.

The feeding of many crops requires timely attention. Both in the vegetable garden and the flower garden intelligent care should be given to this matter. No over-all rule can be set for summer fertilizing; be guided by the needs of various kinds of plants. Roses benefit from fertilizing after the first grand flush of flower is over. Gladioli and Dahlias need similar encouragement when they are half-grown. Many vegetables

old. These measures will prolong the cropping season of both Peas and Sweet Peas. The application of a dilute, quickly available fertilizer also is of benefit to these two crops while they are producing their harvest.

Early June is an appropriate time to sow the seeds of biennials (a list of these was included in "What to Do in May").

Until hot weather arrives (in most localities in July) lawns may be mowed fairly low, but raise

When really hot weather comes, raise the blades of the lawn mower about half an inch so that the grass is not cut as closely as before.

will benefit from fertilizer applications during their growing period. Always water fertilizers in very thoroughly.

It is not too late to fertilize Azaleas and Camellias for the last time.

On the West Coast

Continue to make biweekly plantings of Gladioli to ensure as long a succession of bloom as possible.

Pick faded blooms from Rhododendrons and Azaleas before they begin to form noticeable seed pods.

Keep Dahlias tied to their stakes and disbranched as needed. Cultivate the soil about them shallowly, and mulch it when really warm weather arrives.

In the Northwest, seeds of Beets, Broccoli, Cauliflower, Lettuce, Kohlrabi, Rutabagas and other vegetables required for late harvesting should be sown in June. Sow seeds of Primulas as soon as they are ripe.

Weeding and watering are two tasks that take a good deal of time at this season. Both are well worth all possible effort that can be spent upon them.

Spraying, dusting and baiting to control the

Unwanted Dahlia shoots should be removed while small.

The elimination of weeds is a continuous operation through the summer months.

Faded blooms should be picked off Rhododendrons before seed pods are formed.

various diseases and pests that may be troublesome should be intelligently done. This means that the gardener must be informed about the pests with which he must cope. Seek the advice of your State Agricultural Station if you need help.

WHAT TO DO IN JULY

The Month to Watch for Signs of Drought and Take Measures Against It

The Summer looks out from her brazen tower,
Through the flashing bars of July.
—Francis Thompson

July is a hot and frequently dry month over practically all of North America. At this time many garden tasks are the same in all sections of the United States and Canada.

Everywhere drought is apt to occur, and attention to the matter of supplying water in adequate amounts, when needed, is of paramount importance. Soak the ground deeply when you do water, then give no more for several days—until the plants approach the stage where they will wilt if water is not given.

Special Care. Spring-planted evergreens are particularly likely to suffer if they are permitted to get dry and this is true, too, but to a slightly lesser degree, of spring-planted leaf-losing trees and shrubs.

Areas that are not mulched should be kept cultivated shallowly except where notoriously shallow-rooted plants, such as Azaleas, Rhododendrons, Heathers, Blueberries and Camellias, grow.

Keep faded flowers picked from Snapdragons, Phlox, Delphiniums and other plants. This prevents exhaustion of the plants by seed production and encourages them to keep blooming.

Lawns generally should not be fed at this season for such treatment is likely to encourage weeds rather than grasses, but in dry weather they should be watered regularly to keep them green.

The Compost Pile. Gather all waste vegetable matter that is not likely to harbor soil-borne

Care of flower borders includes removal of faded blooms, weeding, cultivating and staking.

Valuable stores of organic matter for future soil improvement can be accumulated by maintaining a compost heap.

diseases and make it into a compost pile. A good compost pile is a most valuable garden asset, a real conservation measure and a garden economy. Weeds, as well as fallen leaves, grass mowings and waste from the vegetable garden and flower garden, make good compost. It is better not to put woody branches or leaves of evergreens on the compost heap.

Order Your Bulbs Now. Now is the time to think about bulbs that must, or should be, planted early. Do not delay placing your orders for Colchicums, Autumn Crocuses, Sternbergias, Narcissi and Lilies.

Cold Frames

Cold frames require about the same care as during the previous month. At this season they may shelter cool greenhouse plants, such as Cyclamens and Cinerarias, that are grown in them for the summer.

Give Seedlings Attention. Also accommodated in cold frames at this time may be seedlings of biennials and perennials. As soon as these are big enough to handle comfortably, they should be transplanted. Some, such as English Wallflowers and Sweet Williams, will, in the North,

need the protection of a cold frame over winter and others, such as Polyanthus Primroses, will benefit from such an advantage. Seedlings of kinds that are .to receive such shelter should be transplanted directly to beds of fertile soil prepared inside the frames.

See that frames and frame sash are repaired, painted if necessary, and in good order before the winter comes.

In the Greenhouse

Greenhouse work during July is mainly routine in nature. Watering, feeding, spraying, staking and tying will need regular attention. July in a sense marks the end of the greenhouse year; it is very much a between-season period.

Seeds of many annuals for blooming indoors early may be sown now. Kinds to sow include Snapdragons, Stocks, Marigolds, Primulas, Cinerarias, Browallias, Leptosynes, Salpiglossis, Nemesias, annual Chrysanthemums, double Wallflowers, Clarkias and Schizanthus.

Don't Forget These Plants. Chrysanthemums not yet in their final pots or in benches should be potted or planted now.

Cuttings of Poinsettias to provide the main

[1–6]
Vegetables grow quickly in summer and need frequent harvesting

Lettuce

[1–6a]
Beets

[1–6b]
Carrots

[1–6c]
Cabbage

[1–7]
Summer and Fall Garden

Harvesting Fruits

[1–7a]
Cultivating

[1–7b]
Staking

[1–7c]
Planting Bulbs

batch for Christmas flowering may now be inserted. These root best in a close, moist house, with no shade after the first few days.

Newly planted Roses should have the surface of the soil in which they are planted stirred very shallowly at frequent intervals to promote growth. Keep the Rose house humid on clear days. Give old, cut-back bushes a top-dressing of cow manure or of soil and fertilizer, and water it in immediately. As the buds begin to swell, and after they "break," syringe with clear water several times daily.

Carnations planted outdoors should be lifted and planted in the benches at the end of this month or early in August. After planting, shade them for not more than 3-4 days. Support the plants to prevent breaking as soon as they are installed in the benches. Spray with water on bright days and moisten the floors and beneath the benches frequently. Keep the surface soil between the plants shallowly cultivated at frequent intervals.

Keep Careful Watch. Cyclamens at this time should be making fairly rapid growth and Primulas should be coming along nicely. Cinerarias

A standard (tree form) Fuchsia. Now is the time to start cuttings to produce plants like this for next year.

and Calceolarias move rather more slowly during hot weather. Keep a careful watch for insect pests on all of these and take prompt measures to eradicate any that threaten to be troublesome.

If you want standard (tree-trained) Fuchsias, Heliotropes, Lantanas and Geraniums for next year, cuttings should be rooted early this month. Continue to grow the plants without pinching until the stem reaches the desired height, and keep all side shoots pinched out while they are small.

Calla Lilies should be completely dormant now and must not be watered. This is the case, too, with many other South African bulbs such as Lachenalias, Ixias and Sparaxis.

Cuttings of Azaleas may be rooted in a mixture of peat moss and sand. Half-ripened wood should be used for the cuttings.

Now that really hot weather is here, tropical greenhouses may, with advantage, be ventilated much more freely than earlier in the year.

Martha Washington Geraniums should be rested by keeping them quite dry from early July to the middle of August. The plants may occupy a sunny place outdoors during this period.

Repotting of permanent greenhouse plants should be done with discretion. It is important that only those that may be expected to fill the new pots with roots before the onset of winter be accorded this treatment; others may be carried along and kept in good health by fertilizing regularly. Young Boston Ferns are examples of plants that may benefit from a final potting in July.

House Plants

House plants require similar care in July to that described in "What to Do in June." See that they do not suffer for lack of water; but, at the same time, avoid keeping them so constantly saturated that the soil becomes sour and the roots rot off.

Martha Washington Geraniums, Calla Lilies and any other plants that have a season of complete rest in the summer should not be watered now. They may be placed outdoors with their pots turned on their sides.

Leaf cuttings of Gloxinias inserted at this time soon give rise to healthy young plants.

Bearded Irises are now through blooming. July is a good time to divide and replant any that need this attention.

At this time Gloxinias, Achimenes and most of their relatives should be growing nicely; now that really warm weather is here, they may be given more airy locations than earlier. Tuberous Begonias will also respond to more airy conditions.

Cuttings of a great many house plants may still be successfully rooted outdoors as mentioned in the calendar for June. Leaf cuttings of many kinds may be made now.

In the North

Lawns will not need to be mowed as close now as in the early summer. It is better, during very hot weather, to mow at a height of 2 in. rather than to cut the grass shorter.

Wage relentless war on Crab Grass. By the use of selective weed killers and by hand weeding, eliminate this pest before it has a chance to set seeds. Broad-leaved lawn weeds, such as Plantains and Dandelions, may be cleared from the lawn by spraying with a suitable selective weed killer. Take special care that these weed killer sprays do not drift onto nearby garden plants; they will cause considerable havoc if they do.

Bearded Irises may be lifted, divided and replanted any time during the present month, but it is better to wait until the end of July or early

August before so treating Siberian Irises. When dividing these plants, be sure to cut out all diseased portions of the rhizomes. Dust the cut surfaces with powdered sulphur.

Rambler Roses that renew themselves freely by means of strong new shoots, produced from the base of the plants after flowering, may be pruned as soon as the blooming season is through. These and other types of Roses may be

Rambler Roses may now be pruned and their new growths tied in place.

propagated now by means of cuttings set under a mason jar or in a cold frame in a shaded part of the garden.

Madonna Lilies. If it is necessary to transplant Madonna Lilies, do so now. It is better, however, not to move these bulbs unless such a transfer is unavoidable; they thrive best when undisturbed. If new Madonna Lily bulbs are to be planted, place an order with your dealer now for the earliest possible delivery. Remember, when planting, that the tips of Madonna Lily bulbs should be but 2 in. beneath the surface.

The end of July or early August is a good time to divide and transplant Oriental Poppies. Bleeding Heart may also be transplanted and divided then. In each case wait until the foliage has almost died before digging the roots.

Gladioli of quickly maturing varieties may be planted in the early part of the month in many parts of the North; the trick is to get them into the ground sufficiently in advance of killing frost for the flowers to develop. Check the number of days required by various Gladioli varieties and calculate backwards from the expected date of killing frost in your locality.

Young plants of perennials and biennials, seeded earlier, will be ready for transplanting to nursery rows outdoors or to cold frames (depending upon their hardiness) as soon as they have about four leaves and are large enough to handle comfortably. If possible, choose dull, moist weather for doing this work. If it must be done under other conditions, be sure to water the plants well in, keep them shaded, and lightly sprinkle them once or twice a day with water until they get over the ill effects of transplanting.

Pieces of root, each about 2 in. long, of Oriental Poppies, Bleeding Hearts, Anchusas and some other thick-rooted plants, if planted now as root cuttings in sandy, well-drained soil, will each give rise to a sturdy, new young plant.

Madonna Lilies may be transplanted in July or August. These bulbs bloom in June.

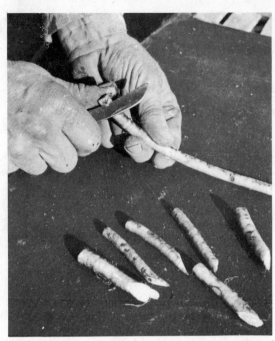

Cuttings of pieces of root of Anchusas, Bleeding Hearts, Oriental Poppies and other plants with thick, fleshy roots may be made and planted now.

Dahlia stems should be tied with soft string before they are damaged by summer storms.

When Dahlias have made sufficient growth, pinch out their growing tips and thin the shoots if the variety and method of culture require this. Except with dwarf varieties, do not allow flower buds to mature until mid-August. Tie the shoots as needed. Begin feeding after the middle of the month.

Remember These Dates. Do not pinch the shoots of hardy Chrysanthemums after the middle of July. These plants should be making good growth now.

Hardy Chrysanthemums, pinched for the last time in late July, soon form sturdy new branches.

The end of July is the ideal time to sow seeds of Pansies and Violas to have good plants in full bloom next spring. English Daisies and Forget-me-nots may still be sown in the early part of the month to bloom next spring.

There is still time to sow the seeds of perennials if you have not done this earlier. The plants that result will be smaller than from earlier sowings and the seedbed may need a little more attention in the matter of watering now that hot weather has arrived, but the plants

Russel Lupines like these will bloom next year from seeds sown in July.

Summer pruning the young shoots of espalier-trained fruit trees.

give good results. In many places these are short-lived perennials and are best discarded after the second season of bloom.

Summer pruning, which consists of shortening the young shoots, of espalier fruits, and shrubs and trees, and of Wisterias, to encourage flowering, should receive attention.

Greenhouse types of Chrysanthemums that are being grown outdoors for early blooms may be caused to bear their flowers six weeks earlier than normal by shading them to exclude all light from 5 P.M. to 8 A.M. for a period of six weeks beginning about mid-July. Special black cloth for shading is procurable from dealers in horticultural supplies. At the end of six weeks of shading the black cloth should be removed.

Special Treatment. Roses should be fertilized, all blind shoots (those that do not end in a flower bud) cut back to a strong leaf bud, and old blossoms removed and the shoots bearing them shortened about halfway back, to a strong leaf bud. Do not cut away more foliage than necessary at this time.

Some annuals, such as Sweet Alyssum and Phlox Drummondii, tend to grow straggly and benefit greatly and bloom better later if they are lightly sheared back after the first flush of bloom is over. Violas also respond to this treatment.

The Vegetable Garden. Sowings of Beans, Corn, Carrots, Leaf Lettuce and Radishes should

raised will be useful for setting out in their flowering locations next spring.

Russell Lupins sown in July, thinned out when the young plants begin to crowd, and allowed to bloom in the place where they are sown

Summer pruning of Wisterias consists of shortening the long, young, viny shoots.

be made before the middle of the month. Head Lettuce may be sown towards the end of the month. Sowings of Rutabagas, Endive and Chinese Cabbage may be made this month.

Young plants of Cabbage, Cauliflower, Kale and Broccoli will be ready for transplanting from the seedbed. As fast as the plants are dug, dip their roots in a thick, creamy mud made by mixing clayey soil with water. This "puddling" preserves the delicate, fine roots from drying during the transplanting operation.

If you plan to make a new lawn this fall, it is not too early to begin getting the ground into condition. Around new homes the soil should be graded and loosened to a depth of 8 in. or more. If necessary, good topsoil should be brought in.

A crop of Buckwheat sown over the area of the lawn-to-be in the first part of July will be ready for turning under in 5-6 weeks and will improve the soil by adding humus to it.

Rye Grass may be sown to hold the soil and make a temporary green carpet. When it is turned under in August it will add some organic

Inserting cuttings of a shrub Potentilla. Most kinds of shrubs can be propagated this way in July.

matter (which soon becomes humus) to the soil.

If the area to be seeded to lawn has been infested with Crab Grass, it is a good plan to work it to the finish grade and then keep it clean of all vegetation until the lawn grass is sown in

Turning under a cover crop of Buckwheat to improve the soil in preparation for sowing a new lawn.

September. By repeated shallow surface cultivation during August and early September, weeds that germinate will be destroyed and a weed-free or nearly weed-free seedbed will be ready for sowing with lawn grass seed.

Outdoor shrubs in great variety are easily rooted from cuttings inserted this month. The cuttings should be prepared from half-ripened shoots—not those that are so soft that they wilt easily. Such cuttings may be rooted in greenhouses, cold frames or under an inverted glass jar outdoors. The atmosphere about them must be humid, and shade from direct sun must be provided. Very little ventilation should be given until the cuttings have rooted.

In the South

"Hulled" seed of Bermuda Grass may still be sown to form lawns. This grass thrives in the hottest weather and may be expected to germinate in about a week.

Iris may now be lifted, divided and transplanted. Oriental Poppies also may be lifted and transplanted and be propagated by rooted cuttings.

Poinsettias in the lower South should be pinched for the last time late this month. Pinching prevents the plants from becoming too long and leggy.

In the vegetable garden, plantings may now be made of Turnips, Rutabagas, Carrots, Beets, Lettuce, Broccoli, Collards, Cabbage and Irish Potatoes. In the lower South, plant Beans, Cowpeas, Peppers, Pumpkins, Rutabagas, and New Zealand Spinach.

Sowing Seeds of Annuals and Perennials. Seeds of fast-growing annuals may now be sown. These include Sweet Alyssum, Marigolds, Nicotianas, Celosias, Calendulas, Balsams, Phlox Drummondii, Ageratums, and Zinnias. In the lower South, plant also Vinca rosea, Coleus, Cosmos, Gaillardia, Morning Glory, Moonflower, Salvia, Sunflower and Tithonia.

Seeds of perennials may now be sown in a cool, partially shaded location. In the lower South, place seeds of Snapdragons, Delphiniums, Pansies and other cool climate kinds in a refrigerator to prechill them prior to sowing in September.

Foxgloves in bloom in early summer. These were raised from seeds sown the previous summer.

For Better Bloom. Keep Chrysanthemums growing by feeding them every 2-3 weeks. See that they are staked and watch them carefully for pests and diseases.

Azaleas, Camellias and Hydrangeas may now be propagated from cuttings inserted in a mixture of sand and peat moss in a shaded cold frame.

Crape Myrtle will remain in bloom longer if faded blooms are picked off promptly.

Give Roses a short rest at this season. Do not water or fertilize them now, but keep them sprayed or dusted to control pests and diseases.

Towards the end of the month or in August sow seeds of biennials such as Foxgloves, Canterbury Bells and Hollyhocks.

On the West Coast

In the milder sections, late winter and spring bloom may be had from annuals sown in late July or early August. Among the kinds to consider are Calendulas, Cornflowers, Stocks, Snapdragons, Iceland Poppies, Forget-me-nots, Linarias, Sweet Peas, Pansies and Primula malacoides.

They Need Attention. Give early-flowering Chrysanthemums their last pinch in the middle of the month, late-flowering varieties towards the end of the month. Keep Carnations pinched until the latter part of August.

After the foliage of Narcissi has died, clean off the tops and do not water the beds (unless they are interplanted with other plants which makes this necessary) so that the bulbs will ripen thoroughly.

Disbud Dahlias if they are being grown for large blooms. Be sure to keep the plants securely tied to their stakes.

The staking of fall-blooming Asters, Heleniums, Boltonias and other tall perennials should receive attention before their stems fall down or become crooked. ·

In the Northwest many early-blooming rock garden plants may be divided and replanted in early July. Creeping Phlox, Aubretias and Armerias are examples of kinds that may be so handled.

The Vegetable Garden. Clear away the vines of early Peas that have finished cropping. Early and midseason vegetable crops of many kinds will now be harvested. Don't allow them to get old and tough before taking them.

Watering if the weather is dry and combating weeds if the season is prevailingly moist will now take up an appreciable proportion of the gardener's time. In neither case will "too little and too late" produce satisfactory results.

WHAT TO DO IN AUGUST

Continue Drought Treatment and Be Alert for Signs of Insects and Diseases

Loud is the summer's busy song:
The smallest breeze can find a tongue,
While insects of each tiny size
Grow teasing with their melodies,
Till noon burns with its blistering breath
Around, and day lies still as death.
—John Clare

The introductory remarks under "What to Do in July" apply with equal force to August. Read them again.

Good garden maintenance is important at this time of the year. A regular spraying and dusting schedule should be followed with crops such as Roses, in which good results depend upon repeated preventive measures. Maintain a very sharp watch for the first sign of attack by pests and diseases on other plants that may need only occasional attention from the sprayer or duster.

Lose no time in placing your orders for bulbs that are to be planted this fall.

Cold Frames

Cold frames will not now be in use, with two exceptions. The first is the cold frame in which cuttings are being rooted; it must be kept close to prevent the cuttings from wilting. The second is the frame in which young biennials are planted; it is not covered with glass sash, and may be protected with slat shades if the plants it shelters are shade-preferring kinds.

In the Greenhouse

In the greenhouse August brings the beginning of a new cycle of activity. Now, many kinds of annuals are sown for winter flowering. Plants such as Calceolarias and Cinerarias, that have been idling rather sullenly through the hot summer weather, get going again when cooler nights come towards the end of the month. The first of the bulbs for winter and spring flowering require potting. Activities to ensure a bountiful supply of blooms throughout the winter and spring are intensified.

Sowing and Potting. Annuals for winter flowering should be sown early in the month.

A flat containing sturdy young Cyclamen plants. Cyclamen seeds are sown in August.

These include those mentioned in "What to Do in July" and, in addition, such items as Godetias, Linarias, Ursinias, Venidiums, Nasturtiums, and Lupines.

Sow Cyclamen seed in light, woodsy soil to produce plants that will bloom in 15-18 months.

Sweet Peas sown about the middle of the month and grown in pots in a cool, sunny greenhouse will produce flowers in time for Christmas, but later sowing is preferable for the chief crop.

Cinerarias sown in early August give excellent 5-6-in. pot specimens for blooming in March.

Potting tubers of white Calla Lilies to give plants for winter blooming.

Freesias, for an early crop, may be potted or planted in flats and placed in a cool, shaded frame until started.

White Calla Lilies should be repotted this month. Until they are well rooted take care not to overwater them.

Pot Easter Lilies as soon as the bulbs become available. Cold-storage bulbs of Lilium speciosum, Lilium tigrinum and other kinds may be potted at two-week intervals from the beginning of August to the middle of September.

Chrysanthemums should be pinched for the last time by the middle of August. Keep the plants staked and neatly tied.

Give Them Special Attention. Buddleia asiatica and Buddleia Farquhari require transplanting into the pots in which they will flower from Christmas on. Keep them staked, well tied and plunged to the rims of their pots in a bed of ashes, sand or soil outdoors until after the first light frost.

Stevias (Piqueria), both the single-flowered and double-flowered kinds, should also be given their final potting in August and be treated as advised above for Buddleia.

Give Carnations their last pinch during the first week of the present month.

Prune, repot and start into growth again Martha Washington Geraniums that have been resting for the past 6 weeks or so.

By the end of the month, Christmas Begonias should be set in the pots in which they are to flower. A light soil, with plenty of decayed manure and leaf mold or other organic material, gives the best results.

Chrysanthemums will benefit from regular feeding from early August until the flower buds begin to show color. Dilute and often is the golden rule here.

Calceolarias of the shrubby kinds may now be propagated to advantage. After they are rooted and potted in a light, humus-rich soil, and begin to get established, grow them as cool as possible with light shade on bright days.

House Plants

House plants that are plunged (buried to the rims of their pots) outdoors should be lifted occasionally and reset in the sand, ash or soil bed after any roots coming through the holes in the bottoms of the pots have been cut off. If plunged plants are allowed to root ouside their pots they will receive a great shock when they are finally lifted and brought indoors, and will almost certainly wilt and lose leaves.

Feed plants that have filled their pots with healthy roots, and that are not dormant or resting, at least once a week and preferably twice a week with dilute liquid fertilizer. See what a difference this makes.

Watch closely for Mealybugs, Thrips, Red Spider Mites and other pests and diseases. If any appear, lose no time in eradicating them. Every plant should be clean of pests when it is taken indoors.

Cuttings of most house plants still root with facility. Plants produced from cuttings taken now will be smaller than those rooted earlier but will still be creditable specimens before winter begins in earnest. Towards the end of the month, cuttings of Wax Begonias, Ageratums, Iresines, Fuchsias, Heliotropes, Coleus, Geraniums, and a number of other tender perennials from the flower garden may be taken and rooted. These, carried through the winter as small plants, will be of useful flowering size next spring or summer, depending upon variety. English Ivy roots with ease now.

Sow seeds, outdoors, of Calendulas, Dwarf

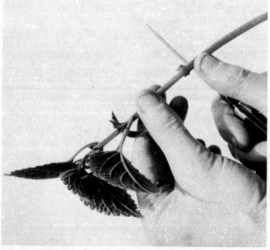

Coleus and many other house plants are easily propagated from cuttings in August.

Marigolds, Nasturtiums, Sweet Alyssum and other favored annuals; these will give plants to be lifted carefully in September, potted, and grown in a cool, sunny window for winter and spring bloom. These seeds should be sown early in the month.

In the North

June-sown perennials will now be ready for transplanting into nursery beds where they will develop into specimens ready for moving to their flowering locations in early fall or next spring.

If Pansy seed was not sown in late July, make no delay in seeding it when August arrives. Use a good strain of seed. English Daisies and Forget-me-nots may be sown at the same time if you overlooked them earlier or if you need more.

New bulbs of Madonna Lilies will be available this month. Plant them as early as possible. The same remarks apply to Colchicums and true autumn-flowering Crocuses.

If Peonies are to be transplanted, or divided and transplanted, the latter part of August or early September is the most favorable time for this work. Dig the plants carefully so that no more roots than absolutely necessary are damaged. Take care that the buds or "eyes" are not more than 2 in. beneath the surface when planting is completed.

Phlox that have finished blooming may be cut back and most surely all faded flower heads should be removed. Late August is a satisfactory time to lift, divide and replant Phlox; it is also a good time to propagate choice kinds by means of root cuttings.

The planting of Japanese and Siberian Irises should be completed without delay.

Cuttings of a great many shrubs may still be rooted in cold frames or under an inverted glass jar in a shaded location outdoors. Many sub-shrubby plants can also be increased with ease in the same way at this time. Here belong Lavender, Santolina, Sage, Thyme, and Helianthemums.

Many rock garden plants and other perennials root readily in cold frames that are kept "close" (closed sufficiently to ensure the atmosphere inside being always humid) and shaded. Belonging in this group of plants are Dianthus, evergreen Candytuft, Arabis, Aubrietias, Sedums, Phlox, Campanulas; Arenarias, Veronicas, Galiums.

Ground covers in variety may be propagated by means of cuttings inserted in cold frames now and treated as advised above for cuttings of shrubs and cuttings of rock garden plants. Pachysandra, Vinca minor, and Euonymus radicans are among the good ground covers that can be increased in this manner.

Lawns. The beginning or middle of the month is none too early to begin getting areas into condition that are to be sown with lawn grass seed next month. After all grading, fertilizing and other preparatory work have been completed, it is well to allow the soil to lie for 4-6 weeks so that it may settle and, more important, so that any weed seeds it contains may germinate. During this waiting period, hoe the surface shallowly at weekly intervals to destroy all young weeds that come up. By this means you will make sure of having a clean, weed-free seedbed.

As soon as the new growth has stiffened, which usually means any time after the middle of the month, evergreens can be transplanted safely. Be sure to water them in thoroughly after they are planted and, if the weather is dry, to soak the soil at weekly intervals.

Winter Rye is an excellent cover crop. Its large seeds are scattered over the soil surface and raked in. If this is done in late summer or early fall, the seeds soon germinate and produce a lush growth.

Newly planted evergreens benefit from having their tops sprayed daily with water and from having the soil about them mulched with compost, peat moss or other suitable material.

In the vegetable garden there is still time in most sections to make sowings of Snap Beans, Spinach, Carrots, Endive, Lettuce and Carrots.

Head Lettuce sown in August and transplanted to cold frames when large enough to handle, and later protected with mats or straw on cold nights, will give fine cuttings almost until Christmas.

Carrots from seed sown early this month, left in the ground and covered with a heavy layer of straw or leaves after the ground freezes, may be dug all winter and will have very much better

Fertilizing a new lawn area in preparation for seeding.

After Onions are harvested they should be spread out in trays in a sunny, dry location so that they may ripen thoroughly before storage.

table qualities than stored Carrots.

The blanching of Celery, either by banking it with soil or wrapping it with heavy paper or cardboard bands, should begin this month.

To Improve the Soil. Sow areas, from which crops have been harvested and cleared, and that are to remain empty, with Winter Rye, merely raking the seed into the surface. This practice conserves fertilizer elements that might otherwise be washed away, adds humus to the soil and improves its texture.

Young Strawberry plants from pots may now be planted in a rich, carefully prepared bed in a sunny position.

Onions should be harvested after their tops turn brown. After they are lifted, allow them to remain on the ground or in some other dry place in full sun for a few days so that they have an opportunity to ripen thoroughly before being stored.

In the South

Cuttings of Hollies as well as of other evergreens such as Abelias, Photinias, Pyracanthas, Barberries, Euonymus, Osmanthus and Privets, may be rooted from cuttings inserted this month

in cold frames or in a sheltered place outdoors. Set the cuttings in a firmly packed mixture of peat moss and sand, or in a bed made by spreading a 2-in. layer of sharp sand over a bed of a mixture of topsoil, peat moss and sand, and packing it firmly. The cuttings must be shaded from direct sun until they are rooted.

A frame filled with rooted Holly cuttings.

At regular intervals during dry weather, do not fail to water thoroughly Azaleas and Camellias, as well as other plants needing this attention.

Seeds of many perennials give satisfaction if sown towards the middle of the month. Start them in a cold frame or shaded spot outdoors where the soil can be kept uniformly moist. Kinds to sow include Columbines, Gaillardias, Pyrethrums, Geums, Gerberas, Shasta Daisies, Hollyhocks, and Veronicas.

Vegetables for fall crops, including Snap Beans, Butter Beans, Beets, Carrots, Cucumbers, Cowpeas, Cabbage, Collards, Kale, Kohlrabi, Rutabagas, Radishes, Turnips, Spinach and Lettuce may be sown. In the lower South, Eggplants, Okra, Peppers, Squash, Tomatoes and Sweet Corn may also be seeded.

Plants of Collards, Cabbage and Tomatoes set out now will provide earlier harvests than will seeds sown at this time. In the upper South,

Tomatoes planted now will not ripen their fruit but will provide green fruits for conserves.

Bulbs to plant now include Madonna Lilies, Sternbergias, Lycoris, Leucojums, Zephyranthes, Freesias, Ornithogalums and Oxalis.

In the lower South, plant bulbs of Easter Lilies and Calla Lilies. The latter need rich soil and partial shade.

Lawns. Do not fertilize lawns this month. Kentucky Blue Grass, the Fescues and most other permanent grasses are semidormant. Cut with the lawn mower blades set at a height of 1½-2 in.

For Best Results. In the lower South, seeds of such annuals as Sweet Alyssum, Baby's Breath, Larkspurs, Sweet Peas, Calendulas, Nasturtiums and Nemophilas may be sown for winter flowers.

Fertilize Roses about the end of the month or early in September. Trim back any rangy shoots but be sparing with the pruning shears at this time.

Irises, both the bearded and Louisiana varieties, may be planted in August.

Spray fruit and nut trees according to recommendations made by your State Agricultural Experiment Station. Follow the suggested schedules carefully.

In the upper South the planting of Peonies may be begun at the end of the month. These plants are not adapted to the warmer parts of the region.

On the West Coast

Intelligent watering, spraying and weeding are the biggest chores of the month. Fertilizing of all plants in need of this aid also demands regular attention. This is the warmest month in California; in the Northwest an appreciable lowering of temperatures may be expected later in the month.

Sow seeds of Primulas, Cinerarias and Pansies to give plants to set out in beds in October to bloom in early spring. Use a woodsy soil, keep it evenly moist and shade the flats.

If you have not yet sowed seeds of annuals for

Lettuce for fall harvesting may be sown now.

winter and early spring blooming, do so early in August.

Keep Fuchsias well watered and spray their foliage with a fine mist regularly in dry weather. Gardenias, Globe Artichokes and many other plants benefit from similar treatment.

Prune Blackberries, Boysenberries and Youngberries as soon as the crops are gathered.

In the Vegetable Garden. Sow Beans, Lettuce and other quick-growing vegetables for fall harvesting.

Prepare ground now in preparation for fall seeding. In southern California, Tomato plants may still be planted in the open garden for the production of fruits to be harvested this fall.

In the Northwest it is time to plant Savoy Cabbage for fall and winter use and to sow seeds of Cabbage to be harvested in spring.

Sow seeds of early-flowering Sweet Peas late in the month in well-prepared trenches in California.

Camellias and Rhododendrons should be well mulched and watered regularly and thoroughly in dry weather. This is necessary to ensure a crop of flower buds for next year's bloom.

In the Northwest, seedlings of young biennials should be transplanted to outdoor nursery beds before the end of the month.

WHAT TO DO IN SEPTEMBER

The Time to Prepare for Harvesting of Crops and to Transplant

O sweet September, thy first breezes bring
The dry leaf's rustle and the squirrel's laughter,
The cool fresh air whence health and vigor spring
And promise of exceeding joy hereafter.
—George Arnold

September brings the beginning of fall and cooler weather. The pattern of our gardening efforts begins to change from emphasis on purely maintenance chores to stressing activities connected with planting and transplanting.

Planting and preparations for planting occupy much of the gardener's time in September, but by no means all. Harvesting fruits, vegetables and flowers needs attention. The upkeep of plants nearing maturity calls for staking, tying, disbudding and other routine work. In many parts of the country tender plants must be brought indoors or otherwise protected against frost. The propagation of numerous kinds of plants is now in full swing.

This is a good time to review the work of the season—to bring one's garden notebook up to date—to evaluate success and failures and to jot down reminders for future years.

Cold Frames

Cold frames now come into their own again. During the seasons of the year when frost threatens at night they are among the most useful adjuncts of a garden, and even in the warmer parts of the year they have many uses. Consider installing a cold frame if you do not already own one.

Deep frames are splendid now for sheltering Chrysanthemums from frost. Potted specimens may be stood in them, or Chrysanthemums growing in outdoor nursery beds may be lifted and planted fairly closely together in them to complete their blooming under the friendly shelter of glass sash. Of course they must be freely ventilated during the day.

Frames containing cuttings of hardy plants, inserted earlier and now rooted, will need ventilating more freely on warm days; even at night, unless severe frost threatens, a little ventilation may be provided. The idea is to grow the young plants "hard" in preparation for winter.

Potted plants of choice rock garden propagations may be plunged to the rims of their pots in a bed of sand or ashes in a cold frame. Set the plants as closely together as possible and make no attempt to protect them with sash or in other ways until much later than this—until after the ground has frozen for the winter.

Newly planted bulbs of Freesias, Roman Hyacinths, Oxalis, and other kinds that are frost-tender but need cool conditions, may be set in cold frames with the surface soil of the pots or flats covered with a layer of moss or peat moss. There, the bulbs will make good root growth. They must be brought inside before the weather becomes so cold that frost penetrates the frame. By placing mats, shutters or straw on the frames at night in cold weather this date can be materially delayed.

Biennials and perennials to be wintered in frames should be kept as hard as possible. Light frost will not harm them. If the frame sash are placed over them before the weather gets quite cold, there is real danger of softening the plants, so that they are likely to be severely harmed when severe cold weather comes later in the winter. This applies to such a comparatively tender plant as the English Wallflower as well as to hardier kinds such as Pansies, Violas, English Daisies, Canterbury Bells, Foxgloves, Forget-me-nots, Siberian Wallflowers and Sweet Williams.

Lettuce, Spinach, and other vegetable crops that are in cold frames should be grown as hard as possible, but should not be subjected to frost. In cold weather, protect the frames at night by covering them with mats, wooden shutters, or in other suitable manner.

Young plants of Foxgloves in a cold frame, where they will remain until the next spring.

In the Greenhouse

In the greenhouse there is much to do in September. Now every square foot of space is fully occupied and, until the Chrysanthemums are through, we must expect to be a bit crowded. Do not make the mistake, however, of crowding plants that simply must have plenty of light and air around them to succeed. Roses, Carnations and Poinsettias belong here.

Temperatures Need Careful Watching. Too much heat can be as disastrous as too little. Cool greenhouse plants in particular are harmed by this. Ventilate greenhouses containing Chrysanthemums, Carnations and most annuals on all possible occasions and to the fullest extent that is practicable.

Most cool greenhouse plants get along well if the night temperature is 45-50 degrees; most warm greenhouse plants, such as Roses, Poinsettias, Gardenias and Christmas Begonias, if the night temperature is 60 degrees. Intermediate greenhouse plants that prosper in a night temperature of about 55 degrees include many Begonias, Christmas Cactus, African Violets, Ferns of many kinds and Shrimp Plants. In all cases the daytime temperatures may be allowed to rise 5-10 degrees or, in very sunny weather, even 15 degrees higher before much ventilation is given.

All tender plants that are to be grown on in the greenhouse should be brought inside before they are touched by frost. Stevias, winter-flowering Buddleias and Chrysanthemums that have been carried outdoors during the summer belong here.

Time to Pot Them. Christmas Cherries and Christmas Peppers that have been planted in the garden in nursery rows should be lifted and carefully potted in the smallest pots that will comfortably contain their roots during the early part of the month. If the ground is dry, soak it thoroughly a few hours before the plants are dug. Keep the newly potted plants in a "close" cold frame or greenhouse for a week or so after potting and then gradually accustom them to more air and light.

Hydrangeas that have been growing in a nursery bed for the summer should be lifted and potted in early September. After potting treat

Lifted from the garden and potted in September, the Christmas Cherry plant is in full fruit at Christmas.

Cuttings of many kinds of tender plants that are used in the garden for summer display should be inserted in the greenhouse propagating bench in September.

them as advised for Christmas Cherries above, then give them all the light and air possible to ripen the wood before they go dormant and are stored in a cool cellar or protected cold frame until forcing time.

September is a good month to pot up Foxgloves, Polyanthus Primroses, Canterbury Bells, English Wallflowers, Hostas, and other hardy biennial and perennial plants that are to be forced into bloom in cool greenhouses during the winter. After potting they should be plunged to the rims of their pots in a bed of ashes or sand in a cold frame. Shade them for a week or two after potting.

Annuals sown earlier for bloom indoors should be potted, or planted in benches, as soon as they are large enough to require these attentions. Space young annuals so that they do not suffer from crowding. Lack of light soon causes them to grow thin and spindly.

Snapdragons benched from 2½-in. pots during the first week in September will produce flowers for Christmas.

Tender Perennials. September, early in the month preferably, is the time to insert cuttings of a great many tender perennials to be grown for use in next year's outside garden or for use in pots indoors. In this category belong Geraniums, Ageratums, Fuchsias, Heliotropes, Lantanas, Acalyphas, Coleus, Begonias, Abutilons, Verbenas, Salvias, and Petunias that are to be grown from cuttings rather than from seeds.

Plants of tender perennials, such as those mentioned in the paragraph above, that are to be carried over winter either for growing into larger specimens or to provide cuttings later, should be potted before frost. Cut them back about halfway and handle them in the way recommended above for Christmas Cherries.

Bulbs. Bulbs for early forcing—Narcissi,

Freesias and many other bulbs that grow in winter and are dormant in summer should now be taken from their resting quarters, potted and started into new growth.

Caladiums that have been grown in pots as summer foliage plants may now be dried off and the pots stored in a cool, dry place for their resting season.

Carnations will now need disbudding.

Carnations will now be carrying a nice crop of flower buds and will need attention in the matters of disbudding and supporting. The plants will benefit from a light fertilizing.

Sweet Peas sown in September and grown

Roman Hyacinths, Prepared Miniature Hyacinths, Freesias and the like—should be potted just as soon as they can be obtained from the dealer.

Bulbs that have been carried over from last year, of kinds that grow in winter and are dormant in summer, will need planting and starting into growth now. Many of these are South African natives. Here belong Lachenalias, Ornithogalums, Tritonias, Sparaxis, Freesias, Babianas, Ixias, Oxalis, and Ferrarias. Newly acquired bulbs of these kinds should be planted and started.

Summer-growing bulbs that rest in winter, that have not already yet died down naturally, should be encouraged to do so by gradually reducing the water supply and finally withholding it. Kinds that may need this treatment include Hippeastrums (Amaryllis), Caladiums, tuberous Begonias, Achimenes, Gloxinias, and Gloriosas.

Don't Neglect Them. Roses planted in the greenhouse in early June should have made good growth and will benefit from feeding regularly from now until mid-November.

The tying and disbudding of Chrysanthemums will require considerable attention at this time. Do not neglect this.

Leaf mold is the result of composting the leaves of deciduous trees. When partly rotted, it may be rubbed through a sieve to produce a flaky product suitable for mixing in potting soils.

under cool, light conditions will produce flowers from January until late spring.

Annuals of all kinds may be sown this month for late winter and spring bloom. Stocks, Snapdragons, Calendulas, Clarkias, Godetias, annual Chrysanthemums, Phlox Drummondii, Mignonette, Nasturtiums, Hunnemannias, Larkspurs, Nicotianas, Felicias, Gaillardias, Coreopsis, Asters, Ursinias, Linarias, Lupines, and many others are worth growing from September-sown seed.

Begin thinking of the soil, leaf mold and other supplies you will need for the greenhouse this winter. The best loam (soil) is formed by stacking, grass sides down, sod grown on good soil. In making the stack alternate 6-in. layers of sod with 3-in. layers of manure or rich compost and spread a good sprinkling of bone meal or superphosphate over each layer. Leave the top of the heap slightly hollow to catch rain.

House Plants

House plants should now be prepared for winter. Examine those that have been indoors all summer and pick off all dead leaves. If the surface of the soil is packed and hard, scrape a little away and replace it with a rich mixture. Sponge the leaves to remove grime and insects. Examine the plants closely for scale insects, mealybugs and other pests, and, if any are present take prompt and effective steps to eradicate them. It is helpful to wash the plants thoroughly with a forceful stream of water that reaches all parts, including the under surface of the leaves, provided care is taken not to break the foliage. Sponging with a good insecticide or spraying with one is also effective.

Plants that have been outdoors for the summer should be inspected and cleaned as recommended above. They should be brought indoors at least two weeks before the furnace is started so that they can accustom themselves to their new environment before they are subjected to the added difficulties of a dry atmosphere.

Try to give each plant the conditions of light and temperature best suited to its kind.

For Early Flowering. Plant Narcissi of the Paper White, Soleil d'Or and Chinese Sacred Lily varieties in bowls of fiber, pebbles and

Bulbs of Paper White Narcissi planted in pebbles and water soon start into growth and bloom within a few weeks.

water, or in pots of soil for early flowering inside. Plant Roman Hyacinths and Prepared Miniature Hyacinths for early flowering.

Bulbs of Hippeastrums, Gloxinias, Caladiums and tuberous Begonias that have not naturally died down by the end of the month should have their water supply gradually reduced to force them to go dormant. After the foliage has died, keep them quite dry until their season of new growth begins.

If you want them to bloom in winter and early spring, young annuals such as Calendulas, Marigolds, Nasturtiums, Petunias and Ageratums should be lifted from the garden early in the month, carefully potted, kept shaded and lightly sprayed with water until they have recovered from the shock of transplanting, and brought into a sunny, cool sunroom from which frost is excluded.

Begonias, Geraniums, Lantanas, Fuchsias, Heliotropes, Abutilons and other plants of like kinds may be dug from the garden, cut about halfway back, potted in containers just large enough to hold their roots, treated after potting as advised for annuals above; they can then be grown in sunny windows to bloom in late winter and spring.

There is still time to root cuttings of many tender perennials including those mentioned in the paragraph above. English Ivy roots easily from cuttings now.

In the North

The planting of evergreens will be in full swing this month. Make sure that newly planted evergreens are soaked immediately after planting. A mulch of compost, peat moss or rotted manure is helpful when placed around evergreens that are newly planted.

If the weather is at all dry, established evergreens will benefit greatly from periodic waterings. They will survive the winter much more surely if they are not subjected to drought during the fall.

Be sure, when watering Rhododendrons and other kinds with a canopy of foliage that shelters the roots, that the roots actually receive a thorough soaking. This is best achieved by let-

September is a fine time to sow new lawns and repair old ones.

ting the hose, soil soaker, or sprinkler run for a long period on the ground beneath the plants.

Newly planted trees and shrubs of all kinds must be watered regularly if dry conditions prevail.

September is the best month in the year in which to sow new lawns. Choose the first week of the month for this work in more northerly sections, the second or third week in the southerly parts of this region. Good soil preparation is a prerequisite to establishing a good lawn.

Choose dull weather to lift and transplant, from the nursery or reserve border to their flowering locations, Chrysanthemums that are to be used as fillers to give a fall display of color. Do this before the flower buds show much color.

New lawn seed should be rolled immediately after the seed is sown.

If carefully handled, Chrysanthemums can be moved with hardly any noticeable ill effects. They must be watered thoroughly immediately after they are planted in their new quarters.

A final clipping may be given to hedges of Privet early in the month.

Important Preparations. If you plan to plant a new perennial bed or border this fall, the ground should be gotten into condition for planting without further loss of time.

Place orders with nurserymen for the perennials you need. Planting of these may begin the end of the month or early in October.

Old perennial beds may be made over in the fall, and, indeed, should be every third or fourth year. Late September or early October is the time to begin. Carefully heel in (plant closely together temporarily in an unused corner) the plants you dig up from the old border; then, after the soil has been deeply dug and enriched, divide and replant those that you are retaining and set out purchased plants and young plants you have raised that are in nursery beds.

Orders for trees and shrubs that are to be set out this fall should be placed without delay and, of course, getting the bulb order off as early as possible is a "must."

Bulbs. With the exception of Tulips, which perhaps are better planted rather late, all bulbs give the best results when they are set in the ground as soon as they can be obtained from the dealer.

Lily bulbs of many kinds may be planted now. Be sure to plant at the depth most suitable for the particular kind. Lilies that produce all their roots from the bases of the bulbs are planted much more shallowly than those which send roots from the bases of the stems which grow from the tips of the bulbs as well as from the bottoms of the bulbs.

Important Points to Remember. Pick Gourds for winter decorations indoors before they are harmed by frost.

When picking Apples, avoid bruising the fruits. They store best in a temperature of about 45 degrees.

Do not cut down the tops of Asparagus until they have been killed by frost. The longer they remain on the plant in a green condition the more food will be stored in the roots to produce next spring's crop.

Except in the colder parts of the North, fall is the preferred rose-planting season. This is the time to place orders for delivery next month. The same is true of hardy fruit trees and bushes.

Bring Them Inside. As soon as their foliage has been slightly frosted, lift and prepare for storage Dahlias, Cannas, tuberous Begonias,

As soon as their foliage has died or been killed by frost, lift the bulbs of Gladioli.

After they have been dried off and their foliage removed, Gladiolus corms may be stored in bags that permit a free circulation of air around the corms.

Gladioli, Tigridias, Montbretias, Tuberoses and other tender bulbs.

Get all plants that need protection under cover before frost comes. If you lift such plants as Begonias, Geraniums and Coleus from beds and window boxes to plant them in pots to keep them over winter, use well-drained pots and light, sandy soil. Cut the plants back about halfway and keep them in a shaded place and moist atmosphere, such as that of a close, protected cold frame, for a couple of weeks until they have gotten over the shock of being dug up.

Plants of Parsley, Chives and some other herbs may be dug from the garden, potted and set in cold frames, cool greenhouses or even in a sun room to provide fresh pickings through the winter.

In the South

Rose beds should be thoroughly gone over in preparation for the fall crop of bloom. Remove any diseased foliage, prune out any weak wood, shorten very vigorous growths back by about one quarter of their length and apply a dressing of fertilizer.

Dahlias and Chrysanthemums should be fertilized lightly to promote growth and good flowers. Keep Dahlias and Chrysanthemums that need this care disbudded.

Plant Them Now. The planting of Camellias, Hollies, Magnolias and other evergreens may receive attention in September.

Many annuals may be sown outdoors for early summer bloom. Place seeds of Calendulas, Snapdragons, Larkspurs and Pansies in a refrigerator for a couple of weeks before sowing them.

In the lower South, Sweet Peas planted in September may be expected to bloom from Christmas on.

Lawns of seed mixtures containing Kentucky Blue Grass, Fescues and Rye Grass may be planted in September in the upper South.

There is still time to plant Calla Lilies in the lower South.

Bulbs that may be planted now are Alliums, Anemones, Baby Gladioli, Camassias, Chionodoxas, Cooperias, Crocuses, Narcissi, Dutch and Spanish Irises, Freesias, Hyacinths, Ixias, Leucojums, Grape Hyacinths, Lycoris, Ornithogalums, Oxalis, Scillas, Ranunculus, Snowdrops and Watsonias.

Tulips for the lower South must be purchased early and placed in cold storage until December to ensure results.

On the West Coast

September brings the need for soil preparation in readiness for fall planting and seeding. Try to

Chives and Parsley potted from the garden and taken indoors, will supply pickings in winter.

Seedlings of late-sown Cinerarias and Primulas will now be ready for transplanting.

keep well ahead with this work.

In the Northwest this is the best time to sow new lawns and to renovate old ones.

In California it is now time to plant out young Stocks, Snapdragons, Pansies and Calendulas. Shade them lightly after planting.

Transplant seedlings of Cinerarias and Primulas into flats of loose, humus-rich soil as soon as they are large enough to handle comfortably. Grow them in a shaded location.

Chrysanthemums require regular applications of fertilizer until the flower buds begin to show color. Keep the soil in which they grow comfortably moist.

Camellias and Roses. Camellia cuttings may be inserted in September; also cuttings of many other evergreens as well as of a great many other plants.

Roses that are lightly pruned now, that have their faded flowers regularly removed and that are fertilized, sprayed and watered regularly, will bear a superior fall crop of blooms and in mild areas will continue producing well into winter.

Some Need More, Some Less. Continue to water Azaleas and Rhododendrons copiously during dry weather.

In southern California go easy on watering and fertilizing subtropical plants such as Citrus, Hibiscus and Tibouchina. Too much attention to these matters may force a soft, late growth that will be unusually susceptible to frost. In dry regions it is important to water freely fruit trees that are now making their buds for next year.

In the Vegetable Garden. In the warmer parts of the West Coast it is possible to have excellent

In mild climates, seeds of Beet and other hardy vegetables may be sown for winter crops.

winter gardens of Beets, Carrots, Radishes, Spinach, Swiss Chard, Turnips, Kohlrabi and some other vegetables by sowing early in September so that the crops are approaching mature size before the coming of cold weather. Seeds of many annual flowers also give good results if sown at the same time.

For Best Results. Hedges of all kinds may receive their final trimming this month.

Japanese Iris and Siberian Iris that have formed large clumps will benefit from being divided and reset. Peonies may also be transplanted and divided.

Plant Narcissi and other spring-flowering bulbs (except Tulips) as early as stock can be obtained from dealers.

In the Northwest there is still time to lift and divide Primrose plants of various kinds which have grown overlarge.

WHAT TO DO IN OCTOBER

The Month for Cleaning Up the Garden and Attending to Bulbs

And when the silver habit of the clouds
Comes down upon the autumn sun, and with
A sobered gladness the old year takes up
His bright inheritance of golden fruits,
A pomp and pageant fill the splendid scene.
—Henry Wadsworth Longfellow

October is clean-up month in the garden. Now is the time to clear away dead stems and trash from the flower garden and vegetable patch. Debris left until spring provides ideal hide-outs for overwintering pests and diseases.

Old trash, such as Corn stalks and Dahlia stems that may harbor insect pests or soil-borne diseases, should be burned, but all other vegetation should be added to the compost pile and turned into valuable organic matter, later to be returned to the soil.

The leaves of deciduous (nonevergreen) trees and shrubs should be carefully collected and either placed on the general compost pile or

A general cleanup of the garden is in order in October.

Leaf raking is an important fall task. The leaves of all deciduous trees and shrubs should be stacked to make leaf mold or added to the compost heap.

stacked separately to make leaf mold. Good leaf mold is valuable indeed as an ingredient of seed and potting soils. If you have a greenhouse or cold frame, or if you raise house plants, you will find it invaluable.

Except, possibly, in the extreme North it is too early to cover plants for the winter but it is a good plan to be locating supplies of salt hay, evergreen branches, litter or whatever other covering materials you plan to use.

Garden construction of most kinds can be undertaken this month—the making of paths, terraces, rock gardens and other features. There is more time for this now than in spring.

Cold Frames

Cold frames will now be chockablock full of plants. Their care does not differ from that detailed for last month. The two points to bear in mind are to protect any frost-tender plants they

contain from being touched with frost, and to grow hardy plants housed in the frames as cool and sturdy as possible.

In the Greenhouse

In the greenhouse the really difficult growing conditions of the hot summer months are now well behind and it is much easier to maintain environments favorable to the growth of plants. October normally is a sunny month, and with good light and favorable temperatures plants prosper.

This is particularly true for cool-climate kinds such as Cinerarias, Primulas, Cyclamens and Calceolarias, as well as for annuals being grown for winter and spring blooom.

Shading should be removed from the roofs of most greenhouses by the end of the month, and for those plants that will stand it, earlier. Nearly all plants indoors require all light possible from now on. Remove the shading gradually; sudden exposure to light much stronger than that to which they have been accustomed can be harmful.

Ventilate on really warm days, and the ventilators of cool houses should be opened as freely as possible whenever this may be done without harm to the plants. Guard against sweeping cold drafts being directed onto tender growth.

Watering. As the days shorten, watering in the greenhouse needs more careful attention. Overwatering must be guarded against, yet plants in need must not be permitted to suffer from lack of moisture. So far as is practicable, complete all watering in the forenoon and only give water later in the day in cases of clear need. Take great care that foliage is not wetted on dull days, or so late in the day that it will not dry before dusk.

In the Chrysanthemum greenhouse a drier atmosphere must be maintained than earlier, otherwise Mildew disease is apt to spread rapidly, particularly if the plants are at all crowded.

Continue to feed Chrysanthemums with soluble fertilizers until the color of the petals shows. Do not crowd the plants more than absolutely necessary, otherwise their lower leaves will yellow.

Christmas Begonias will begin producing flower buds. These should be picked off while quite small, until 5-6 weeks before the plants are wanted in full bloom. Careful staking and neat tying are essential if these plants are to look their best.

Do not spray Christmas Begonias overhead any more but dampen the benches between the pots frequently to maintain a humid atmosphere. Wet the floors and other surfaces in the Begonia greenhouse from time to time for the same purpose.

Nerines in choice variety bloom in the fall and are accommodating plants well suited to the amateur's greenhouse. A greenhouse from which frost is just kept suits them. Too-high temperatures, particularly at night, are ruinous. Now that these plants are growing freely they will need an abundance of water and regular fertilizing from the time the flowers fade until the bulbs go naturally to rest in spring.

Cyclamens. Allow Cyclamens to come into bloom as fast as they naturally form flowers; if it is important to have them later, the season of bloom can be somewhat delayed by picking off the earliest flower buds.

Cyclamens that are to be flowered in March should be transferred to their flowering pots by the end of October.

Don't Neglect These Plants. Poinsettias need all possible sunshine. Do not crowd them. Keep the night temperature at 55-58 degrees, the day temperature not above 65 degrees. Avoid drafts.

Seeds of Calendulas and Stocks sown now will provide plants that flower in March. This is a good month to sow seeds of Larkspur and Schizanthus. Snapdragons sown now will give plants to set in benches after the Chrysanthemums are through.

Cinerarias make roots rapidly now and must not be allowed to become pot-bound until they are in their final containers. They may need potting into larger pots as frequently as every 2-3 weeks at this season.

Hydrangeas, lifted and potted earlier, should be placed in a cool, airy place where they will get light but will not be subjected to frost. Never permit the soil to dry out while the plants are in storage.

Freesias and other bulbs requiring similar treatment such as Lachenalias, Ixias, Babianas and Sparaxis, that have been in cold frames will be well started into growth before the end of the month. They must be brought into a cool, sunny greenhouse before there is any danger of their being frosted.

Potting Hyacinth bulbs for forcing.

Hardy Bulbs. This is the important month for planting Dutch bulbs and other hardy kinds for forcing into bloom during the winter and spring. Hyacinths, Daffodils and other Narcissi, Tulips, Dutch and Spanish Irises and such lesser bulbs as Scillas, Crocuses, Grape Hyacinths, Chionodoxas, and Snowdrops are included here. So are many Lilies.

All hardy bulbs, after planting, must either be buried outdoors or placed in a root cellar or other cool place for several weeks before they are brought into the greenhouse. It is most important that they form good root systems in temperatures approximating 40 degrees before they are subjected to higher temperatures to force them into bloom.

When potting hardy bulbs for forcing, and when planting them in flats, use a well-drained soil and well-drained containers.

House Plants

House plants require more careful attention in all matters affecting their growth as days become shorter, light less intense, and the indoor atmosphere in most rooms drier and less satisfactory for the growth of plants.

Plants stood on shallow, broad trays filled with pebbles, cinders, sand or moss that is kept always moist, benefit from the humidity provided by the moist surface. Where many plants are

Special care in watering house plants is now important. The soil of most kinds should be kept moderately moist at all times.

grown together in a window they are apt to be more successful than solitary specimens because the moisture given off by a lot of foliage moistens the air locally.

Except in the case of plants that are dormant, and are without foliage, keep the soil of all house plants evenly moist, but not constantly saturated. When you give water provide enough to saturate the entire body of soil thoroughly, then give no more until it is nearly dry again.

With Cacti and other succulents be particularly careful not to overwater, but do not allow them to dry completely. In their desert homes these plants extend their roots for unbelievable distances and are usually able to obtain a little moisture from the soil or from dews. When a Cactus is grown in a pot indoors, these natural sources are not available to the plant; you must apply water to the soil occasionally even in winter.

The Christmas Cactus will bloom more surely if you rest it from early October until mid-November by keeping it in a fairly cool room and giving it little or no water.

In the North

Lifting Bulbs. In the North the lifting of summer-flowering bulbs should not be long delayed. Most kinds may be left until they are touched with frost, and those that retain their foliage in a green condition until late should certainly be so handled; however, if killing frost is late in coming, bulbs whose foliage has yellowed may be dug before frost, dried and prepared for storage in a manner appropriate to their kind. Tuberous Begonias and Gladioli are examples of this latter group that often turn yellow and need lifting before frost.

Carefully inspect all bulbs lifted for storage and discard any that are diseased. When digging, be careful not to spear the bulbs with the prong of a fork or in other ways damage them. Every wound affords a chance for disease organisms to enter. When digging Ismenes (Peruvian Daffodils), take special care not to break the roots more than is absolutely necessary.

Lift Tuberose bulbs in clumps and do not divide them until planting time or plant them next year without dividing.

Montbretias, too, should be lifted in clumps (unless they are to be left outdoors under a heavy mulch) and stored in slightly moist soil that is not permitted to quite dry out during the winter.

In many sections, killing frost will not have arrived by the beginning of the month and there is still time to bring in tender plants from the outdoors; but there is not much time—delay no longer.

Planting Time. This is a great planting season. Bulbs of many kinds should be set in the earth now and the planting of deciduous (winter leaf-losing) trees and shrubs should be at its height. Fruit trees and bushes and Roses also may be planted. It is getting late to transplant ever-greens; if you intend to move any this fall, do so early in the present month.

With the exception of Tulips, which many gardeners prefer to set out in early November, all bulbs planted in fall are better for being placed in the ground as early as possible. Nothing is gained, and something may be lost, by keeping them out of the earth longer then necessary. Keep in mind that bulbs root downwards; the quality of the soil beneath them is more important than that of the soil above them.

When planting trees and shrubs, remember the supreme importance of good soil preparation. These plants are quite permanent installations. Once they are established, you cannot improve the subsurface layers of soil; all you can do is add fertilizers, etc., at the top. Make the holes considerably larger than the spread of the roots and sufficiently deep to set the tree or shrub very slightly deeper than it was previously. Improve the soil in the bottom of the hole by forking it deeply and adding generous amounts of manure, compost or other suitable organic matter, and some bone meal. Most trees and shrubs, as well as Roses and fruit trees and bushes, flourish in well-drained soil only; if water seeps into the planting holes and they remain partly filled, the need for drainage is indicated. Pack the soil firmly about the roots of trees and shrubs when planting them.

In very cold, northerly sections the planting of Roses is best done in spring, but, in many parts of the North, fall planting is much to be preferred.

A few trees and shrubs, notably those with fleshy roots, such as Magnolias and any that are slightly tender, such as Albizzias, are better when spring-planted; but the vast majority of trees and shrubs thrive if planted at the season when they lose their leaves, and the gardener usually has more time to do a good job of planting in October than he has in spring.

In the vegetable garden, Parsnips, Jerusalem Artichokes, Salsify and Carrots may be left in the ground all winter. If this plan is followed, cover them with a heavy layer of leaves or straw so that the ground will not freeze hard enough to make digging in severe weather impossible.

Dig the roots of Witloof Chicory and set them in boxes of sand or sandy soil in a well-protected frame or root cellar until they are needed for forcing.

Celery lifted from the garden and planted closely together in a protected cold frame, well watered and kept dark, will provide good table material for a long time.

Parsley plants dug very carefully and planted in pots and plunged in a cold frame, or planted directly in sandy soil in the bottom of the frame and well watered and shaded for a week or two, will soon recover and will give good picking in spring. Chives may be handled in similar manner.

Vegetables in winter storage require different conditions. Many keep best in a humid atmosphere with the temperature between 35-40 degrees. Here belong Potatoes, Beets, Carrots, Parsnips, Salsify, Turnips, Winter Radishes, Cabbage and Celery. Others, such as Squash, and Pumpkins, keep best in temperatures of 40-60 degrees with a dry atmosphere. Onions and dry Beans store best in a dry atmosphere where the temperature approximates 32 degrees.

Roses. Just before the ground freezes for the winter, hill soil about the bases of the Roses. If the bushes are planted close together, the best plan is to bring the soil from an outside source, but if they are widely spaced sufficient soil can be pulled from the surface of the bed to mound about the Roses. The roots of the Roses must not be exposed. Hill soil to a minimum height of eight inches. Before hilling soil about Hybrid Tea and Floribunda Roses, cut back any tall growths to a height of 24-30 in.

Protect standard (tree type) Roses by laying them down and covering them with soil, or by any other approved method; do the same for Climbing Roses in sections where they are not reliably winter-hardy.

Young trees and newly planted trees may be girdled by rabbits during the winter. To prevent this, surround the lower parts of the trunks to a height of 3-4 ft. with closely woven wire netting.

Garden Equipment. Take in all garden furniture and, when outdoor work slackens, repair and paint it in preparation for spring.

Clean and put away in dry storage all garden tools and equipment that are no longer needed. Sprayers, lawn mowers, fertilizer spreaders, wheelbarrows, etc., should all be carefully cleaned and their unpainted steel and iron surfaces wiped with an oiled rag as an extra precaution against rust. Hand tools should be carefully cleaned and similarly protected.

Wind your hoses on reels or other devices that prevent kinking and place them in storage away from furnaces or other sources of dry heat.

Protect Your Strawberries and Raspberries. When an inch or two of frost is in the ground, and before the night temperatures drop to 20 degrees, cover the Strawberry bed with clean straw, salt hay or dry leaves to a depth of 3-4 in.

A heavy mulch placed around Raspberries now is beneficial.

Lawns. Keep leaves raked from the lawn. Do not permit them to gather in areas and mat down. If grass continues to grow, mow it but do not cut to a height lower than two inches.

Boxwood and other evergreens are much less likely to suffer from winter injury if the surface of the soil around them, for the distance the roots spread, is protected with a heavy mulch of littery manure, leaves, straw, salt hay or peat moss before the ground freezes, and if the bushes have been copiously watered regularly during dry fall weather. If the soil is now dry, soak it deeply around evergreens.

Chrysanthemums. Now that outdoor Chrysanthemums are at their gorgeous best, it is a good time to visit public displays, nurseries and private gardens where they are grown, as well as Chrysanthemum Flower Shows, in order to become acquainted with the best and most useful varieties.

After Chrysanthemums are killed by frost, cut them down in preparation for winter. Make sure that all are correctly and clearly labeled. It is annoying not to know the names of the plants in your garden.

All tools should be thoroughly cleaned and their metal parts wiped with an oily rag before they are stored for the winter.

Chrysanthemums bloom outdoors in October. This is the time to select varieties for next year's garden.

In cold localities and on heavy soils, Chrysanthemums may need the protection of a cold frame to live through the winter. Where this is desirable, dig the plants up and plant them in the frame when they are through blooming.

In the South

Roses should be in good bloom this month. Fertilizing should be discontinued except in the lower South where the bushes should be given one good feeding, be mulched and brought into the winter in full bloom. If the finest blooms are wanted, disbudding of Hybrid Tea varieties should receive attention.

Rye Grass may now be sown for winter lawns. Where this is sown over lawns of permanent Bermuda Grass, do not scatter the seed too thickly. Five pounds of Rye Grass seed to each 1,000 sq. ft. is sufficient. The seeding rate, for temporary lawns that are to consist entirely of Rye Grass, is 10 lb. to each 1,000 sq. ft.

Camellia cuttings taken this month and planted in a cold frame or greenhouse should give good results. Seeds of Camellias, which are now ripe, may also be sown in a cold frame. The seeds will germinate next spring. Protect them from rodents. This may be done by lining the frame with fine wire mesh or hardware cloth, extending 6-8 in. into the ground.

Tubers of Ranunculus and Poppy (St. Brigid and similar types) Anemones are to be planted this month in good, sandy, woodsy soil that is well drained.

Young Azaleas raised from cuttings inserted earlier will probably be well enough rooted by now to be planted individually in 3-in. pots. Use a sandy, peaty soil and, after potting, plunge the pots nearly to their rims in peat moss in a cold frame.

No more pruning than absolutely necessary should be done until spring. Seed pods not wanted for decoration or propagation should be removed promptly.

Spring bulbs to plant include all of those mentioned in "What to Do in September." In the lower South, Narcissi of the Paper White, Soleil d'Or and Chinese Sacred Lily varieties thrive. Gloriosas, Alstroemerias and Gladioli may also be planted in the lower South.

Perennials of almost all kinds that require dividing or transplanting may be given attention. Plant new perennials. Give late-flowering Chrysanthemums an application of fertilizer before their flower buds show color.

Perennials that are through blooming should be cleaned. Cut back stems and tops and, if these are diseased, burn them; otherwise they may be consigned to the compost heap. Good sanitation in the garden is important. This is an appropriate season to give the matter attention.

Prepare soil now, and prepare it deeply and generously, for planting Sweet Peas next month.

Do not be in too much of a hurry to plant Roses even though they are obtainable from dealers. November or December is time enough to plant. You may, however, to good advantage, get the beds ready at your earliest convenience.

Easter Lilies and other kinds of these beautiful bulbous plants may be set in the ground as soon as their bulbs are obtainable from dealers.

In many parts of the South, October is likely to be a notably dry month. Be sure to water regularly and abundantly all plants that require moisture. Camellias, Azaleas and other evergreens are vulnerable to dryness. Newly planted plants soon suffer if watering is neglected. Seedbeds including newly seeded lawns must not be permitted to become dry.

Order fruit trees, Roses and ornamental trees and shrubs required for November and December planting.

On the West Coast

October is an active planting month. Bulbs for spring bloom should be gotten into the ground with a minimum of delay; perennials of all kinds may be set out; the planting of evergreens may proceed.

In California this is an ideal time to start new lawns and improve old ones.

Cool-season vegetables such as Lettuce, Peas, Turnips, Rutabagas, Kohlrabi, Carrots and Kale may be sown in mild-climate areas; Cabbage, Cauliflower and Broccoli plants may be set out.

Poppy Anemones of the St. Brigid and similar types, Persian Ranunculus and winter-blooming

Young plants of Cabbage. Cauliflower and Broccoli may now be set out.

tonias, Babianas, Watsonias, Lachenalias and Gloriosas and Ixias.

Pot or tub subtropical plants for use indoors in regions where they are likely to suffer seriously during the winter.

Cuttings of Roses may be rooted in October.

Summer bulbs such as Gladioli, tuberous Begonias and Tigridias that are to be stored over winter should be lifted now and prepared for storage.

Plants of Snapdragons, Pansies, Stocks and other annuals may still be set out in milder regions.

Sow seeds of wild flowers after the ground has been well moistened by heavy rains.

Renovate Bermuda Grass lawns by raking out the old grass, fertilizing or top-dressing and watering freely.

Oxalis may now be planted, and, in regions where they are hardy, such bulbs as Freesias, Tri-

WHAT TO DO IN NOVEMBER
When Most Outdoor Garden Activity Ends, But Greenhouse Work Continues

When chill November's surly blasts
Made fields and forests bare.
—Robert Burns

In all sections of the United States and Canada pressure of garden work now lets up somewhat, and in the coldest parts practically ceases. The gardener easily keeps busy, unless, and until, freezing of the soil puts an end to nearly all outdoor activities; then, if he has a greenhouse, he finds plenty to do indoors.

Always there is need to look after bulbs and other plants in storage, to care for equipment, to bring one's notebook up to date and to catch up on garden reading.

Cold Frames

Cold frames should be made snug for the winter. A light cover of salt hay or leaves scattered inside the frame over perennials and biennials gives added protection from low temperatures and helps, by shading the soil, to keep the root temperatures fairly uniform.

When cold frames are located in a sheltered

After the ground has frozen, spread a light covering of salt hay or of dry leaves over plants in cold frames to give additional protection to the plants inside.

To protect somewhat tender plants cold frames may be insulated by building an outer frame of boards around them and packing the space between with straw, hay or leaves.

place and well banked around with leaves, straw or other insulating material, and covered on cold nights with thick mats or wooden shutters, comparatively tender plants can be overwintered satisfactorily even in cold sections of the country. Frames less well-protected are suitable for hardy plants such as most flower garden biennials.

Ventilate with judgment, avoiding extremes of cold and warmth, remembering that on sunny days the temperature under a glass sash can soon get too high if ventilation is not provided.

Sweet Peas sown this month in pots plunged to their rims in a bed of sand, ashes or peat moss in a cold frame, and then covered with a mulch of an inch or two of peat moss, will give fine plants for setting out in the open garden in early spring and will bear early flowers.

Chrysanthemums, Kniphofias and any other perennials that are needed for early spring propagation, or that are slightly tender, winter well in cold frames if set in very sandy soil and watered in immediately.

In the Greenhouse

If this was not done in summer, you may find opportunity to give the structure a thorough cleaning after the Chrysanthemums are finished. All woodwork should be scrubbed, all glass washed down, brickwork and stonework whitewashed, debris removed from under the benches and new ashes or gravel placed there. Gravel on benches on which pots stand should be washed or replaced with new material.

Now that the sun's light is less brilliant and is still diminishing in intensity, shade on the greenhouse is no longer required. Even the most tender plants will benefit from full exposure after the end of November.

The increased use of fire heat necessary to maintain adequate temperatures increases the problem of maintaining within the greenhouse a sufficiently humid atmosphere. This is particularly true where tropical plants are grown. Wetting the paths and under the benches several times a day is a necessity in such houses. No such regular damping is required in houses where cool-temperature plants are grown, but occasional dampings on sunny days are usually advantageous.

It is not too late to pot Tulips and Hyacinths for late flowering; hardy Lilies potted at this

Christmas Begonias may be propagated from leaf cuttings taken off before the plants are used for display.

time, carried in a cold frame and protected with a heavy layer of leaves, salt hay or straw, and brought into the greenhouse after they are well rooted, will provide good plants to bloom in late spring.

Leaf cuttings taken from Christmas Begonias should be inserted in sand in a warm propagating case now to provide plants that will bloom next year. They will root more readily if the temperature of the sand is about 75 degrees— five degrees warmer than the air. Avoid overwatering the leaf cuttings.

As soon as bench-grown Chrysanthemums are out of the way, you may plant out from small pots Snapdragons and Calendulas, both of which thrive in old Chrysanthemum soil. Other possibilities are Stocks, Leptosynes and winter-flowering Pansies.

Do not let moisture collect in the centers of plants of Primula malacoides. If you do, they are very likely to rot.

For Early Blooms. Paper White and Soleil d'Or Narcissi that have made good root growth may be brought at intervals of 10-14 days into a 50-degree night temperature greenhouse. Under these conditions they will soon bloom. Roman Hyacinths handled in the same way will bloom for Christmas.

Retarded Lily of the Valley pips, potted or planted in boxes and placed in a 50-60-degree night temperature, will bloom in 3-4 weeks.

Give all plants plenty of room at this season. If you crowd them unduly they will shade each other and become weak and spindly.

House Plants

House plants during the present month need routine attention in the matter of watering. Take care that none get so dry that their leaves wilt or their stems shrivel, but refrain from watering so often that the soil is kept in a constant boglike condition.

Go very easy with fertilizing now. Most plants will not need that attention, but pot-bound old foliage plants with plenty of leaves, such as Ferns, Dracaenas, Fatshederas and Philodendrons, may be given dilute liquid fertilizer twice a month.

Light and Heat. At night it is apt to be very much colder close to a window than it is towards the center of the room. Move tender plants away from windows on cold nights, or pull down the shades and place a few sheets of paper between the window and the plants.

See that your plants get all possible sunlight now. Keep them away from hot radiators and other sources of dry heat.

Cold drafts are extremely bad for house plants. Some, such as Poinsettias, drop leaves at once if they are exposed, others show no immediate effect but are permanently harmed.

Long spindly growth is a sure indication that your plants are getting insufficient light, that the temperatures are too high, or that both conditions prevail.

In the North

November may be regarded as the first of the winter months; in some sections really severe weather is sure to come, and in others it may.

Hurry to complete all planting operations. Trees, shrubs, Roses, perennials and bulbs that are to be planted this fall and are not yet in their places should be set out without delay.

Tulips should be planted in early November. Set them at an even depth in a well-dug and fertilized soil that is in a nice, crumbly condition.

If you have ordered Lily bulbs for planting outdoors, and they may not arrive before the

November is the ideal time in most sections to plant Tulip bulbs.

ground freezes hard, cover the area where they are to go with a thick layer of leaves, straw or salt hay, with a few planks or branches placed on top, to prevent its blowing away. This will keep the ground soft and make late planting easily possible.

The fall cleanup of the garden should be completed. Assemble all plant wastes that are suitable for converting into compost and form them into neat heaps. Fallen leaves may be used in the general compost pile or be segregated and converted into leaf mold (which is compost made from the leaves of nonevergreen trees, without the inclusion of any other plant materials). Do not add tough evergreen leaves, such as those of Rhododendrons or Pines, to the leaf-mold pile, and only in small amounts, if at all, to the general compost pile.

Clean gutters and drains of fallen leaves that may impede their functions. Do not permit leaves to lie for long periods in masses on the lawn.

Drain garden pools before frost. Tropical Wa-ter Lilies and other tender aquatics should have been taken indoors before this. Hardy Water Lilies may be carried over winter by removing the tubs containing them (without disturbing the roots in the soil) to a cool cellar; or by leaving them in their tubs in the bottom of the drained pool and covering them with 2-3 ft. of leaves or straw with boards on top of them; or by burying them in their containers in the garden, covering them with a foot of soil and a good mulch of leaves or straw. The idea is to keep them cool and moist and to prevent frost from reaching them.

Proceed with basic soil-improvement work until frost makes further effort impossible. Fall digging or plowing of land not sown to Winter Rye, provided the surface is left in rough clods, is particularly beneficial to heavy (clayey) soil. This is a good time to turn under coarse organic material. Fresh manure, Corn stalks, half-rotted leaves, partly decayed compost, etc., can all be buried now with good effect. Such material does not have to be nearly as decomposed now as it

A good start for spring planting may be had by spading the ground in the fall.

should be for incorporating with the soil in spring.

Cuttings from Trees and Shrubs. The propagation of many kinds of evergreens, such as Yews, Boxwood, English Ivy, Hollies, Junipers and Aucubas, by means of cuttings inserted in a propagating bench in a cool greenhouse, may be undertaken now with every prospect of success. Take the cuttings before really severe freezing weather.

Hardwood cuttings of all kinds of deciduous trees and shrubs susceptible to that method of propagation—and most kinds are—may be made this month, tied in bundles and buried in sand in a cold frame or outdoors. In early spring they are taken from the sand and planted outdoors in nursery rows.

Protection from Wind and Sun. In many areas it is necessary to provide special protection against sweeping wind and intense winter sun for slightly tender evergreens such as Boxwood, and for newly planted evergreens. It is well to install such protection before the ground freezes too hard and before damaging winds can do their harm. Screens of burlap or branches of Pine or other suitable evergreens, stuck into the

The surface of ground turned over in fall should be left rough so that the maximum benefit of winter frost is received.

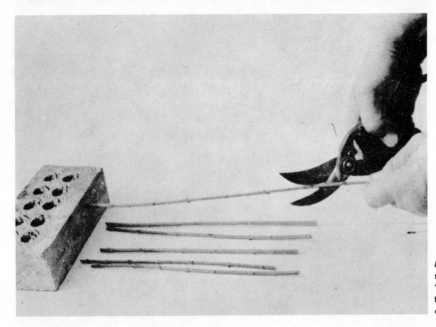

Making hardwood cuttings of shrubs. The brick is used as a "stop" against which the ends of the cuttings are placed while they are cut in equal lengths.

ground about the plants to be protected, are satisfactory. These types of protection are especially useful for evergreens planted in drafty locations near buildings. Such protection is an addition to the mulching mentioned under "What to Do in October."

Applying Mulches. After the ground is frozen to a depth of 3-4 in., a mulch of littery manure,

Before the ground freezes solidly, protective screens of burlap should be placed around evergreens likely to suffer from winter sun and wind.

leaves or other suitable material should be placed on beds of Hybrid Tea and Floribunda Roses as well as other kinds that are somewhat tender. This mulch should cover the mounds of soil hilled about the Roses for winter protection and fill the hollows between as well.

Do not make the mistake of applying winter protection to Roses, perennials and other plants too early. Many beginners labor under the delusion that the chief purpose of winter mulches is to keep the plants warm. Actually, it is to keep the soil temperatures as uniform as possible, to prevent rapid and violent fluctuations, and to reduce the danger of root breakage and other damage that result from alternate freezing and thawing.

Winter protective mulches should be put on after a continued cold spell sets in and after the ground is frozen to a depth of 3-4 in. Don't cover plants at the first cold "snap."

Just when to apply winter covering will depend upon locality and prevailing weather conditions. It is better to be somewhat late than too early. Make sure in advance that you have covering material at hand to be put on when needed —this month, next month or, perhaps, not until the beginning of January.

Cover lightly rather than heavily and use material that admits air and will not pack down

Salt hay, spread out and weighted down with pieces of brushwood, is an excellent winter protection for rock-garden plants.

tightly under the influence of rain and snow. Salt hay, littery manure, cut Corn stalks and dry leaves are good covers. Branches of evergreens are excellent for laying over perennials that retain their foliage all winter, such as Dianthus, evergreen Candytuft and Alyssum saxatile. Take great care not to cover the centers of leaf-retaining plants that form rosettes such as Foxgloves and Canterbury Bells.

Pruning. If you find it necessary to prune a sizable branch from a tree at this time of the year, it is well to leave a stub several inches long; remove this in early spring and then paint the cut with tree wound paint.

In the South

In the South this is a busy month. Preparations for the fall planting of trees and shrubs are under way. Bulbs not yet in the ground should be planted at once (except Tulips, in sections where refrigerated bulbs must be used).

Send away orders for trees, shrubs, fruit trees and bushes, and Roses that are to be planted late this month or next month.

November and the following month are good times to plant all kinds of fruit trees and bushes in the South.

Perennials of nearly all kinds can be set out and can be divided and transplanted in November.

As soon as early-flowering Camellias are through blooming, as they soon will be in the lower South, give them an application of a specially prepared Camellia fertilizer or some other approved kind.

Begin mowing newly planted Rye Grass that has been overplanted on permanent lawns, or that has been seeded to give pure Rye Grass lawns, as soon as it is 2 in. high. Use a sharp mower.

Hardwood cuttings of many shrubs and trees may be planted now in a cold frame or directly outdoors.

Lifting a large Day Lily plant preparatory to dividing and replanting it.

Two spading forks, pushed back to back into the root clump and then pried apart, provide an effective way of dividing many perennials.

Divisions of a Day Lily ready for replanting.

In the Vegetable Garden. In the lower South, sow Carrots, Beets, Broccoli, Cabbage, Brussels Sprouts, Celery, Collards, Swiss Chard, Kale, Lettuce, Onions, English Peas, Radishes, Rutabagas, Parsley and Turnips for harvesting in winter and early spring.

In the middle South, sow Lettuce, Radishes, Spinach, Endive, Cabbage, and Kale. Plant Onion sets and young plants of Cabbage and Collards, as well as Asparagus.

In the upper South, Lettuce, Cabbage and Onion seed may be sown in cold frames to give plants for transplanting to the garden later. Asparagus, Rhubarb, Onion sets, Radishes and Spinach may be planted and sown in the open garden.

Annual flowers in great variety may be seeded in the lower South. In other sections outdoor sowings of hardier kinds made late enough so that they will not germinate until early spring, are in order. Kinds to sow include Larkspurs, Sweet Peas, Poppies, Phlox Drummondii and Cornflowers. Pansy seed sown now, after having been kept in the refrigerator for a week or two, will give plants that will flower in early spring. Sow them in a cool, shaded frame.

On the West Coast

On the West Coast, bulb planting may be continued. In many parts it is now time to set out deciduous trees and shrubs including fruits and Roses.

In colder sections, thought must be given to affording protection to plants that are likely to be harmed by low temperatures.

In the northern parts, sow seeds of hardy annuals where they are to bloom. Cut back Snapdragon plants and leave them to bloom a second year.

In the Northwest a thorough cleanup of the garden should be undertaken in preparation for winter.

Continue to prepare ground for fall and spring planting as long as conditions permit.

If rains are late in California, do not fail to water liberally all actively growing plants, particularly Roses and Camellias.

Sowings of Peas, Lettuce, Beets, Turnips and

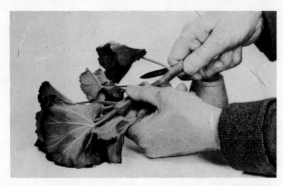

Cuttings of Geraniums and many other tender perennials made now and inserted in a greenhouse propagating bed root readily.

Rutabagas may be made in southern California.

Cuttings of Geraniums, Heliotropes, Coleus, Lobelias and many other plants root easily now in a greenhouse or frame.

In California, sow Sweet Peas, plant out Cinerarias, Primulas, Pansies, and other plants for winter display. Stake Snapdragons and Stocks.

Keep after slugs and snails. Repeated baiting produces the best results. Watch out for other diseases and pests. Garden sanitation—the removal of dead foliage and blossoms and other debris—is an important contribution to pest control.

WHAT TO DO IN DECEMBER

At Last the Gardener May Relax and Enjoy His Garden Library

Autumn to winter, winter into spring,
Spring into summer, summer into fall,
So rolls the changing year, and so we change;
Motion so swift, we know not that we move.
—Dinah Mulock Craik

The gardener can now take things easier than during almost any other month. Once the outdoor garden is buttoned up for winter, there is little to do outside in northern gardens, and even in the southern United States tasks are less numerous and usually less pressing than at most other times.

This is a good time to catch up on horticultural reading. Enjoy your garden library. Acquaint yourself with the new books offered. Visit your public library and look over their stock of garden books—and don't neglect the older ones. There is a mine of good information contained in the best old books.

Check to make sure that you are subscribing to one or more gardening magazines and, for Christmas, why not give garden books and subscriptions to garden magazines to your friends who are horticulturally minded?

Cold Frames

Cold frames require careful attention. Snow that falls on them forms a good protective blanket. Do not remove it so long as the weather is cold. In mild weather, airing frames is important. Prop the sash up a few inches at their lee end for an hour or so whenever possible.

Watering should be done if the soil is approaching a too-dry condition, but only during spells of warm weather, and then, if possible, during the morning.

When the sash are not covered with snow, see that coverings are placed over those at night that require this added protection.

In the Greenhouse

Poinsettias will be in full flower fairly early in the month. The night temperature in which these plants are grown may now be dropped to 55 degrees but not lower.

When preparing Poinsettias for Christmas use, a few branches of Mountain Laurel stuck into the pots or pans will provide foliage if the Poinsettia leaves have dropped off the lower parts of the stems.

Easter Lilies may be planted this month. Time

needed to produce flowers depends somewhat upon variety and temperature at which they are grown; but most take about a hundred days from planting to bloom in a warm greenhouse.

Hyacinths, Tulips and Narcissi that were specially prepared for early forcing by the grower before they were purchased and were bought as "precooled" bulbs may be brought into the greenhouse from the plunging bed in the cold frame or outdoors at any time now. Keep the pots in complete darkness for a week after bringing them indoors, to induce longer stems. Place Hyacinths in light when the shoots are 5 in. tall, Tulips and Narcissi when they are 3 in. tall.

Carnation cuttings inserted now will give plants in 4-in. pots by June, ready for planting in benches. The strongest side shoots on the flower stems make the best cuttings. Shade the newly planted cuttings for 3-4 weeks after planting.

More About Temperatures. The temperatures in greenhouses where tropical plants are grown may be kept somewhat lower now than earlier in the year. A night temperature of 58-60 with a 5-10 degree rise during the daytime, and a little more when the weather is sunny, is sufficient.

A 45-degree night temperature is ample for Carnations and cool greenhouse annuals. Primulas and Cinerarias also thrive under this condition, as do Christmas Cherries, Christmas Peppers, winter-flowering Buddleias, and Freesias.

Not much potting will be necessary this month but annuals, including Cinerarias, Primulas and Calceolarias, that are needed for late winter bloom, should be placed in containers of the size that will accommodate them in the flowering stage.

Plants of Chrysanthemums that are through blooming and that are needed for stock should be cut back and kept "on the dry side" in a cool light greenhouse to give cuttings later. Spray with an insecticide to keep them free of insects.

Sow seed of Stocks to give flowers in late winter.

House Plants

Plants with large leaves and smooth foliage such as Philodendrons, Dracaenas, Palms, Rub-

ber Plants, Fatshederas and English Ivy benefit greatly if, at intervals, their leaves are washed on both sides with a sponge dipped in soapy water and squeezed out. This removes grime and lets the pores of the leaf "breathe" more freely.

Examine Hippeastrum (Amaryllis) bulbs and, as soon as a new growth is detected pushing out from near the tips, soak the soil in water, top-dress or repot, according to the needs of the individual bulb, and place in a sunny position where the temperature is about 70 degrees. Repeat this with other Hippeastrum bulbs whenever they show signs of starting into new growth, as they will do at intervals during the next two months or so.

Hoya carnosa at this time of the year should be kept in a cool situation with the soil nearly, but not quite, dry.

Begin watering plants of the Christmas Cactus with fair freedom onwards from the beginning of the month. Keep them in full sun in a moderately warm room.

Terrariums that receive direct sunshine soon become overheated, and drops of moisture form on the inside of the glass. At the first sign of this, ventilate the terrarium more freely.

Seeds of Grapefruit or Orange, sown in well-drained pots of sandy soil as they are taken fresh from the fruit without drying, soon produce attractive green-leaved plants.

Poinsettias and other Christmas gift plants should be watered regularly, kept out of drafts and not exposed to either excessively low or excessively high temperatures.

Gift plants received at Christmas should be carefully tended to get the most value from them. Keep them out of drafts and away from cold windows at night and water them often enough to keep their soil always moist but not constantly saturated.

In the North

In the North, outdoor work is at a minimum. Read "What to Do in November" to be sure that you have not overlooked details concerned with putting the garden to bed. Everything should be snug and shipshape before the severest weather arrives, but do not put winter covering in place too early—not before the ground is frozen to a depth of 3-4 in., which in mild parts of your region may mean not until after Christmas.

It is well to make sure that sizable, newly planted trees are secured with guy wires to pegs driven well into the ground to prevent them from being blown over or loosened by winter storms. Thread the wire through a piece of old hose where it passes around the trunk or the branch of a tree.

Pruning. Where old, overgrown shrubs are in need of renovation, corrective pruning may be begun and continued, whenever weather permits, until new growth begins in spring.

Grapes may be pruned now, except in extremely cold regions, where they are likely to be partly killed back in winter. In such areas it is better to delay pruning until February or even March.

If catalogues are desired from either foreign or domestic seedsmen or nurserymen, and you are not on their mailing lists, request them without further delay.

In the South

The tasks to be done this month vary considerably with the locality. In the upper South the work to be done does not differ materially from that which needs doing in gardens in the North, except that it is practicable to keep on with planting and to continue turning over ground in readiness for spring, and to push on with garden construction work until a later date. In the lower South, December is an active planting and seeding season.

Trees, Shrubs, and Vines. Roses, trees, ornamental and fruit-bearing trees and shrubs, and Grape vines may be set out this month.

Evergreens may now be transplanted. After they are moved, water them thoroughly and mulch the soil around them.

Hardwood cuttings of deciduous (winter leaf-losing) shrubs may be made and planted in a sheltered border or buried in sand, to be taken out and planted in nursery rows in spring. Among kinds that can easily be increased in this manner are Flowering Almond, Forsythia, Privet, Philadelphus, Crape Myrtle, Currants and Weigela. Cuttings of broad-leaved evergreens may also be made.

Compost Piles. Do not omit building all waste vegetable matter that does not contain soil-borne pests or diseases (and these are few in number) into compost piles. The addition of organic matter is of tremendous benefit to almost all garden soils, and compost forms an excellent source of supply.

Annuals and Tulips. In the warmer parts of the South, sowings of all kinds of annuals may be made; but in the upper South, outdoor seed sowing is now at a standstill.

Tulips may be planted. Those that have been refrigerated (as they must be if they are to be successful in the warmer sections) should be planted upon receipt from the dealer, or be stored in the refrigerator until you do plant them.

Dormant spraying to combat scale insects and certain other pests and diseases may now be given attention. Do not spray if there is danger of the temperature dropping below freezing. Consult your State Agricultural Experiment Station regarding sprays to use.

Pruning and Lawn Care. Pruning may be done. Do not prune spring-flowering shrubs at this time except where a real rejuvenation job is called for and you are prepared to sacrifice spring bloom for a year.

Keep lawns of Rye Grass fairly closely cut, especially where the Rye Grass was sown on top of permanent summer lawn grasses.

If Dahlias have not been dug and stored, give

attention to this matter during December.

On the West Coast

December is a month with comparatively little to do in gardens in northern sections; but further south there is plenty of activity.

When fruit trees have dropped their leaves they may be given a first dormant spray.

Pruning fruit trees and ornamentals that lose their leaves may start as soon as the trees become dormant.

Hardwood cuttings of a great many shrubs, including Roses, may be planted in nursery rows this month.

This is an excellent period in most sections to plant trees and shrubs.

Planting Time. In gardens where winters are mild, set out plants of Canterbury Bells, Foxgloves, Columbines, Carnations, Snapdragons, Stocks, Cinerarias, Primulas, Shasta Daisies and others.

Calla Lilies and Amaryllis may be planted now. This is about the last chance to plant bulbs of true Lilies. Plant Gladioli in warm regions. Plant Ranunculus and Anemone tubers to pro-

Deciduous trees and shrubs of all kinds may be pruned after they have shed their leaves.

vide a succession of flowers to follow those planted earlier.

In California, lift Dahlias and keep them in a cool, dry place until spring. Begin to prepare beds for Rose planting.

New Illustrated Encyclopedia of Gardening – Unabridged

❁

AARON'S BEARD. The name of an evergreen ground cover (Hypericum calycinum) which bears, in summer, large yellow flowers with somewhat beardlike stamens. Cymbalaria muralis and Saxifraga sarmentosa also are sometimes known by this name.

ABACA. See Musa textilis.

ABELE TREE. See Populus alba.

ABELIA (Abe'lia). Attractive leaf-losing or evergreen flowering shrubs which are natives of China, Japan, the Himalayas and Mexico and belong to the Honeysuckle family, Caprifoliaceae. They were named in honor of Dr. Clarke Abel, a physician attached to the British Embassy in China early in the 19th century.

Where and When to Plant. Abelias are suitable for foundation plantings, shrub borders, beds and hedges. Planting is best done in spring or early fall. Abelias flourish in any ordinary soil. The most suitable soil is well-drained loam with the addition of leaf mold, compost or peat moss.
They stand part-day shade but prefer full sun.

Pruning and Taking Cuttings. Pruning is done in spring by cutting out the old shoots or branches, those which have bloomed, together with dead branches and weak twigs, leaving the fresh young shoots uncut to provide blossoms. Even if the shrubs are pruned to the ground, as they must be if the shoots are winterkilled and the roots are alive, flowers will appear the same year on new shoots that spring from the roots. Stock may be increased by taking cuttings of the half-ripened or semiwoody shoots of the current year's growth in July or August. The cuttings, about 3 in. long, should be planted in sand, vermiculite or perlite in a propagating greenhouse, cold frame or under a bell jar. A close atmosphere must be maintained for four or five weeks to encourage the cuttings to form roots.

When well rooted, the cuttings are potted singly in 3-in. pots filled with loam, leaf mold and sand, are kept in a cold frame for the winter and planted out of doors in spring. Propagation may also be carried out by layering the lower branches in spring.

The hardiest kind is Abelia grandiflora, or Glossy Abelia. It is a hybrid between A. chinensis and A. uniflora and is a splendid flowering shrub, 3-6 ft. high, with white, pink-tinged flowers from July to October; its foliage is handsome. In fairly mild climates it is partially evergreen. Abelia Edward Goucher (a hybrid between A. grandiflora and A. Schumannii) is 4-5 ft. tall and is intermediate in habit between its parents. It is semievergreen and from July to October bears rather large, lavender-pink flowers that resemble somewhat those of A. grandiflora. Slightly less hardy than A. grandiflora, it may be grown outdoors in climates similar to that found as far north as New York City.

Still more tender and adapted for milder sections only are the Chinese A. Schumannii and the Mexican A. floribunda. The former is semievergreen, 5 ft. tall, and has lavender-pink flowers in summer and fall. The latter is evergreen, 5-6 ft. tall, and bears large, pink blossoms in summer.

ABELIOPHYLLUM DISTICHUM (Abeliophyll'um). A leaf-losing shrub native to Korea and hardy in sheltered places as far north as New York City. It belongs to the Olive family, Oleaceae. The name Abeliophyllum refers to the abelia-like leaves. The shrub grows about 3 ft. high, with slender, twiggy branches and opposite leaves. The fragrant white flowers, about ½ inch across, borne in small clusters very early in spring, occur on the previous year's growth. Cut sprays open well indoors.

Planting and Pruning. Plant in early autumn

1

or early spring in well-drained, loamy soil. Stock may be increased by cuttings, 3-4 in. long, set in sandy soil in a close frame in July, or by layering the lower branches in early spring. The only pruning needed is to thin out the older wood immediately after flowering, every 4 or 5 years. This shrub is sometimes called White Forsythia.

One of the earliest shrubs to bloom in spring, the White Forsythia, Abeliophyllum distichum, is an attractive and unusual fragrant-flowered kind of easy culture.

ABERIA. See Dovyalis.

ABIES—*Fir* (A'bies). Hardy evergreen trees which are valued for planting on the lawn and in other places where their graceful and symmetrical form may be fully displayed. They are natives of Europe, North America, northern Asia and northern Africa, and belong to the Pinaceae, a section of the Conifer family, Coniferae. The name Abies is derived from *abeo*, to spring up, to rise, and refers to the upright growth of the trees. Most of them ultimately develop into trees 80 ft. or more high. In their native habitats they may reach a height of 200 ft. or more.

Where and When to Plant. Firs are easily grown in deep, moist, well-drained soil and a pure atmosphere. The majority are not suitable for dry soil, for wind-swept positions, or for the smoke-laden atmosphere near large towns. Early

fall and spring are the best times for planting.

How to Prune. Firs are so symmetrical in growth that comparatively little attention in regard to pruning is necessary. Only one leader or main central shoot should be allowed to grow; if upright side shoots develop as rival leaders they must be cut away. In the event of the leading shoot being broken it is useless to tie up a side branch with the idea of forming a new, erect leader. The damaged top must be cut out and, when new young shoots develop, the strongest and best-placed one should be left to grow to form the new leader and the others should be removed.

Raising Trees from Seeds and Cuttings. Seeds provide the best means of raising young Fir trees. The seeds are sown thinly in late spring out of doors or earlier in a cool greenhouse. The shoots of rare kinds may be grafted on seedlings of a common kind under glass in winter or spring; for these purposes, only the shoots at the top of the tree should be used. Grafts made from the side branches often remain dwarfed and rarely make satisfactory trees. Young Firs are very light-sensitive, and should be shaded from strong sun until they are two or three years old.

Abies homolepis, the Nikko Fir, is one of the hardiest kinds and the best for planting in town gardens.

Principal Firs. Only a few Firs really thrive in the climate of northeastern America, but many prosper in the moister Pacific coast area. Abies concolor (White or Colorado Fir) is perhaps the best for the East, growing into a tall, symmetrical specimen, handsome with its soft grayish or glaucous leaves. Two from Japan seem to grow as well. A. homolepis (Nikko Fir) develops into a wider specimen than A. concolor and has very dark green leaves which are silvery beneath. A. Veitchii is more compact, and has very handsome, lustrous, dark green leaves which are very silvery beneath. A. Nordmanniana, (Caucasian Fir) is hardy in the most favored parts of New England. It forms a narrow specimen, attractive with shining, green leaves which are silvery beneath. Abies cilicica is somewhat similar in appearance but has grayer bark that becomes scaly with age. A. cephalonica (Greek Fir) has sharp-pointed leaves that are likely to scorch in winter in climates north of New York City. A. Pinsapo, the Spanish Fir, is hardy in sheltered places in southern New England.

Abies alba (Silver Fir), a native of Europe, A. grandis (Giant Fir), a native of the Far West, and A. nobilis (Noble Fir), from the same section, develop into handsome, large specimens in their natural surroundings, but do not grow well in the eastern United States. A. Fraseri (Southern Balsam Fir) is hardy in the North and is a better tree in cultivation than A. balsamea, the common Balsam Fir of the North. A. amabilis, (Cascade Fir) is distinguished by gray bark with white blotches and shining, dark green leaves with broad, white bands beneath; it is hardy only in favored spots in the East.

Newer Kinds. Several Firs, introduced from Asia in recent years, promise to do fairly well in the more favored parts of New York and southern New England. Abies Fargesii has mahogany-purple shoots and long, very dark leaves, silvery beneath; A. Forrestii has reddish-brown shoots and lustrous leaves; A. koreana (Korean Fir) has rather small, dark green leaves, also silvery beneath, and bears purple cones with white bracts which mature earlier than those of most Firs; A. recurvata has leaves bright to bluish-green above, pale green beneath; A. squamata has bluish-green leaves with white bands beneath and purplish-brown flaky bark.

Economic Uses. The wood of several of the Firs is of considerable value. It is odorless, from white to yellow, or sometimes reddish-brown in color, soft and easy to work, finishes with a smooth surface and takes paint well. It has many uses: for the indoor finish of houses, the commoner kinds of carpentry, match wood, box boards, paper pulp and wood wool. Its odorless character makes it an excellent wood for boxes for absorbent products, such as butter, cheese, lard and bacon.

Firs may be distinguished from Spruces by their upright cones; cones of Spruces are pendent.

Canada balsam and Strasbourg turpentine are obtained from bark blisters of A. balsamea and A. alba, respectively. These substances are used for varnishes, mounting microscopic specimens and in medical practice. The most important timber producers are the European A. alba, western North American A. grandis, A. nobilis and A. magnifica, and eastern North American A. balsamea.

ABRONIA—Sand Verbena (Abro'nia). Half-hardy, trailing annual or perennial plants, bearing, during summer, verbena-like flowers of various colors. They grow wild in western North America and belong to the family Nyctaginaceae. The word Abronia is derived from *abros*, delicate, and refers to the bracts surrounding the flower.

Abronias are chiefly valuable for the fronts of flower beds and borders, and for the rock garden, where they should be planted in spring in a sunny location in well-drained sandy loam. Al-

The Sand Verbena, Abronia umbellata, has pink flowers. It grows well in sandy soil in sunny locations.

though perennials, they are generally raised each year from seeds, which germinate very slowly unless soaked in water for 24 hours before sowing.

When to Sow Seeds. In mild regions the seeds are sown in September out of doors. Where winters are harsher they are sown indoors in late winter. The resulting seedlings are transplanted into flats filled with loam, leaf mold and sand, and in May are planted where they are to flower in summer. An alternative method is to sow directly outdoors in early spring. The perennial kinds can be propagated also by cuttings in March-April, made from the fresh shoots on old plants which have been kept in a frostproof greenhouse during the winter. They are inserted in beds of sand or sandy soil in a frame which is kept close for a few weeks.

The chief kinds are Abronia latifolia (A. arenaria), which has kidney-shaped leaves and fragrant lemon-yellow flowers; A. maritima, prostrate, flowers dark red; and A. umbellata, which bears pink flowers and is the most commonly cultivated.

ABRUS PRECATORIUS—*Necklace Plant, Rosary Pea, Crab's Eyes* (A'brus). A tropical climbing plant from the East Indies; it has pinnate leaves, and ornamental seeds, and belongs to the Pea family, Leguminosae. Abrus, which is derived from *abros,* soft, alludes to the delicate or soft leaves. This plant needs a minimum winter greenhouse temperature of 60 degrees, and is grown in large pots in a compost of

half loam and half peat with sand added. Hot, moist conditions are essential. It can be grown outdoors in southern Florida. It can be increased by seeds, or by cuttings set in a warm-greenhouse propagating case in spring.

The small seeds are red, with a single black spot on each, this peculiar coloring having led to the name of Crab's-Eyes. They are in demand for the manufacture of necklaces, fancy bags, rosaries, and the like.

ABSINTHIUM. See Artemisia Absinthium.

ABUTILON—*Flowering Maple* (Abu'tilon). Tender shrubs with large ornamental leaves and attractive bell-shaped pendulous flowers in summer and autumn. They are natives of Brazil, India and tropical Asia, and belong to the Mallow family, Malvaceae. Abutilon is derived

Hybrid Abutilons bear attractive flowers over a long period of time. They are suitable for planting in summer beds and window boxes and for growing in indoor window gardens.

from an Arabic word for a Mallow. Abutilon vitifolium and A. megapotamicum (also called A. vexillarium) are the hardiest; they are cultivated outdoors in the south of England. The others cannot stand frost and must be grown in a greenhouse having a minimum winter temperature of 50 degrees, except in favored climates such as that of California where they may be grown in the open garden. When grown in pots they are invaluable for window gardens and for decorating greenhouses. In summer they make a good display when planted in sunny outdoor flower beds and in window boxes. The variegated-leaved varieties are especially suitable for these purposes.

Summer Management. Abutilons require a rich soil of two thirds loam and one third leaf mold and decayed manure. Repotting is done in spring as soon as new growth commences, the plants being transferred to slightly larger pots. They are kept in a warm, moist atmosphere for a few weeks and syringed frequently. When well rooted, they delight in full sunlight and a free circulation of air. Abundance of water is required during the summer, and a biweekly application of liquid fertilizer is beneficial; the lower leaves will fall if the roots lack nourishment.

Winter Management. During the winter the soil must be kept drier, but the stems must not be allowed to shrivel through lack of moisture. Plants growing in tubs or in beds of soil in the greenhouse are kept healthy and vigorous by removing some of the topsoil in spring and replacing it with the mixture advised for potting.

How and When to Prune. When the Abutilon is grown as a climbing plant, the side shoots on the main branches are cut back in March to within two or three buds of the base of the previous summer's growth, and old, weakly branches are cut off. During the summer, the new shoots are tied to the wire supports as they progress. Plants in pots are pruned in March (the shoots of the previous year's growth being shortened by half), and kept warm and moist—temperature, 55 to 60 degrees F. When fresh growth begins they are repotted.

Taking Cuttings. Cuttings will form roots at almost any time of the year; they should be inserted in March to produce pot plants for winter and autumn decoration, and in August to supply plants for summer bedding out of doors the following year. Side shoots, about 3 in. long, are torn off with a "heel" or piece of the old branch, or failing a supply of these, the tips of the shoots are taken as cuttings. If they are placed in a propagating case in a warm greenhouse, roots will form in three or four weeks. The rooted cuttings are potted, first in 3-in., and later into larger pots. They will bloom well in 6 or 7 in. containers. Abutilons grown from cuttings in August are, when rooted, potted in 3-in. pots in which they remain until February, when they are repotted in 5-in. pots. They are hardened off and planted out when the weather is warm and settled.

Abutilons may also be propagated from seeds sown in pots of finely sifted soil in spring in a temperature of 55 degrees. The seedlings are potted and treated in the same way as cuttings, but they will not flower until the following year.

The Chief Kinds. Abutilon striatum Thompsonii has large green and yellow leaves and orange-colored flowers. This variegation is actually caused by a virus (see Virus), and when a shoot is grafted on a green stock, the latter becomes infected and produces variegated leaves, too. A. Savitzii has smaller, green and white leaves. A. megapotamicum has slender stems clothed with small, green and yellow leaves and bears pendulous, yellow and scarlet flowers. These three kinds are often used in summer flower beds for their colored leaves.

There are numerous named hybrids of Abutilon with large, handsome flowers. The best of these are Boule de Neige, white; Delicatum, rose; Louis van Houtte, purple; and Queen of the Yellows, yellow. They bloom freely, are very attractive, and may be grown as climbing plants or in pots.

Abutilon vitifolium, a shrub from Chile, may reach a height of 15 ft.; it has large leaves and lovely pale violet-blue flowers in summer. It is suitable for permanent planting out of doors in mild climates, and should be set in a sunny place in well-drained, loamy soil. It is not always long-lived, but is easily raised from seed. There is a white variety (album).

Several Abutilons produce useful fiber between the bark and wood of the stems. One of the most useful is A. Theophrastii, the Chinese Hemp or Indian Mallow, a small bush found in China and naturalized in North America.

ACACIA—*Wattle, Mimosa* (Aca′cia). Tender trees and shrubs with ornamental foliage and attractive yellow flowers in spring. Acacias are much grown out of doors in California and elsewhere where winters are mild. In more severe climates, some are grown in greenhouses. The word Acacia is derived from *akakia,* the Egyptian name for thorn, and refers to the thorns borne by some kinds.

About four hundred Acacias are known and

A typical spray of the yellow-flowered Acacia Baileyana. This, one of the most beautiful Acacias, has bluish foliage. It is suitable for growing in greenhouses in pots, tubs and beds and for planting outdoors in mild climates.

about one quarter of these are reported to be in cultivation in the United States. They belong to the Pea family, Leguminosae, and are chiefly natives of Australia.

All Acacias bear clusters of yellow flowers, most of which are in small, fluffy balls. Acacia decurrens variety dealbata is the kind commonly cut and sold under the name Mimosa.

Greenhouse Management. When grown in pots Acacias must be kept in the greenhouse—temperature, 45-50 degrees F.—from October to May. During the remainder of the year they should be placed in a sunny position out of doors, the pots plunged to the rims in ashes; this treatment ripens the shoots which will bloom the following spring. Repotting should be done as soon as the flowers have faded, using a compost of equal parts of peat and loam and a free scattering of coarse sand. The soil must be made firm. After potting, syringe the plants frequently and keep the greenhouse close and moist until new growth commences. Then gradually ventilate more freely and in early June set the plants out of doors. The soil must be kept moist.

Sowing Seeds. Acacias can be propagated by sowing seeds in spring and summer. As the seeds have very hard skins they must be chipped with a penknife, taking care not to damage the "eye," and soaked in warm water for 24 hours before sowing. They should be set ½ in. deep in well-drained pots filled with sandy loam and peat in

equal parts; the pots are placed in a propagating case in the greenhouse, and covered with glass to keep the soil moist. When the seedlings appear, the pots containing them should be placed on the open greenhouse bench for a few weeks and then they should be potted separately in 3-in. pots in sandy loam and peat moss with sand added.

Taking Cuttings. Propagation is also effected by cuttings inserted during June–July when the shoots are semiwoody. Short side shoots are torn off with a piece of the branch attached, inserted in pots of the soil mixture mentioned, and covered with a bell jar which must be wiped inside every morning. When the cuttings are rooted they are hardened off as are for seedlings.

How and When to Prune. The young plants should be shortened to 3 in. as soon as they are about 4 in. high. The side shoots which develop must also be cut back similarly to produce plants with several branches. Acacias required for draping pillars or the greenhouse roof should be planted in a bed of sandy, peaty loam and the shoots tied to wires or other supports. These must be pruned annually by cutting out some of the weaker shoots and shortening the side branches when the flowers have faded. Plants grown in small pots for decorative purposes should be pruned by shortening the shoots to about half their length after flowering.

The Best Kinds. The following are the best Acacias. Those most suitable for cultivation in flowerpots are A. armata, with oval leaves and balls of yellow flowers; A. Drummondii, with clover-like leaves and cylinder-shaped heads of lemon-colored flowers; A. platyptera, with long, flat, leafless branches and deep-yellow flowers; A. longifolia with yellow flowers in loose spikes; and A. cultriformis, which has round heads of yellow flowers. By annual pruning when the blooms have faded these plants can be grown in 5-in. or 6-in. flowerpots.

Acacia decurrens, A. decurrens dealbata, A. Baileyana, A. verticillata, A. pubescens, and A. Riceana, all with yellow flowers, do not bloom freely unless allowed to develop fully with little or no pruning; they are, therefore, planted to cover pillars in the greenhouse, are grown in large tubs, or are planted outdoors where climate permits. Others that are grown in

[1–8]
Glossy Abelia (Abelia grandiflora)

[1–8a]
Mimosa (Acacia)

[1–9]
Japanese Maple
(Acer palmatum atropurpureum)

[1–9a]
Silver Maple (Acer saccharinum)

the warmer parts of the United States are A. auriculaeformis, A. macrantha, and A. Farnesiana, the latter a shrub especially adapted for seaside planting, and one of the few Acacias that thrive in Florida. For the plant sometimes called Acacia lophantha, see Albizzia.

Economic Uses. Some Acacias are valued for timber, for the tannin contained in bark or wood, and for gum which exudes from stems and branches; and a perfume is obtained from the flowers of one. The wood of several is hard and durable, and is used abroad for building, making furniture, tool handles, turnery and many other purposes. A few useful kinds are Myall Wood (A. homalophylla), Australian Blackwood (A. melanoxylon), Silver Wattle (A. decurrens dealbata), and Raspberry Jam Wood (A. acuminata). Most of the Australian Acacias contain tannin in the bark, and the bark is exploited under the name of Wattle Bark. Acacia decurrens dealbata, A. pycnantha and A. mollissima are popular kinds used for tanning purposes.

Gum Arabic is a gum that exudes from the stems and branches of A. nilotica, a tree found wild in the dry regions of tropical Africa and India. This and other Acacia gums are used in dyeing and printing, and as a basis for mucilage. A choice perfume is obtained from the flowers of A. Farnesiana, which is cultivated commercially in the south of France.

ACACIA, BLACK. See Robinia Pseudoacacia.
ACACIA, FALSE. See Robinia Pseudoacacia.
ACACIA, ROSE. See Robinia hispida.
ACAENA—*New Zealand Bur* (Acae'na). Dwarf trailing plants, more or less evergreen, useful in the rock garden, or for setting in the chinks of paved paths or between flagstones; they are more attractive in fruit than in flower, and spread quickly. Some are winter hardy as far north as New York City in sheltered positions, or with light covering, and some succeed further north; but they are more reliable in milder climates. The name Acaena is derived from *akaina,* a thorn. Acaena belongs to the Rose family, Rosaceae, and is allied to Geum.

The flowers have no petals, and are small and crowded in erect, terminal spikes or heads. The calyx is usually armed with spines. The fruits, as well as the leaves of some Acaenas, turn a beau-

Acaena novae-zelandiae, a New Zealand Bur, is a pretty foliage plant for the rock garden and for planting in crevices between flagstones.

tiful color in the summer and autumn, and remain attractive during early winter. Most are natives of New Zealand or South America.

Planting and Propagation. These plants succeed in ordinary, well-drained soil; sand or grit should be added to heavy soils. They are planted in early fall or in spring. Increase may also be obtained by lifting and dividing the plants at those seasons and separating them into small pieces and replanting. Cuttings may be inserted in sand or in sandy soil in a frame in June–July. Seeds also provide a ready means of increase.

The best of all is Acaena microphylla, which forms a dense carpet, about ½ in. high, of bronze-green leaves; it is in full beauty in summer and fall when the bright crimson spines of the small fruits or burs are at their best. Although this Acaena will thrive in either wet or dry ground, the spines color most brilliantly when the plants are in light, sandy soil. Acaena novae-zealandiae is similar in appearance, but has barbed spines. The gray-leaved Acaena Buchananii is very attractive; so also is A. adscendens, which has bronze leaves and prostrate shoots which rise at the tips. A. pulchella has bronze-green leaves. A. ovalifolia, which grows 9 in. high and has bright green fernlike leaves and purplish burs, thrives under trees. A. Sanguisorbae light green, fernlike leaves.

ACALYPHA (Acaly'pha). Tender shrubs

which, when grown indoors, need a minimum winter temperature of 55 degrees. In the far South they are permanent outdoor subjects; in the North, colored-leaved kinds are used for summer beds outdoors. They are mostly natives

The Chenille Plant, Acalypha hispida, bears long tassels of bright red flowers in summer and autumn. It may be grown in greenhouses and, in the far South, outdoors.

of the tropics, and belong to the Spurge family Euphorbiaceae. The name is derived from an ancient Greek name for a Nettle.

The only one worth cultivating for its flowers is the Chenille Plant, Acalypha hispida (A. Sanderiana); in summer and fall this bears long tassels of bright-red flowers which resemble Love-Lies-Bleeding. The plants may be "grown on" for several years to form large specimens, but new plants are usually raised annually from cuttings; they then grow 2-3 ft. high. There is a creamy-white flowered variety, alba. Other kinds are grown for their ornamental leaves: Acalypha Godseffiana, leaves green, with cream-white margins and its variety heterophylla with much-divided leaves of the same coloring; and the Copper Leaf, A. Wilkesiana, varieties of which include, musaica, green and red, Macafeana, red, crimson and bronze, macrophylla, russet-brown, obovata, bronze-green with pink edges, and marginata, pink-edged leaves.

When to Take Cuttings. Cuttings of the colored-leaved kinds root easily at any time. September-rooted cuttings yield good plants for planting in the garden the following summer. Pinch the young plants once or twice to promote bushiness. Old plants of A. hispida grown indoors should be cut down to within 12 in. of the base in February, and syringed frequently to start them into growth. When the fresh shoots are about three inches long, they should be pulled off with a "heel" or piece of the old branch attached and inserted in a propagating case in the hothouse, kept close until rooted, and then gradually hardened off by ventilating the glass case. The rooted cuttings are potted in 4-in. pots, then into 6-in., and subsequently into 8-in. pots. The shoots must not be pinched or pruned. The best potting compost consists of two parts fibrous loam, one part leaf mold, and one part well-decayed manure.

The greenhouse must be kept moist and the plants syringed frequently, but after the flower spikes have developed, cooler and drier conditions are necessary. Special care should be taken to prevent moisture from lodging in the flower spikes as they are liable to damp off. Water freely spring through fall, moderately in winter. when it becomes quite dry.

ACANTHOCALYCIUM (Acanthocaly'cium). A group of South American Cacti closely related to Echinopsis and requiring the same general cultural treatment.

The chief kinds, all from the Argentine, are A. spiniflorum, pink; A. thionanthum, yellow; and A. violaceum, pale violet.

ACANTHOCEREUS (Acanthoce'reus). Previously named Cereus pentagonus, this night-blooming Cactus from Central America is of trailing habit, with 3- or 5-angled stems furnished with spines and bearing large, funnel-shaped, white flowers. It belongs to the family Cactaceae, and the name indicates a spiny Cactus. For cultivation see Cactus.

ACANTHOLIMON—*Prickly Thrift* (Acantholi'mon). Low-growing, slow-growing, hardy evergreen perennial plants suitable for the rock garden or rock walls. They grow wild in eastern Europe and Asia Minor and belong to the Thrift family, Plumbaginaceae. The flowers, which open in July, are like those of Thrift, but the leaves differ in being sharply pointed. Acantholimon means spiny Sea Lavender (the plant is allied to the Sea Lavender, or Limonium).

Planting and Propagation. Acantholimon must be planted in early fall or spring, in a sunny place, and needs well-drained, loamy soil, containing sand and limestone chips. It dislikes being disturbed. The best method of propagation is by working plenty of sandy soil into the leafy tufts in late summer, having previously torn some of the branches at a joint so as partly to sever them; water should then be given to settle the soil. By spring many of the branches will have rooted.

Cuttings are uncertain; the best time to take them is in August and September. The shoots should be torn off with a "heel" or piece of the woody part and inserted in sand or in sandy soil in a cold frame or cool greenhouse. Acantholimon is not easily raised from seeds, but these may be sown in pots of sifted sandy soil set in a frame in spring.

The loveliest Prickly Thrift is Acantholimon venustum; it bears rose-pink flowers on spikes 5 to 6 in. high, and has gray-green prickly leaves in compact cushions. A. glumaceum bears rose-colored flowers. A. acerosum has white flowers and grayish leaves.

ACANTHOPANAX (Acanthopa'nax). Hardy, ornamental shrubs or small trees from China and Japan, which belong to the Aralia or Ginseng family, Araliaceae. They often have large leaves and the inconspicuous summer flowers are followed by black ivylike fruits in autumn. Acanthopanax is derived from *acanthos,* a thorn, and Panax, the name of a genus of plants.

Planting and Propagation. These shrubs should be planted in fall or spring in deep. loamy soil. Propagation is by cuttings inserted in sandy soil in a cold frame in August, or suckers (rooted side pieces) may be removed and planted in autumn or spring. Plants can also be raised from seeds sown out of doors in autumn.

The chief kind is A. Sieboldianus (A. pentaphyllus, Aralia pentaphylla), a good, hardy, thorny shrub, to 10 ft. tall, leaves dark green, each divided into 5-7 leaflets; stands sun or shade; may be sheared to form a good impenetrable hedge; disease and pest free; and does

well under city conditions.

ACANTHOPHYLLUM (Acanthophyll'um). Perhaps not in cultivation. Plants grown under this name are usually Dianthus Noeanus, which see.

ACANTHUS—*Bear's Breech* (Acan'thus). Perennial plants having ornamental leaves and spikes of white or purplish flowers. Most kinds bloom in summer. Hardy in the North only if well protected in winter. They grow wild in southern Europe and in Africa and belong to the family Acanthaceae. The name is derived from *acanthos,* a spine, an indication of the spiny

Acanthus montanus, a handsome subshrubby plant suitable for growing outdoors in warm climates and in greenhouses.

leaves of some kinds. The leaves of Acanthus may have served as models for designs used in the ornamentation of pillars in Corinthian architecture.

When to Plant—Suitable Soil. These plants will flourish in a sunny or slightly shady place, in well-drained, ordinary soil; they should not be planted in heavy ground until this has been made suitable by adding leaf mold or compost and sand freely. They become established slowly, dislike being disturbed and should not be transplanted unnecessarily. In California they sometimes become so well established that they are something of a nuisance because of their spreading habit. Planting is best done in the spring.

Acanthus are suitable for planting·in perennial borders, at the fringes of woodlands and at the fronts of shrub beds where bold foliage effects are desired.

If an increased stock is required, the plants may be lifted in March and separated into rooted pieces for replanting. Seeds may also be sown in a greenhouse in March—temperature 50 degrees—but the seedlings grow slowly. They should be placed singly in small pots when an inch or so high and kept in a cold frame until large enough to plant out.

The chief kinds are Acanthus longifolius, 3-4 ft., purplish-rose; A. mollis, 3 ft., rose or white, and its broad-leaved variety, latifolius, 4 ft.; and A. spinosus, 2-3 ft., with spiny leaves and pur-

plish flowers. All bloom in July–August. A. montanus is a West African species sometimes grown in tropical greenhouses and perhaps suitable for outdoor cultivation in the far South. It has 10-in. spikes of rose-tinted flowers, and is 3 ft. tall. It blooms in spring.

ACAULIS. A botanical term meaning without a stem, e.g., Gentiana acaulis.

ACCENT PLANTS. Plants, contrasting strongly with their surroundings, that are planted singly or in small groups to provide emphasis in the garden picture. Usually they are of distinct form or coloring, as, for example, are the Italian Cypress and the Atlantic Cedar. They should be used with restraint.

ACER or MAPLE

Handsome Shade Trees and Smaller Kinds
with Richly Colored Foliage

The Acers (A'cer) are hardy and ornamental trees, varying greatly in height, from dwarf Japanese Maples which are only 2-3 ft. high to some of the North American kinds which reach a height of 100 ft. or more. They are natives of various parts of Europe, Asia and North America, and belong to the family Aceraceae. The word *acer* is the Latin name for Maple.

All the commonly cultivated Acers are leaf-losing trees, most being hardy in the North. They are extensively employed as shade trees for planting home grounds, parks and streets.

The Flowers and Winged Seeds. Most of the Maples have clusters of small greenish-white or yellow flowers; in some kinds they are reddish or reddish-purple. While not outstanding as flowering trees, many of them are attractive when in bloom in early spring before the leaves unfold. Notable in this respect are Acer rubrum and Acer Opalus. The flowers are followed by clusters of winged fruits popularly called "keys," which aid in the dispersal of the seeds by wind. The fruits or seed vessels of most kinds are not showy, but there are exceptions, as, for example, the scarlet-fruited Sycamore Maple, A. Pseudo-Platanus erythrocarpum.

Beautiful Autumn Tints. The chief beauty, however, of the Maples is in the lobed leaves,

which, in some kinds, are attractive from early spring until late autumn. In some kinds the unfolding leaves are beautiful in spring; in others

The flowers of many Maples are attractive in spring before the leaves open. These are the reddish flowers of Acer rubrum, the Red, Scarlet, or Swamp Maple.

they are attractive during the summer, but Maples display their chief splendor in autumn, when the leaves are tinted with yellow, red and gold. A few Maples have colored markings on the trunks and larger branches; these are most conspicuous when the trees are leafless in winter. These kinds are worth planting for their beauty at that season of the year.

Easily Grown Trees. The cultivation of Acers presents no problems except in very acid soil. They are easily grown in ordinary soil; but poor, sandy land should be enriched with manure and loam. Planting is best done in fall or spring, but it may be carried on throughout the dormant

Acer saccharum, the Sugar or Rock Maple, in summer. This is one of the most splendid native trees of eastern North America. Its foliage colors are magnificent in fall. It is the source of maple sugar.

season when weather conditions permit. Even large specimens may be transplanted with little fear of loss. Most Maples thrive best in an open, sunny situation. Japanese Maples are liable to be damaged by sun scorch in late spring, particularly in exposed gardens. Plant them where they are not exposed to sweeping winds and keep their roots mulched. The Japanese Maples may be grown in pots for decoration of the greenhouse in spring and they are excellent tub plants.

Pruning and Propagation. Pruning is only necessary for the purpose of thinning out crowded branches and shortening very long ones which tend to spoil the shape of the tree. This work should be done during summer. Seeds,

sown when ripe in autumn in a sheltered place out of doors, or in a cold frame, provide the best means of raising young plants. Next to this in point of value is the practice of layering; branches which can be bent down conveniently are pegged in the ground in summer, or they may be air-layered. Grafting may be done in March, or budding in July, seedlings of one of the common kinds being used as stocks.

Principal American Maples. Acer macrophyllum (Oregon Maple) grows up to 100 ft. tall; it has yellow fragrant flowers, and leaves that measure a foot or more across. The leaves turn bright orange in fall. It is a good street tree in coastal towns of the Northwest. A. Negundo, the Box Elder, grows quickly to a spreading tree 50 ft. high or more. It is very hardy and drought-resistant. Its leaves are pinnate, with three or more leaflets, and resemble those of the Ash. Varieties of A. Negundo with gold and silver leaf-variegation are sometimes cultivated. A. pennsylvanicum (Moosewood) is a small tree that thrives in cool, shady places; its large, light green leaves turn a clear yellow in the fall. Its distinctive

In winter the branches of the Sugar Maple, Acer saccharum, form a handsome pattern against the sky.

twigs and branchlets are light green, striped white. A. rubrum, the Red, Scarlet or Swamp Maple, grows into a large tree that is handsome the year around. In winter the gray beechlike bark of the upper parts is attractive; in spring its red flowers and keys (seeds), in summer its bright green leaves, and in fall the gorgeous red and yellow shades of its foliage, are arresting. A. rubrum is a good street tree, although it is native to swamps. The variety A. rubrum columnare grows into a narrow, upright tree of distinctive habit. A. saccharinum, Silver or White Maple, soon grows into a large, handsome, wide-spreading tree. Its deeply lobed leaves are silvery beneath and turn a clear yellow in fall. In A. saccharinum laciniatum, Wiers Maple, the much-dissected leaves are borne on pendulous branches. In the variety pyramidale of A. saccharinum the branches are upright and form a somewhat narrow tree. The Silver Maples have brittle wood. A. saccharum, Sugar or Rock Maple, is a magnificent tree in size and form, elegant in flower and wonderful in its fall coloring of red, orange and yellow shades. A. saccharum monumentale, Sentry Maple, is a valuable, upright, narrow variety. A. spicatum, Mountain Maple, develops into a large bush or small tree with flowers that are borne in narrow spikes and are followed by bright red keys in summer; the leaves turn orange and scarlet in fall.

Principal Exotic Maples. A. Buergerianum, Trident Maple, is an attractive, small tree with 3-lobed leaves. A. campestre, Hedge Maple, grows into a round-headed tree up to 50 ft. with slightly corky branchlets. It is useful as a tall screen. A. Davidii grows to 50 ft. tall and is handsome in the fall when its leaves turn yellow and purple, and in winter because of its shiny, white-striped branchlets. A. ginnala, Amur Maple, is a large shrub or small tree, very hardy, and showy in the fall with orange and crimson leaves. A. griseum, Paperbark Maple, is a small tree remarkable for its cinnamon-brown, flaky bark. A. nikoense grows to 40 ft. and is showy in fall because of its scarlet foliage.

A. platanoides, Norway Maple, is a favorite street tree that is showy in spring with greenish-yellow flowers, which appear before the leaves. Numerous forms are known that show leaf and growth variations. The leaves of the variety

Schwedleri open red and change to dark-green later. The newer variety, Crimson King, keeps its rich purplish-red coloring uniform throughout the season. The growth habits of the varieties columnare and globosum are well indicated by their names. A peculiar variety is cucullatum, Eagle Claw Maple, which has short, crimped leaf lobes; it is rarely seen. A. Pseudo-Platanus, Sycamore Maple, is a tall, rugged tree, good for city and seaside planting. Numerous varieties are known that differ in their leaf coloring. Very attractive is the variety erythrocarpum, which has smaller, shiny leaves and bright red keys. A. tataricum, Tatarian Maple, is a very hardy shrub or small tree, with bright green leaves turning yellow in the fall. This kind is conspicuous in late summer because of its keys.

Japanese Maples are varied and beautiful shrubs or small trees. They are forms of A. palmatum and A. japonicum. Some of the most attractive varieties of A. palmatum are atropurpureum, deep purple; aureum, yellow; dissectum, with green, finely cut leaves; ornatum, with deep red leaves, finely cut; roseo-marginatum,

The Japanese Maples are slow-growing, hardy small trees, ideal for planting as specimens because of their dainty foliage which colors brilliantly in fall. This fine specimen of Acer palmatum is located at Mount Vernon, New York.

which has deeply cut leaves that are edged with pink; rubrum, with large leaves that are red when young and change to almost green later. A. japonicum has leaves each with seven or more lobes; they are bright green, but turn crimson in fall. The variety aconitifolium, Fernleaf Maple, has deeply divided green leaves that turn ruby red in fall; the leaves of aureum remain yellow throughout the season. Seedlings of Japanese Maples are likely to vary in form and color from the parent plants.

Economic Uses. The wood of the Sycamore Maple (Acer Pseudo-Platanus) is white, of clean appearance, works well and finishes with a good surface; in Europe it is used in making rollers for washing and calico printing machines, and for various kitchen and dairy requisites that require constant washing or scrubbing.

Several North American Maples are extremely valuable for their lumber. The lumber trade recognizes two distinct types—Hard Maple and Soft Maple. The former is the wood of the Sugar Maple (A. saccharum), and the latter of the Red Maple (A. rubrum), and the Silver Maple (A. saccharinum). The wood is used for furniture, flooring and many other purposes. Some wood of A. saccharum is very prettily marked, and names such as Bird's-eye Maple and Fiddleback Maple are applied to distinct types; they are used for cabinetwork and furniture. The wood of the Norway Maple (A. platanoides), Oregon Maple (A. macrophyllum), and of other species is also of value. Maple sugar and syrup are obtained by boiling and evaporating the sap of the Sugar Maple.

ACERANTHUS DIPHYLLUS—*Maplewort* (Aceranth'us). Hardy, herbaceous perennial, native of Japan, belonging to the Barberry family, Berberidaceae, and closely allied to Epimedium. It is about 6 in. tall and bears small white flowers in spring. Its foliage is attractive. The name is derived from the Greek *a*, not, *ceras*, horn or spur and *anthos*, a flower. It refers to the fact that, unlike the flowers of the nearly related genus Epimedium, those of Aceranthus do not have spurs.

A Good Ground Cover. Aceranthus forms a good, low ground cover for lightly shaded places in rock gardens and elsewhere. It prefers a woodsy soil, not excessively dry. Plant in early fall or spring, 9-10 in. apart. Propagate by division at planting time.

ACHILLEA—*Milfoil, Yarrow* (Achille'a). Hardy perennial plants suitable for the herbaceous border and the rock garden; they are easily

grown and most of them will flourish in poor soil. They vary in height from 6 in. to 3 ft., have attractive, somewhat fernlike leaves, and bear

Achillea millefolium Fire King, a showy plant for the perennial border.

Achillea tomentosa is an easily grown plant that bears flattish heads of yellow flowers in early summer.

clusters of single, or double, small, daisy-like flowers in summer. Most of them grow wild in the countries of southern Europe. They belong to the Daisy family, Compositae. Achillea commemorates Achilles, the Greek hero.

For the Flower Border. The tall kinds are excellent for the herbaceous border where they should be planted in autumn or in early spring, in ordinary soil. They spread quickly and are easily propagated by detaching rooted pieces in autumn or spring. The plants are of loose habit of growth, and the stems must be carefully supported by stakes in early summer.

The double white varieties of Achillea Ptarmica, named The Pearl and Snowball, 2-3 ft. high, with small flowers borne profusely in loose

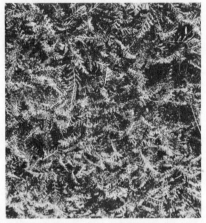

Common Yarrow, Achillea Millefolium, is a good substitute for lawn grass. It thrives in sunny, dry locations.

sprays, are favorites for the herbaceous border and for cutting from June till August. The colored varieties of A. Millefolium, the common weed called Yarrow, especially Cerise Queen, rose-red, 2 ft., and rosea, pink, 2 ft., are good for the front of the border. A. filipendulina (A. Eupatorium) grows 3-4 ft. tall and bears large heads of bright yellow flowers. Especially good varieties of this are Gold Plate, golden-yellow, and Coronation Gold with exceptionally large heads. A. Taygetea, 18 in. tall, has yellow flowers and does well in hot, dry situations.

For the Rock Garden. The rock garden kinds are pretty, low-growing plants with gray leaves and white or yellow flowers in small, flat bunches or corymbs. Many are listed but few are of real decorative value. They should be planted in autumn or in spring, in poor, sandy or stony, loamy soil, in a dry, sunny place; the addition of a little lime is beneficial.

The best rock garden kinds are Achillea ageratifolia, 6 in., with gray-white leaves and white flowers, and its variety Aizoon, which is similar; A. Clavennae and A. umbellata, which have

Old clumps of Yarrow, dug from lawns or waste places, may be split into small pieces, each with some roots.

The divisions, planted about six inches apart, soon grow together and form a close mat. Spring or early fall is the best planting time.

gray-white leaves and white flowers; A. tomentosa, 10-12 in., with green leaves and yellow flowers; A. rupestris, 4 in., with green leaves and white flowers; and the hybrid named King Edward, sulphur-yellow, 9 in. All bloom in June-July. Cuttings of young shoots should be taken in summer or division of old plants done in spring or fall.

For Lawns. As a grass substitute on hot, dry

banks and similar locations, Common Yarrow, A. Millefolium, is excellent.

ACHIMENES (Achime′nes). Greenhouse and window garden plants of slender growth, with brightly colored, funnel-shaped flowers in summer; they are suitable for cultivation in flowerpots or suspended baskets in a greenhouse having a temperature of 55-60 degrees. They belong to the Gesneria family, Gesneriaceae, and are found wild in Mexico and Guatemala. Achimenes is derived from *chemaino,* a word meaning to suffer from cold.

The Best Potting Compost. The commonly cultivated Achimenes have small, scaly tubers or tubercles; these should be potted late in February, four or five in a 3-in. pot, in a compost of loam and leaf mold or peat moss with a free scattering of sand; or, they may be set in a flat of this soil and potted separately in small pots when growth has begun. In a temperature of 60 degrees they soon start into growth if the soil is

In February, at the end of their resting season, Achimenes are removed from their pots.

The wormlike, scaly tubers are picked from the soil and may be replanted whole or broken in pieces to secure increase.

Achimenes, with flowers in a wide range of colors, are delightful tuberous-rooted plants for the greenhouse.

kept moist. When the small pots are fairly full of roots the plants must be repotted in 5- or 6-in. pots, or set in wire baskets lined with moss, using a compost of equal parts of loam and leaf mold or peat moss with the addition of sand and a little, thoroughly decayed, dry manure. Care must be taken not to overwater until the plants have become well rooted; on the other hand, the soil should not be allowed to become dry.

Management in Summer. During the summer months, Achimenes need shade from bright sunshine, and, until the plants begin to flower, the greenhouse must be kept moist. After flowering begins, keep the air drier and grow the plants in

When the newly planted tubers have developed shoots two to three inches high they are planted, several together, in the containers in which they are to bloom.

as cool an atmosphere as possible, so long as the temperature does not fall below 55 degrees. If grown in flowerpots, the plants ought to be supported by thin stakes or the shoots will fall over. If grown in wire baskets, a few of the shoots should be tied to small thin stakes to keep them upright, the remainder being allowed to fall over the sides of the basket.

Management in Winter. When the flowers have faded and the leaves begin to wither, watering must be discontinued gradually, and finally, when the leaves have fallen, the tops should be cut off and the soil left dry. Throughout the winter months the roots are left in the pots or baskets in a minimum temperature of 50 degrees. Towards the end of February the roots or tubercles are taken out of the pots or baskets and are repotted in the way described.

Beautiful Flower Colors. The original species or wild types of Achimenes are grown by specialists only; usually preference is given to the numerous, large-flowered varieties which have been raised by seedsmen. The colors of the blooms range from white through rose, salmon blush, pale mauve, pink, salmon and carmine. The dwarf type of Achimenes, which is of more compact growth than the ordinary kinds, is especially well suited to the needs of amateurs.

Achimenes can be raised from seeds sown in finely sifted sandy soil placed in a propagating case in a heated greenhouse in February. The plants will not bloom until the following year. They are more usually increased by division of the tubers, by cuttings of the young shoots in spring and by leaf cuttings in summer.

ACHRAS ZAPOTA—*Marmalade Plum, Sapodilla, Sapote* (Ach'ras). An evergreen tree of tropical Central America, sometimes grown in southern Florida for its edible fruit and also as an ornamental. This tree is the source of chicle, which is the basis of chewing gum.

ACHYRANTHES (Achyran'thes). Plants commonly grown under this name belong correctly in Alternanthera and Iresine, which see.

ACIDANTHERA (Acidanthe'ra). Tender African bulbs (corms) belonging to the Iris family, Iridaceae. Acidanthera is from *akis,* a point, and *anthera,* an anther. They need the same treatment as Gladiolus but demand a longer growing season. For this reason, in the North it

is best to plant several together in large tubs or pots, to be grown outdoors in the summer, and brought into a cool greenhouse before frost. They bloom in late fall.

The bulbs are potted in spring in a mixture of loam two thirds, and leaf mold one third, with a scattering of sand. When the flowers are gone and the leaves fade, watering should be discontinued, the soil being kept dry through the winter until the bulbs are repotted. Propagation is carried out by removing the small bulbs or offsets when repotting.

Acidanthera bicolor, with white and purple flowers, and its variety Murielae, a vigorous form, both fragrant, are the hardiest, and may be planted permanently outdoors in mild climates.

ACID PHOSPHATE. A name sometimes applied to superphosphate. See Fertilizers and Manures.

ACID SOIL PLANTS. This is a term used to designate plants that are believed to need acid soil for their successful growth and will not thrive on soils that have an alkaline reaction. Plants that grow successfully on alkaline soils, but will not live or thrive on those that exhibit an acid reaction, are termed Alkaline Soil Plants.

A great deal of investigation of the special requirements of particular plants with regard to their acid or alkaline soil preferences has been carried out during the last two decades, and much has been written on this subject. More has been published about plants that prefer acid soils than about those that require an alkaline reaction; and often too much emphasis has been placed upon the importance of the careful regulation of soil acidity or alkalinity as a practical factor in garden cultivation. It is increasingly clear that the data published so far are not so conclusive as one would wish.

More recent studies of soils in relation to their physical and chemical make-up render it evident that the interactions of some of the soil elements may be as important as their actual presence or absence; this is particularly true of those that influence the balance between iron and nitrogen. If this balance is not satisfactory, symptoms may be produced in the plants that closely resemble those caused by disease organisms.

The published lists of plants believed to

require specific soil reactions are commonly divided into four sections: those that prefer or tolerate strongly acid soil conditions; those that prefer mildly acid conditions; those that thrive best in neutral soils; and those that need or tolerate strongly alkaline soils.

In reading published lists one is usually impressed by the fact that most of the plants reported on are not commonly grown in gardens. If the matter is pursued further, one is likely to find that opinions have changed about some of the plants originally assigned specific places in the acid-alkaline range of tolerance. Examples of these are Bearded Iris and American Holly, Ilex opaca.

It may be dangerous to attempt to reduce the available data to a rule of thumb generalization that will apply to all cultivated plants; but for the home gardener the old idea that a well-prepared soil of neutral cr nearly neutral reaction is the best for the great majority of the plants he grows comes closest to the truth.

A soil of this type will normally have to be modified sharply only for members of the Heath family and the Blueberry family, and not even all of these are so strongly acid-loving as once reported, although none is strictly a lover of alkaline soils.

Throughout this Encyclopedia, where acid or alkaline soil preferences are of significance, they are given in the cultural directions.

ACINETA (Acine'ta). Summer-flowering Orchids from tropical America, which there grow wild on trees. In North America they are suitable for cultivating only in a hothouse. Acineta is derived from the Greek word *akineta,* meaning immovable; the flowers are remarkable for their rigidity and thick, waxlike texture. These plants belong to the family Orchidaceae.

All these orchids have ribbed, flatly conical pseudobulbs, surmounted by two or three large, ribbed leaves, and bear drooping spikes of blossoms.

Details of Cultivation. In winter, when the plants are dormant, they should be kept in a temperature of about 60 degrees F., and at that season need watering only occasionally. They are most conveniently grown in teakwood baskets with large pieces of flowerpot placed at the bottom to keep the compost in position.

The potting compost should consist of chopped osmunda fiber or of Fir bark. Rebasketing is carried out in early spring, or, as with the majority of Orchids, as soon as fresh root growth begins. The summer temperature should not fall below 65 degrees at night and should be at least 5 to 10 degrees higher in the daytime. A humid atmosphere is necessary.

The Chief Kinds. The favorite kind is Acineta superba. The flower spikes are two feet or so long and bear seven or more slightly fragrant, fleshy flowers, fawn-yellow, spotted with red.

Mexico is the home of Acineta chrysantha, a golden-flowered, scented Orchid. Acineta Barkeri is very similar in appearance. So peculiar, almost grotesque, are the flowers of Acineta that whenever seen they invariably attract and arouse interest among garden lovers.

ACOKANTHERA—*Winter Sweet, Bushman's Poison* (Acokan'thera). Attractive evergreen shrubs or small trees, native of South Africa,

Acidanthera bicolor is a South African bulbous plant that bears attractive fragrant flowers.

which belong to the Dogbane family, the Apocynaceae. The name refers to the shape of the anthers. Suitable for garden planting in southern Florida and California; for greenhouses elsewhere.

These shrubs, when grown in pots and tubs, thrive best in a compost of loam with the addition of a little well-decayed leaf mold, manure, and sand, and benefit by weekly applications of dilute liquid fertilizer in summer. Repotting should be done in spring. The best means of increasing the stock is to insert cuttings in spring or early summer in a propagating case in a greenhouse—temperature 50-55 degrees.

The shrubs flower from February to April. When the blooms have faded, pruning is done by shortening the longest shoots and removing thin, weak twigs. When the new shoots are 1-2 in. long repotting should be carried out if necessary. The temperature of the greenhouse at night in winter should not fall below 45-50 degrees.

Acokanthera spectabilis is known as the Winter Sweet because of the jasmine-like fragrance of the white blossoms borne in long sprays in early spring. These are sometimes followed by blackish-purple fruits the size of a small olive, each containing one large nutlike seed.

A. venenata is the Bushman's Poison of South Africa, so named because of a poison natives extract from the bark. The clusters of white or rose-tinted flowers are borne in the axils of the leaves towards the ends of the shoots from February to April.

ACONITE. See Aconitum.

ACONITE, WINTER. See Eranthis.

ACONITUM—Monkshood (Aconi'tum). Hardy, herbaceous, perennial plants, 3-5 ft. high, which bear helmet-shaped flowers in summer and early autumn. They belong to the Buttercup family, Ranunculaceae. The common Monkshood, Aconitum Napellus, grows wild in various parts of Europe; other Monkshoods are natives of European countries, China and North America.

The thick, fleshy roots are poisonous and if flowers are grown in a vegetable garden Monkshood ought never to be included.

For Sunny or Shady Places. Monkshoods thrive in rich, deeply prepared soil in a sunny or shaded place and may be planted in fall or early spring. They need good drainage but will not stand dryness. If they are in a sunny location, be sure that they are kept well watered. They are suitable for the back of the herbaceous border, or for the wild and woodland garden. They can be increased by lifting and separating the roots in autumn or spring, and by sowing seeds in flats of fine soil placed in a frame in March–April. The seedlings are planted in a nursery border out of doors when large enough to be moved. Established Monkshoods resent disturbance. Do not transplant unless necessary.

The Chief Kinds. The common Monkshood (Aconitum Napellus), 4-5 ft., has dull blue flowers in July–August; the blue and white variety, bicolor, the white variety, alba, and Spark's variety, indigo, are more attractive. A. Wilsonii, 5 ft., bears dark violet-blue flowers in September; A. Fischeri, 3 ft., and A. autumnale, 4 ft., have blue flowers in September; A. lycoctonum, Wolfsbane, 2 ft., pale yellow and A. Hemsleyanum, a clinging or twining plant, 6 ft., violet blooms in July–August. A. uncinatum, 5 ft., blue, is a semiclimbing native of eastern North American woodlands. It needs shade and moisture.

Economic Uses. Although poisonous, several of the Monkshoods have valuable medicinal properties when used with knowledge. The common Aconite or Monkshood (A. Napellus) is one of the most important kinds and is grown commercially.

ACORN. The fruit of the Oak tree.

ACORUS—Sweet Flag (Ac'orus). Handsome, herbaceous, aquatic and bog plants, belonging to the Arum family, Araceae, which are suitable for planting in shallow water and wet places near the edge of a garden pool or pond. The common Acorus Calamus has long, sword-shaped leaves, which give off a strong scent when bruised, and bears small yellow flowers in summer. The word Acorus is derived from kore, a pupil, and refers to the supposed ophthalmic virtues of the plant.

Plant in Shallow Water. They are of the easiest possible cultivation. The rhizomes or root stocks of A. Calamus should be planted in ordinary soil, in water not deeper than 8 or 10 in., in fall or spring. They spread quickly and care must be taken to keep them within bounds by reducing the size of the clumps in spring. For purposes of propagation the rootstocks are lifted, divided and replanted in spring or fall. A. gramineus should be planted in boggy places in spring or early fall.

The chief kinds are Acorus Calamus, Sweet

Flag, 3 ft., native of Europe, its variety variegatus, which has green and yellow leaves, and A. gramineus, a dwarf Japanese plant with narrow, grasslike leaves. A. gramineus, its variegated variety, and its dwarf variety pusillus, are often grown in pots as house plants.

ACRE. An area of land; 4,480 square yards or 43,560 square feet.

ACRIS. A botanical term meaning acrid, bitter or sharp—e.g., Ranunculus acris.

ACROCLINIUM. See Helipterum roseum.

ACROCOMIA—*Gru-Gru* (Acroco'mia). Tropical American feather-leaved palms suitable for outdoor planting in the warmest parts of North America only. The name is derived from *akros,* top, and *kome,* tuft, and describes the arrangement of the leaves at the top of the trunk.

These palms thrive best in sandy soils that are fairly moist. They are propagated by suckers and by seeds. The species in cultivation are not well determined botanically. They probably include A. aculeata, A. armentalis and A. Totai, the latter perhaps the hardiest.

ACROSTICHUM (Acros'tichum). Swamp Ferns which are widely distributed in tropical countries. The different kinds vary greatly in form and size; some have undivided fronds while those of others are finely divided; some are but 6 in. high, others grow to 3 ft. and a few are of climbing habit. They belong to the botanical family Polypodiaceae.

For the Greenhouse. They require a minimum winter temperature of 55 degrees. A compost of equal parts of peat, loam and leaf mold with sand added, suits them. Repotting should be done in March when new fronds are forming. During the summer, water must be given freely; in fact it is best to stand the pots in shallow water, the atmosphere being kept moist and the greenhouse shaded; but in winter somewhat drier conditions should be maintained, though the soil must be kept moderately moist.

Increasing the Plants. Propagation is effected by dividing the clumps at potting time or by sowing spores in spring and summer (see Ferns). The chief kinds are A. aureum and A. daneaefolium, with erect fronds 6-12 ft. long.

ACTAEA—*Baneberry* (Actae'a). Hardy, herbaceous, perennial plants, 18 in. high, with attractive fernlike leaves, and spikes of small white

flowers in May, followed by red, white or blue berries which are poisonous. They grow wild in North America, Asia and Europe and belong to the Buttercup family, Ranunculaceae. The word Actaea indicates the elder-like leaflets, and is derived from *aktea,* the Elder.

The Red Baneberry, Actaea rubra, retains its clusters of brightly colored berries for several weeks.

Plant in Partial Shade. These plants are suitable for a partially shaded place and thrive in woodsy soil or in ordinary soil with which leaf mold has been plentifully mixed. Planting is done in early fall or spring. Propagation is by seeds sown in light soil out of doors in early summer, the seedlings being afterwards pricked out 6 in. apart in a nursery bed or shaded frame bed, and the plants put in their final locations in autumn. Clumps may be lifted, separated and replanted in spring. These are excellent plants for the woodland garden.

The chief kinds are A. rubra, Red Baneberry or Red Cohosh, with white flowers and red berries, and A. pachypoda (A. alba), White Baneberry or White Cohosh, with white flowers and white berries. Both grow 18-24 in. tall.

ACTINEA (Actine'a). Low, hardy, western American herbaceous plants that belong to the Daisy family, Compositae, and are sometimes cultivated in rock gardens and wild gardens. The name is derived from *aktin,* a ray.

Actineas thrive in well-drained, gritty soils in full sun. They may be propagated by seeds or by division. The best known are A. acaulis, 6 in., yellow; A. grandiflora (Rydbergia grandiflora), 6-9 in., yellow; and A. herbacea, 8-10 in. yellow.

ACTINIDIA (Actinid'ia). Hardy and tender climbers, natives of China, northern India and Japan, which are useful for covering walls, fences, arches and arbors or porches. They belong to the family Dilleniaceae. The name Actinidia is derived from *aktin,* a ray, and refers to the styles of the flower which radiate like the spokes of a wheel.

Planting and Pruning. These plants thrive in ordinary, well-drained, garden soil which has been deeply dug and enriched with decayed manure, together with a little leaf mold and peat if available. Fall and spring are the best seasons for planting. A little pruning is done in summer to thin and regulate the long, trailing shoots, but most of the pruning is done in spring, before new growth begins; old, weak and superfluous shoots are then cut off.

When to Take Cuttings. Propagation is best carried out by taking cuttings of semiwoody shoots of the current year's growth, and inserting them in July in a frame or under a hand light in a sheltered border. Propagation can also be carried out in summer by layering the ends of trailing branches. Sometimes a plant grown on a sunny wall produces fruits within which, when ripe, will be found seeds. These germinate in two or three months if sown in February in pots of sandy soil in a greenhouse in a temperature of about 50 degrees. Male and female flowers are usually borne on different plants; so in order to obtain fruits, plants of both sexes must be planted.

Kinds. A. arguta, Tara Vine, is a vigorous grower 40 ft. tall or more, hardy in the North. It has large, dark green leaves, and clusters of whitish flowers which are slightly fragrant. The female plants produce greenish-yellow fruits resembling Gooseberries. A. chinensis is very handsome and vigorous but too tender to be reliable in gardens north of Washington, D.C. The flowers change from cream white to buff-yellow, and the fruits have a Gooseberry-like flavor. A. Kolomitka rarely grows more than 15 ft. tall. Its small white flowers are

slightly fragrant. Its chief interest lies in the pink and white variegated leaves of the male plants. A. polygama, Silver Vine, is a moderate grower with a fascination for cats. It has white, fragrant flowers and yellow fruit. Young leaves of male plants have a silvery appearance. A. Kolkomitka and A. polygama are hardy.

Economic Use. The fruits of Actinidia chinensis are used for food in China.

ACTINOPHLOEUS MACARTHURI—*Cluster Palm* (Actinophloe'us). A handsome, feather-leaved palm that produces several erect trunks to a height of about 10 ft. It is a native of Australia. Its name is derived from *aktin,* a ray, and, probably, *phloeus,* bark.

In southern Florida, this palm thrives outdoors in part shade. It is a good decorative plant for growing in tubs and pots, is easily raised from seeds, and thrives in well-drained, fertile soil.

When grown in pots and tubs water freely and fertilize regularly from spring through fall, but less copiously during winter. Repot in spring but only when the containers become so crowded with roots that it is evident that the specimen is suffering because of this conditions.

ACULEATUS. A botanical term meaning prickly—e.g., Ruscus aculeatus (Butcher's Broom), a shrub which has prickly branches.

ACUMINATE. A botanical term applied to leaves and other parts that taper gradually to a slender tip.

ACUTE. Means sharply pointed when used as a botanical term.

ADA AURANTIACA (A'da). The botanical name of an orchid, of the family Orchidaceae, which grows wild in Colombia. It bears orange-scarlet flowers in spring, and is suitable for cultivation in a greenhouse having a minimum temperature of 50-55 degrees. The plant is of compact growth; the small pseudobulbs are almost hidden by the sheathing, strap-shaped, evergreen leaves. The flowers, which may number as many as fifteen in each inflorescence, are on erect, or arching, spikes 12 to 15 in. high, and last a long time in beauty. This orchid is said to have been named in compliment to a lady named Ada.

Details of Management. The treatment is similar to that needed by Odontoglossum crispum. Both these orchids can be grown together as they thrive in a moist atmosphere, and a summer temperature as near 60 degrees as conditions allow.

Shading should be given from the end of February onwards. In autumn the plants should be fully exposed to the light. Except in severe weather, the top ventilators must be opened daily, but at all times draughts should be avoided.

These orchids may be potted in osmunda fiber or in Fir bark. In either case perfect drainage must be provided. Repotting should take place in September. As small a pot or deep pan as possible should be used; a plant large enough to produce two or three flower spikes can be grown in a 5-in. pot; the oldest pseudobulbs are placed against the edge, thus giving room for the development of the young growths.

Annual repotting is not necessary, but twice in each year the plants should be examined and any alien mosses removed from the compost, and weak places made good. As the plants grow throughout most of the year, the roots must be kept moist even in winter, but naturally less water is then required.

ADAM-AND-EVE. See Aplectrum.

ADAM'S LABURNUM. Laburnocytisus Adamii, which see.

ADAM'S-NEEDLE. Yucca filamentosa, which see.

ADDER'S-TONGUE. See Erythronium.

ADDER'S-TONGUE FERN. See Ophioglossum.

ADENANTHERA PAVONINA—*Red Sandalwood Tree* (Adenanthe'ra). A tropical Asiatic tree to 60 ft. tall that belongs to the Pea family, Leguminosae. The name Adenanthera has reference to the gland-tipped anthers. This tree is only suitable for cultivating in the far South.

Propagation is by seeds, which should be soaked in hot water before sowing. The attractive red and yellow flowers are followed by pods containing bright-red seeds (the Circassian Seeds of commerce), which are used for making necklaces and other decorative articles.

ADENOPHORA—*Grand Bellflower, Ladybell* (Adenoph'ora). Hardy, herbaceous, perennial, summer-blooming plants, 18-24. in. high, which are closely related to Campanula. They grow wild in many parts of the world—Siberia, China, Turkestan, and belong to the Bellflower family, Campanulaceae. Adenophora is derived from *aden,* a gland, and *phoreo,* to bear, and refers to the nectary in the flower.

Dislike Being Transplanted. They should be planted in spring in a sunny border in light loamy soil; heavy soils can be made suitable by the addition of compost or peat moss and sand. These plants dislike being disturbed and should not be transplanted unless it is really necessary.

Propagation is by seeds sown in autumn or early spring in a cold frame. The seedlings should be potted singly in small pots, kept in a frame for the winter and planted out in spring.

The chief kinds are Adenophora Bulleyana, 3-4 ft., pale blue; A. lilifolia, 18 in., pale blue, fragrant; A. Potaninii, 2-3 ft., purple. All have bell-shaped flowers and bloom in summer.

ADHATODA (Adhato'da). Tropical shrubs of the Acanthus family, Acanthaceae. Natives of Asia, Africa and South America. The name is a native Brazilian one.

The chief kind is A. cydoniifolia, a semi-climber with clusters of showy white and purple flowers. Adhatodas require the same culture as Jacobinias.

ADIANTUM or MAIDENHAIR FERN
Beautiful and Easy-to-Grow Foliage Plants for the
Greenhouse and Outdoor Garden

There are many kinds of Adiantum or Maidenhair Fern (Adiantum): most are natives of tropical countries, but two are hardy and can be grown out of doors in the North. Adiantum belongs to the family Polypodiaceae. The name is derived from *adiantos,* dry, and refers to the

way in which water runs off the fronds.

Hints on Management. The tender kinds require a semishaded, heated greenhouse where the light is diffused, but not too dull. Strong sunlight is detrimental as it scorches the young fronds, and dense shade induces the formation of very weak growth. A minimum temperature of 50-55 degrees is suitable. The atmosphere must be kept moist during the growing season. The fronds should not be syringed, as the moisture collects between the young ones, and causes them to damp off. Maidenhair Fern can be grown indoors in a shady window, but usually the plants deteriorate after a few months unless they are returned to a warm, moist greenhouse for a time or are enclosed by a terrarium.

Varieties of the popular Adiantum cuneatum are among the most beautiful of greenhouse Ferns. This is A. cuneatum variety Wrightii.

An ideal soil consists of equal parts of peat moss, leaf mold, and loam with a free scattering of coarse sand, and a few small pieces of charcoal.

When to Repot. Repotting is done in March or April as soon as the young fronds begin to uncurl. The crocks and loose soil are removed with a pointed stick, and the plants are repotted in slightly larger pots. The compost should be pressed firm with the fingers, not rammed with a potting stick.

By repotting the plants year after year, large specimens can be grown in 10-in. pots, but smaller plants in 5-in. pots are the most serviceable. When in larger pots, Maidenhair Ferns can be kept vigorous for several years by top-dressing with fresh compost in March and feeding with diluted, weak, liquid fertilizer weekly from May until August.

On the approach of autumn, water must be given less frequently. From September to March very little water is required, as this is their resting period, but the soil must not be allowed to

become very dry.

Propagation by Division. Maidenhair Ferns can be increased by division or by spores. Division is done in the spring, as soon as the fronds commence to uncurl, the plant being separated into two or three pieces; these are repotted separately in pots of suitable size. If a large number is required, the soil is washed away from the roots and the plants are separated into single rooted pieces which are laid in a flower pan of

The American Maidenhair Fern, Adiantum pedatum, a beautiful hardy plant for cool, moist, shaded places.

moist sand, and placed in a propagating case; when well rooted they are potted separately in 2-in. pots.

How to Sow Fern Spores. Propagation by spores is an easy and reliable method. A frond is gathered when the spore cases, found on the back of the frond, are dark brown; this is placed in a paper bag. In twelve hours the ripe spores will fall to the bottom of the bag as a fine dust. Finely sifted potting soil is then sterilized by heat (see Soil Sterilization). It is important, too, that the pots or pans to be used are sterilized. Drainage is placed in the bottom of the pot or pan and it is then filled with soil, pressed moderately firm and made quite level. The spores are then sown thinly over the surface and are lightly pressed in with a piece of board. They are not covered with soil. After sowing, the pot or pan is covered with a sheet of glass, and set in a saucer kept full of water. If the pots are placed in a shaded greenhouse—temperature 55-60 degrees—a green mosslike growth will appear in a month. In a few more weeks it will be possible to distinguish the thin, green, heart-shaped

[1–10]
cidanthera bicolor

[1–10a]
Aechmea fulgens

1–10b]
eruvian Lily (Alstroemeria aurantiaca hybrid)

[1–10c]
Poppy Anemones (Anemone coronaria varieties)

[1-11]
Silk Tree or Mimosa (Albizzia Julibrissin)

[1-11a]
Japanese Angelica Tree (Aralia elata)

structures or prothalli, from which the young fern plants eventually develop. As soon as the miniature fronds are discernible, small clumps of the prothalli are set 1 in. apart in pans of finely sifted compost, and kept shaded and moist. Before they become crowded they are potted separately in 2-in. pots, and, when well rooted, into larger ones.

The favorite kind is Adiantum cuneatum or Delta Maidenhair Fern, from Brazil, with many attractive varieties, e.g., elegantissimum, gracillimum, grande and Pocottii. They make ideal pot plants, and the fronds are useful for decorative purposes when cut. The oldest fronds are most suitable for cutting; the young ones droop quickly. They should be immersed in water for 24 hours before use.

Other kinds of Maidenhair Fern are A. macrophyllum, which has very large pinnules (leaflets), and A. tenerum Farleyense, a most beautiful fern having large fronds on stalks from 18 in. to 2 ft. long. The latter needs a warmer greenhouse than the others mentioned—a minimum temperature of 60 degrees.

The hardy Maidenhair Fern, Adiantum pedatum, of North America, has graceful fronds 18-24 in. long; it will thrive in a shady place in garden soil, which has been made woodsy by the addition of leaf mold and sand. It likes a rich soil that is well drained but always moist. A mulch of leaf mold encourages it to thrive. Excellent for massing in cool, shady places in the wild garden, rock garden and elsewhere, Adiantum Capillus-Veneris grows wild in North America, Europe and South America. It should be planted in shady crevices in a mixture of loam, leaf mold, peat and sand. These hardy ferns may be planted in September, October or in early spring.

ADINA RUBELLA (Adi'na). An interesting leaf-losing Chinese shrub, hardy in sheltered places north to the vicinity of New York City and flowering freely over a long period in summer. Adina is from *adinos*, crowded, and refers to the arrangement of the flowers in tight, globular heads.

Adina thrives in any well-drained soil in a sunny situation, and is easily propagated from leafy cuttings of half-ripened shoots in summer. Its flowers are white or pale lavender-pink and

Adina rubella, an unusual fragrant-flowered shrub, is hardy in sheltered places as far north as New York City.

are fragrant. Adina belongs in the Madder family, Rubiaceae.

ADLUMIA FUNGOSA—*Climbing Fumitory, Allegheny Vine* (Adlu'mia). A hardy climbing plant, native of North America, which belongs to the Fumitory family, Fumariaceae. It has pretty, fernlike leaves, reaches a height of 12 ft. or more, climbs by means of leafstalks, and is suitable for the woodland garden. The large clusters of white or purplish, tube-shaped flowers are in full beauty in June–July. This plant was named in memory of Dr. Adlum. It was previously called A. cirrhosa.

When to Sow and Plant. Adlumia needs a shady location, well sheltered from wind, and fairly light, well-drained, moist, cool soil. It should be planted out of doors in spring. It is a biennial, and dies after it has flowered. To maintain a supply of plants, it is necessary to sow seeds every year. Often self-sown seedlings volunteer and so maintain the planting.

ADOBE LILY. See Fritillaria pluriflora.

ADOBE SOIL. A clayey type of soil that occurs in arid regions of the Southwest.

ADONIDIA MERRILLII—*Manila Palm* (Adonid'ia). An attractive, slender-trunked, feather-leaved palm from the Philippines suitable for planting in the far South. It grows 20-25 ft. tall. The species was named in honor of Dr. E. D. Merrill, an American botanist famous for his studies of Philippine plants.

The bright red fruits, borne in clusters, are highly ornamental. Seeds provide a ready means of increase.

ADONIS—*Pheasant's-eye, Flower of Adonis* (Ado'nis). Hardy herbaceous plants, with fern-like leaves and buttercup-like flowers, suitable for the rock garden and herbaceous border. One kind grows wild in Manchuria, and others are

The red, summer-flowering annual Pheasant's-eye, Adonis aestivalis.

found in various parts of Europe. They belong to the Buttercup family, Ranunculaceae. The legend runs that this plant sprang from the blood of Adonis when he was wounded by a wild animal.

When to Plant—Suitable Soil. These plants like a sandy soil enriched with leaf mold or compost. They may be set in a sunny or slightly shaded place. Planting of perennial kinds is done in spring or fall. The best method of propagation is by lifting the plants in October, separating them into pieces, and replanting. Seeds may be sown out of doors or in a cold frame in the fine sandy soil in September but they are usually very slow in germinating.

The best perennial kinds are Adonis

amurensis, 12 in., white, yellow, pink and red, spring; A. pyrenaica, 12-18 in., yellow, June–July; and the Spring Adonis, A. vernalis, yellow, spring.

The hardy annual kinds are attractive, early summer-flowering plants suitable for a sunny border; the seeds may be sown out of doors in September, or March–April, if the plants are to bloom in July–July; the seedlings are thinned to about 8 in. apart.

The best of the annuals are Adonis aestivalis, the Summer Adonis, 12-15 in., with deep red flowers, and A. annua, (A. autumnalis), the Autumn Adonis, 12-15 in., with bright red blooms.

ADROMISCHUS (Adromis'chus). Tender succulent South African plants of rather slow growth, often with attractively marked leaves. They belong in the botanical family Crassulaceae and are closely allied to Cotyledon. The name comes from *adros,* strong, and *miskos,* a flower stem, referring to the stout flower stems.

Adromischus needs the same culture as Echeveria, which see. Among the better-known kinds are A. clavifolius, A. Cooperi, A. hemisphaericus, A. maculatus, and A. rhombifolius.

ADVENTITIOUS. A botanical term used chiefly in reference to roots or buds which appear in other than the ordinary positions. For instance, aerial roots, which often develop on the branches of a vine grown under glass, are adventitious roots.

AECHMEA (Aech'mea). Hothouse and house plants, from tropical America, which bloom chiefly in summer and autumn and need a minimum winter temperature of 55 degrees when grown under glass. They are distinct from most plants as the tough, spine-edged leaves arise from the rootstock and overlap each other to form a long tube from the inside of which the flower spike emerges. The botanical name Aechmea, derived from *aichme,* a point, has reference to the pointed calyx. Aechmea belongs to the family Bromeliaceae.

These plants are grown in a compost of half osmunda fiber and half leaf mold, with a little sand and charcoal. During summer they require abundance of moisture both in the soil and in the atmosphere. Less water is required during the winter months. Light shade from strong summer sun is desirable.

To increase the stock, the sucker growths which push up from the bases of the plants are taken off with a sharp knife in March and inserted in small pots of sandy peat in a propa-

Aechmea miniata has attractive foliage and flowers, the latter followed by berry-like fruits which remain in good condition for a long period.

gating case. When rooted, they are placed in larger pots. Established specimens flourish for several years with an annual top-dressing.

The chief kinds are: A. fulgens, with green leaves, scarlet and blue flowers; A. fulgens discolor, similar but with maroon leaves; A. miniata, has green leaves and red and blue flowers; A. miniata discolor, similar but leaves green above and maroon beneath; A. fasciata, leaves green with white bands, pink flower head, blue flowers; A. marmorata, with mottled leaves, pink bracts, blue petals; A. Racinae, leaves green, flowers red, yellow and black; A. Foster's Favorite, wine-red leaves, red and blue flowers. They reach a height of 12 in. or more. Colored bracts add much to the beauty of some kinds.

AEGLE MARMELOS—*Bael Fruit* (Ae'gle). This citrus-like shrub or small tree from India, belonging to the family Rutaceae, is sometimes grown in the warmer parts of the Citrus Belt. It has trifoliate leaves and greenish-yellow, hard-shelled fruits, the pulp of which is edible and is used in preparing drinks.

AEGOPODIUM—*Goutweed, Bishop's Weed* (Aegopo'dium). Low, hardy, creeping perennials belonging to the Carrot family, Umbelliferae. Aegopodium is derived from *aix,* goat, and *podion,* a little foot.

The Goutweed has a limited use in places where its tendency to crowd out other plants is not disadvantageous. It roots deeply and is difficult to eradicate when once established and so should never be planted in rock gardens or in other places where it may do harm by spreading over choicer plants. It may be used in a limited way as a ground cover in shady areas; it prefers a moist soil.

Propagation is rapidly effected by division of the roots in spring or fall. The variegated form, A. Podagraria variegata, is the only one that is usually considered worth planting; it is less vigorous and invasive than the green-leaved A. Podagraria.

AEONIUM (Aeo'nium). A group of mostly succulent subshrubs closely related to Sempervivum and sometimes included under that name. They are natives of the Canary Islands, Cape Verde Islands, Madeira and parts of North Africa. The name was used by Dioscorides for A. arboreum.

Aeoniums are cultivated chiefly by fanciers of succulent plants. They are good window garden subjects, and in dry, warm climates, such as that of the Southwest, are well adapted for planting outdoors.

Culture. These plants thrive best in a porous, well-drained soil that is not excessively rich. They appreciate a liberal proportion of limestone chips and sand in the soil mixture. They should be repotted or planted just as new growth begins, which is usually in late summer.

After repotting, water should be given with caution at first—just enough to keep the soil barely moist—but, as roots penetrate the new soil and leaf development becomes active, more generous amounts will be needed and throughout the season of active growth the soil should be kept fairly moist.

At the end of the growing season, in late spring, watering should be gradually reduced and the soil kept nearly dry throughout the summer.

Aeoniums need full sun, an airy, buoyant atmosphere, and, when grown indoors, a minimum night temperature of about 50 degrees with a rise of 5-15 degrees permitted during the daytime. At times of the year when normal outdoor temperatures exceed these minimums, the outdoor temperatures are satisfactory.

Propagation is easily effected by means of cuttings inserted in sand at the beginning of the growing season, and by seeds sown in light, sandy soil.

Kinds. Among the most popular kinds are A. arboreum, a 3-ft.-tall plant with golden-yellow flowers and foliage that turns bronzy-purple in fall; A. arboreum foliis purpureis, similar but with dark purple leaves; A. canariense, which attains a height of about 1½ ft. and has whitish or yellowish flowers; and A. tabulaeforme, a curious and beautiful kind that forms great flat discs, each composed of many green leaves, and which has pale yellow flowers. Many other kinds, including a number of hybrids, are grown by specialists. Among these is A. Manriqueorum, a 6 ft.-tall kind with bright yellow flowers.

AERATION OF THE SOIL. The importance of adequate aeration of the soil can hardly be overstated. The spaces between the fine particles of soil are occupied partly by films of water and

If a special implement or tool is not available, lawns may be aerated by spiking them with a spading fork.

partly by air. The air contains oxygen which is so necessary for the healthy growth of all the roots. Experiments have shown that if the oxygen is driven out by waterlogging or other methods, the roots of most plants quickly rot and die. Bog and aquatic plants are especially adapted to live in water-saturated soil.

Aeration also greatly affects the fertility of the soil. The bacteria which inhabit it are constantly decomposing manure and vegetable matter, and, in this way, they release elements which sustain plant growth. Most bacteria cannot do their work in the absence of oxygen; in fact, if this gas is absent, another group of soil organisms known as denitrifying bacteria release the nitrogen as nitrogen gas; this passes away into the air and is lost as far as the plants are concerned.

The aim of all cultivation should, therefore, be to allow free access of air to the soil—i.e., to render it reasonably open in texture. Sandy soils are well aerated, but most garden soils require deep digging, or its mechanical equivalent, occasionally. The addition of stable manure and vegetable refuse assists in the aeration of heavy soils and so, also, may the intelligent use of synthetic soil conditioners, such as Krillium, and of coarse ashes and sand. Permanently waterlogged land must be drained before it can be rendered fit for most trees and plants. Lawns are benefited by spiking in spring to let air into the soil.

AERIAL ROOT. A root which develops on the stems or shoots of a plant and helps to sustain it by absorbing moisture from the air. Many orchids have aerial roots.

AERIDES—Air Plant (Aerid'es). Beautiful East Indian summer-flowering evergreen orchids of the family Orchidaceae; most must be grown in a greenhouse having a minimum winter temperature of 60 degrees. They have woody stems furnished with dark-green leaves arranged in opposite rows; the flower racemes develop in the axils of the leaves. The name Aerides is derived from aer, the air. The plants are epiphytal—they grow wild on trees.

The winter temperature should not be less than 60 degrees at night, rising higher in the day. In summer it should be 65-70 degrees at night, and may reach tropical heat in sunny weather in the day. A moist atmosphere is essential and shading is required during the summer.

Aerides longicornu has drooping spikes of fragrant rosy-purple flowers in summer.

Details of Management. Wooden orchid baskets are often used for Aerides, but flowerpots are to be preferred as, when repotting is necessary, the clinging roots cannot be easily removed from wood; if they cling to the pot, this can be broken and the pieces, with roots attached, placed in the new pot. Osmunda fiber forms a satisfactory potting compost for Aerides and they may also be grown quite well in Fir bark and in other barks suitable for Orchids. In potting, place a few crocks in the bottom of the pot, set the stem on them, carefully working the roots inside the pot, and fill the spaces with the compost, pressed firmly with a blunt stick. As the plant will reach a height of 2 ft. it is often necessary to place a bamboo cane in the pot for support. In April, and again at the end of August, some of the old compost should be removed and be replaced by fresh.

If this detail is attended to, repotting is not necessary until the plant stem has become bare of leaves at the base. When that happens, the leafy top of the stem may be cut off in spring, providing there are roots on it, and be potted. The bottom part of the plant may then be repotted. Water should be given throughout the year. In summer the compost should never be dry, but less water is required in winter.

The most popular kind is Aerides odoratum, 2-3 ft., with long arching spikes of very fragrant,

white and amethyst-colored flowers. A. odoratum majus (A. virens) is similar but has longer flower racemes and the blossoms are less strongly scented. Others are A. Lawrenceae, and A. quinquevulnerum, white and amethyst purple; and A. Lawrenceae Sanderianum, cream white and crimson. Aerides crispum has large fragrant flowers, pale rose and amethyst, on arching spikes 2-3 ft. long. A. Fieldingii is of similar coloring. All need the same conditions—a warm, moist greenhouse in which a minimum winter temperature of 60 degrees F. is maintained.

Cooler conditions are needed by Aerides vandarum, one of the most sweetly scented of orchids; it reaches a height of 3-4 ft., but is of such slender growth as to need the support of a stick. The white, rose-flushed flowers open in autumn, winter, or early spring; they are in short spikes, each spike usually bearing not more than three blossoms. A winter temperature of 55 degrees is high enough.

AERIDOVANDA. A group of bigeneric hybrid Orchids between Aerides and Vanda. They require the same culture as Vanda. Aeridovanda Mundayi has flowers that are white tinged with lilac.

AESCHYNANTHUS. See Trichosporum.

AESCULUS—*Horse Chestnut, Buckeye* (Aes'-culus). They are natives of Europe, North America and Asia, and belong to the family Hippocastanaceae. The name Aesculus is a Latin name for a tree, probably some kind of Oak.

Horse Chestnuts and Buckeyes are handsome ornamentals much favored for planting in gardens and parks and along roadsides. They thrive best in deep, fertile, fairly moist soils. In dry locations some kinds, especially the Common Horse Chestnut, A. Hippocastanum, and its varieties, are particularly likely to suffer in summer from a disfiguring physiological leaf scorch disease.

When to Plant. Horse Chestnuts and Buckeyes may be planted at any convenient time during fall or spring, provided the weather is mild and the ground not sodden. They possess an abundance of fibrous roots and can be transplanted easily and safely even when large.

The flowers of the common Horse Chestnut, Aesculus Hippocastanum, are attractive in spring.

The flower spikes are succeeded by conspicuous thorny fruits.

best raised from seeds, but when these are not available, grafting in spring or budding in July is practiced, seedlings of the common Horse Chestnut being used as stocks. For the Buckeyes, A. octandra makes a better stock. Grafting and budding may be done out of doors; the young trees used as stocks must be planted at least six months in advance. The seeds should be sown out of doors as soon as fully ripe, or they may be stratified and sown in spring; being fleshy, they soon shrivel and lose their vitality if kept in a dry room.

Pruning is best done in late winter or spring, for at that time the trees are leafless, and it is much easier to see which branches will benefit by being thinned out because of overcrowding, or if it is necessary to shorten any of them in order to ensure a well-balanced tree. It is important for a period of some years to see that each young tree is limited to one strong, outstanding, central growth to form the leading shoot.

The Common Horse Chestnut. The best known kind is Aesculus Hippocastanum, the Common Horse Chestnut. It has digitate leaves and in May bears spikes of white, yellow-blotched blooms, tinged with red; these are followed by clusters of green prickly fruits enclosing the seeds.

The double-flowered variety called flore pleno, is not only a beautiful tree, but is better adapted for planting in public parks and open spaces than the single-flowered kind because it does not produce fruits, which have such an attraction for children, who may damage the trees with sticks and stones when the fruits are nearing maturity.

The Red Horse Chestnut. Aesculus carnea, the Red Horse Chestnut, is a tree of rounded form, 25-50 ft. high, with showy, rose-red flowers in May. Though of hybrid origin (A. Hippocastanum x A. Pavia). It comes true or nearly true from seeds; the seedlings do not revert to one or other of the parents, as is usual with hybrids. A variety named Briotii has deeper colored, almost crimson, flowers. Yet another variety, A. carnea plantierensis, which is called the Damask Horsechestnut, has white-tinged-pink flowers. This variety does not produce fruits.

The Red Buckeye (A. Pavia) is a large bush or small tree, 12-30 ft. high, native of the southeastern United States but hardy as far north as southern New England. The tubular red flowers are produced in loose clusters in May and early June. Variety atrosanguinea has deeper colored flowers. It is typical of a group of North American trees that were at one time distinguished under the generic name of Pavia.

The Sweet Buckeye (A. octandra) is native from Pennsylvania to Georgia and Illinois. It develops into a round-headed tree 60 or more ft. high, with erect panicles of yellow flowers in May and June. This tree is not so attractive as the Common Horse Chestnut.

The Himalayan or Indian Horse Chestnut, (A. indica) has flowers similar in color to those of the Common Horse Chestnut but the spikes are longer and the rich, dark-green foliage is more attractive. Its greatest value lies in the fact that the trees are in full beauty at the end of June and early July, six weeks later than the Common Horse Chestnut. It is hardy in mild climates only.

The California Buckeye (A. californica) is a round-headed tree that grows to a height of about 40 ft. It has white or pale pink flowers. This kind is hardy in mild climates only.

For Small Gardens. In small gardens the Bottle-brush Buckeye (A. parviflora) is worthy of a place; it grows 7-10 ft. high, and the white flowers are freely produced in late July and during August. It is a native of the southeastern United States but is hardy further North. It spreads by means of sucker growths from the ground and is easily increased by detaching and planting these in March. It forms a large, billowy shrub and is excellent for planting as a lawn specimen where it has sufficient room to display its beauty. Similar in habit is A. splen-

Long spikes of white flowers decorate the Bottle-brush Buckeye in July and August. This is a native of the northeastern United States.

dens, a species native from Alabama to Mississippi and Louisiana, and hardy possibly as far north as Washington, D.C. It has red flowers and is the most handsome of the Buckeyes.

Economic Uses. The wood of Aesculus, or Horse Chestnut, is white and clean if cut when the sap is down (in winter), but it is neither strong nor durable in exposed places. It is used for toys, kitchen and dairy requisites.

AESTIVALIS. Flowering in summer; from the Latin, *aestas,* summer.

AESTIVATION. A botanical term denoting the arrangement of the flower petals in the bud. The aestivation is said to be revolute if the margins of the petals roll outwards, involute if they roll inwards.

AETHIONEMA—*Stone Cress* (Aethione'ma). Hardy perennial rock garden plants, 6-12 in. high, with wiry, trailing stems and pretty candytuft-like flowers in May–June. They belong to the Mustard family, Cruciferae, and are natives of Persia, Armenia, and other eastern countries. The botanical name is derived from *aitho,* to scorch, and *nema,* filament.

When to Plant and Take Cuttings. These beautiful little plants should be set out in early fall or spring in sandy or stony, loamy soil on a dryish sunny slope in the rock garden; there

The Bottle-brush Buckeye, Aesculus parviflora, is a shrubby species that grows 7 to 10 ft. high.

Aethionema Warley Rose, forming large cushions smothered with heads of bright rose-pink flowers in spring, is one of the most reliable of all sun-loving rock-garden plants.

they form bushy plants and will last for many years without renewal. It is beneficial to shorten the shoots slightly when the flowers are over. They are usually propagated by cuttings made from the new shoots which grow soon after the plants have been trimmed after flowering; if placed in pots or a bed of sifted sandy soil in a

The charming pink-flowered Lebanon Candytuft, Aethionema pulchellum.

shaded frame, kept close, the cuttings will form roots in a few weeks.

When well rooted they should be potted singly in small pots in loam and leaf mold with a scattering of sand, and grown in a cold frame until September; then they may be planted in the rock garden. Or they can be kept in pots in the frame until spring, and then planted out. Aethionema may be raised from seeds sown in pots of sandy soil in a cold frame in September.

Kinds: Aethionema pulchellum, pink; A. grandiflorum, rose color; A. armenum, rose color; A. Warley Rose, bright rose; A. coridifolium, pink; A. iberideum, white; A. saxatile, pink.

AFFINIS. A botanical term meaning similar to or related to.

AFRICAN DAISY. Name applied to Arctotis, Dimorphotheca, Gazania and Gerbera.

AFRICAN HEMP. See Sparmannia.

AFRICAN LILY. See Agapanthus.

AFRICAN MARIGOLD. See Tagetes.

AFRICAN MILKBUSH. See Synadenium.

AFRICAN TULIP TREE. Spathodea campanulata, which see.

AFRICAN VIOLET. See Saintpaulia.

AGAPANTHUS AFRICANUS—*African Lily, Lily of the Nile* (Agapan'thus). A small group of tender herbaceous plants which have fleshy or tuberous rootstocks and long, strap-shaped leaves, and bear large umbels of blue, purple-blue or white flowers on top of long, stout stems in summer. They are natives of South Africa and belong to the Lily family, Liliaceae. The name is derived from *agape,* love, and *anthos,* flower.

These plants are commonly grown in large wooden tubs; flowerpots are unsuitable, as the vigorous roots soon crack them. They are placed out of doors in a sunny or slightly shady situation after the weather is warm and settled; they are brought into a cool greenhouse, light cellar or porch, before frost threatens, where they are kept for the rest of the year. In mild climates they thrive out of doors the year around and are suitable for planting in beds and borders.

Cultivation and Soil Compost. The tubs must have a sufficient number of holes in the bottom to enable surplus water to drain away freely. A 3-in. layer of broken crocks is put in and covered with pieces of turf. Enough soil is then set on the turf to ensure that when potting is completed the topmost roots are an inch or so below the surface. The remainder of the soil is added and made firm. Two parts loam, one part leaf mold, and one part well-decayed manure make an ideal soil mixture. During summer these plants need a good deal of water, but in winter the soil is only watered occasionally to prevent its becoming very dry. They may remain in the same tub for many years. Liquid fertilizer should be applied weekly in summer.

Another method of cultivation is to plant out of doors in May and lift and store in the autumn.

Propagation is effected by division of the clumps in April. They are lifted, soaked in water for a few hours to wash away the soil, and the rhizomes are cut through with a knife so that each part has a few roots. They are potted in 6-in. pots and, later on, in larger ones. Plants which have become well-rooted in 8-in. pots should next be planted in tubs 18-24 in. in diameter. Plants may also be raised from seeds sown in the greenhouse in spring, the seedlings being repotted until they are large enough to be placed in tubs. They will not bloom until three years old.

Kinds. Much confusion exists regarding the correct naming of Agapanthus. Plants formerly known as A. umbellatus, and still frequently grown in gardens under that name, are known to represent at least three species, A. africanus, A. campanulatus and A. orientalis. The last named is the most common in cultivation and occurs in several varieties.

A. africanus (A. umbellata variety minor) has leaves 4-10 in. long and deep blue-violet flowers on stalks 10-20 in. long. A. campanulatus (A. umbellata variety Mooreanus) grows to a height of 18 in. or less and has sky-blue flowers. This is the hardiest kind. It may be grown outdoors as far north as Washington, D.C., and even somewhat farther north in very sheltered locations. A. caulescens has a short but distinct, erect, above-ground stem. Its stamens protrude from the flowers. Except for these features it resembles A. africanus. A. inapertus has drooping blue flowers on stalks that may be 4 ft. high. It has a stout, creeping rootstock. A. longispathus is similar to A. orientalis but has smaller flowers and is deciduous (loses its foliage in winter).

A. orientalis has evergreen leaves up to 30 in. long and large clusters of flowers on scapes 2-3 ft. high. The flowers are normally medium blue but two white-flowered varieties, albus and maximum albus, are known. A. orientalis variety pallidus has pale blue flowers, A. orientalis variety Leichtlinii somewhat deeper blue flowers, and in A. orientalis variety giganteus the flowers are dark blue. The last-named variety is very robust, attains a height of 3-4 ft. and has up to

200 flowers in each cluster. A. orientalis variety aurivittatus has its leaves striped lengthwise with yellow. A. orientalis variety variegatus has leaves shorter than those of the green-leaved A. orientalis and almost entirely white with but a few longitudinal bands of green. A. orientalis varieties maximus and monstrosus are especially vigorous varieties that are larger in all their parts than the typical A. orientalis. A. orientalis variety flore-pleno has double flowers which remain attractive for a long period.

A. pendulus resembles A. inapertus but its flowers are narrower in their mouths and are rich purple.

AGAPETES BUXIFOLIA (Agape′tes). A tender evergreen shrub from northern India, which bears red, tube-shaped flowers in spring.

Agapanthus campanulatus, low growing and blue-flowered, is one of the hardiest kinds.

It belongs to the Heath family, Ericaceae. Agapetes is derived from the Greek *agapetos,* meaning beloved.

Although little known in America, this species would seem to have value for planting outdoors in mild sections. In Europe, it is grown in greenhouses and, by annual pruning, the plants can be sufficiently dwarfed to flower in 5- or 6-in. pots. Large specimens are obtained by repotting in larger pots when they are well rooted in the small ones. Each year after flowering the branches are cut back by half. In a warm, moist greenhouse—temperature 60 degrees—new shoots soon form. When these are about an inch long the plants are repotted in slightly larger pots. A soil of two parts peat, one part loam, and some sand is used and must be made firm. When well rooted, they are gradually inured to full sunlight and are ventilated more freely. The soil must be kept moist; prolonged dryness is very harmful. In winter less water is needed, and care must be taken to prevent the compost from becoming sour through overwatering. A temperature of 45-50 degrees during the winter is suitable.

Propagation is effected by inserting cuttings in August or September in a mixture of peat moss and sand. The cuttings are covered with a bell jar until they are rooted. When 3 in. high the tips of the plants are pinched off and the resultant side shoots are treated similarly.

AGARICUS CAMPESTRIS. The botanical name of one of the Mushrooms. For details of cultivation see Mushroom.

AGARITA. See Mahonia.

AGASTACHE (Agas'tache). Hardy tall herbs, native to North America, and belonging to the Mint family, Labiatae. The name is derived from *aga,* very much, and *stachys,* a spike of wheat; it refers to the many-flowered spikes.

Agastaches are propagated by seeds, which are produced freely, and by division in spring. They are sometimes grown in flower borders and in wild gardens. The chief kinds are: A. nepetoides, up to 5 ft. tall, with dense 18-in. spikes of greenish-yellow flowers in July; and A. urticifolia, about 3 ft. tall, with shorter spikes of rose to violet flowers.

AGATHAEA. Felicia amelloides, which see.

AGATHIS—*Dammar Pine* (Ag'athis). Tall evergreen trees from Australia and Malaya that are sometimes planted in southern California and in Florida. They belong to the Monkey Puzzle Tree family, Araucariaceae. The most commonly cultivated are A. robusta, the Queensland Kauri, and A. alba. Agathis is from the Greek *agathos,* a ball of thread, and refers to the form of the catkin.

AGATHOSMA (Agathos'ma). Low evergreen shrubs from South Africa suitable for growing outdoors in warm climates, or as cool greenhouse pot plants elsewhere. They belong to the Rue family, Rutaceae, and thrive in sandy, peaty soil that never becomes excessively dry.

The name is derived from *agathos,* pleasant and *osma,* smell.

Propagation is by cuttings of half-ripened shoots in summer. The plants should be sheared after flowering, to induce bushiness. A. villosa, flowers light purple, is the commonest; A. Ventenatiana, flowers white, lilac or purple, is also grown.

AGATI GRANDIFLORA (Aga'ti). An Asiatic tree, handsome in growth and attractive in bloom. It belongs to the Pea family, Leguminosae, attains a height of about 40 ft., grows quickly, but is short-lived. It is a tropical species.

Its white, pink or red flowers are succeeded by pods. The young fruits, flowers and foliage are edible. Sometimes called Sesbania grandiflora.

AGAVE—*Century Plant* (Aga've). Distinctive ornamental succulent plants suitable for planting out of doors in mild climates, especially in

Agaves are natives of the warmer and drier parts of the Western Hemisphere. Here Agave atrovirens luxuriates in a greenhouse at The New York Botanical Garden.

Agave striata has much narrower leaves than most kinds. Its greenish flowers are in elegant spikes.

desert and semidesert regions; for cultivating in greenhouses; and, in small sizes, as house plants elsewhere. Where winters are severe, they can be used in the garden in summer, the pots being sunk to the rims in beds and borders; large plants in pots or tubs are often placed on steps

The Century Plant, Agave americana, flowers at long intervals only. After blooming, the plant dies. Rarely do plants live to be 100 years old before blooming.

and terraces. The Agaves belong to the Amaryllis family, Amaryllidaceae, and most of them are natives of Mexico; some grow wild in the West Indies and a few in the United States. The name Agave is derived from the Greek *agavos*, meaning admirable.

Some Kinds Perish After Flowering. The name Century Plant was given to the large kinds of Agave because they grow very slowly; many years, though rarely a hundred years, may pass before a plant reaches maturity and produces a flower spike. The leaves of Agaves form rosettes, the plants usually having little if any stem, but sometimes developing well-defined trunks several feet tall, as does A. attenuata. The flowers are usually in tall, branched spikes. After flowering, most of the Agaves die, though suckers may develop at the base. A few Agaves, those of smaller growth, produce flowers fairly regularly and continue to live.

The Best Potting Compost. Agaves need a very

porous soil compost and firm potting. A suitable soil mixture consists of two parts fibrous loam, one part broken bricks, and one part sand with a little bone meal and dried cow manure added.

March and April are the best months for repotting, but as these plants are of slow growth and thrive best in comparatively small pots, repotting is not usually necessary for several years, especially when the plants are large.

Plenty of drainage should be placed in the bottom of the pot or tub, as the plants benefit by liberal supplies of water during the summer, but little is required during winter.

Propagation. Seeds, suckers and plantlets provide the means of increasing Agaves. Many kinds perish after they have flowered and ripened seeds. Sometimes suckers develop around the base of old plants; in some cases plantlets develop on old flowering stems. These can be taken off and potted. If such shoots are not produced, propagation must be by seeds, which should be sown, when ripe, in pots of sandy soil.

The Favorite Kind. The best-known Agave and the kind which is most extensively cultivated is Agave americana, the common Century Plant. It will withstand more neglect than most plants because of its thick, green leaves. It has characteristic beauty as it develops slowly from a small plant into a noble specimen, with leaves 3-6 ft. long and 6-9 in. wide. Only after many years does it bloom. The flower spike, 15-25 ft. high, is covered with dense clusters of comparatively small, yellowish-green flowers. In the variety variegata the leaves are margined with yellow. In the variety picta, the yellow color is down the center of the leaf and the margins are green. Agave americana is sometimes called American Aloe.

There are numerous other Agaves, of which these are some of the best: A. albicans, A. atrovirens, A. ferox, A. filifera, A. Kerchovei, A. noli-tangere, A. Salmiana, A. scabra, A. striata, A. stricta, and A. Victoriae-Reginae.

Economic Uses. Agaves produce excellent fiber in their leaves; this really provides the strengthening element which enables the massive leaves to retain their rigidity. A few kinds have been selected as being superior to others, either for the production, or ease of extraction, of the fiber. The two principal ones are A. sisalana, producing the Sisal Hemp of commerce, and A. fourcroydes, from which the Henequen, or Yucatan Hemp, is obtained. The Mexican beverages pulque and mescal are derived chiefly from A. atrovirens.

AGERATUM (Agera'tum). Medium- and low-growing tender plants from Mexico, with small heads of fluffy, lavender-blue, white or pinkish flowers, used chiefly for edging or carpeting sum-

Ageratum is ideal for summer flower beds.

mer flower beds, for window and porch boxes, and in borders. They belong to the Daisy family, Compositae. The word Ageratum is derived from *a*, not, and *geras*, old, and indicates the lasting character of the flowers.

When to Sow Seeds. Seeds are sown in flower pans or flats filled with light, sandy compost in a warm greenhouse, temperature 55-60 degrees, in late winter or spring, eight to ten weeks before the plants are wanted for setting out in the outdoor garden. The seeds are scattered thinly on the surface and covered with a light soil covering and sheets of paper or pieces of glass, until germination takes place. When an inch or so high, the seedlings are pricked out about 2 in. apart in flats filled with half loam and half leaf mold, with sand added. In about ten days, the tips are pinched off to ensure branched plants. Two or three weeks before planting outside, the flats of seedlings are placed in a cold frame and are gradually hardened off.

Instead of being grown in flats, the seedlings

may be potted separately in 3-in. pots. They are set 6 to 9 in. apart in the flower beds. Ageratums can also be grown from seeds sown directly outdoors in early spring. Plants so raised bloom a little later than those started earlier indoors. If the dead blooms are removed as they fade, the flowering season will be prolonged.

AGERATUM, HARDY. See Eupatorium coelestinum.

AGGREGATE. A term applied to shingle, coarse gravel, crushed bricks, and the like, used for mixing with sand and cement to form concrete.

AGLAONEMA (Aglaone'ma). Evergreen foliage plants from tropical Asia and Africa, cultivated in pots for house and greenhouse decoration. Aglaonema is from *aglaos*, bright, and *nema*, a thread, perhaps having reference to the shining stamens. It belongs to the Arum family, Araceae.

Flowers sometimes appear on cultivated specimens of Aglaonema modestum, the Chinese Evergreen. Their similarity to those of the Calla Lily indicates the botanical relationships of these plants.

Aglaonemas require the same cultural conditions as Dieffenbachia, which see. One, A. modestum, is much cultivated under the name Chinese Evergreen (although actually a native of the Philippines); it thrives in poorly lighted places and will grow for long periods in water

Aglaonema pictum has prettily variegated foliage. This native of Malaya is an attractive house plant.

without soil. A. costatum is a very low kind, well suited for terrariums. Other attractive kinds are A. commutatum, A. Roebelinii, A. oblongifolium, A. oblongifolium variety Curtisii, A. pictum, A. pictum variety tricolor, A. angustifolium, A. siamense, A. simplex, A. pseudo-bracteatum and A. marantifolium variety tricolor.

AGRICULTURE, THE UNITED STATES DEPARTMENT OF. This important department of the federal government is headed by the Secretary of Agriculture. It is concerned chiefly with the progress and development of agriculture in the United States, but devotes considerable attention to horticulture and to the investigation of problems concerned with ornamental plants. Its headquarters are at Washington, D.C.

The United States Department of Agriculture is responsible for the publication of many leaflets, bulletins, and circulars that deal with subjects of interest to the gardener. Some of these may be had free from the Division of Publications, Office of Information, United States Department of Agriculture, Washington 25, D.C.; others can be obtained at modest prices from the Superintendent of Documents, Government Printing Office, Washington 25, D.C.

AGROSTEMMA—*Corn Cockle* (Agrostem'-ma). The annual Agrostemma Githago, with grayish, silky-haired leaves and stems, is the

Corn Cockle, selected strains of which, with showy, rose-red flowers, are sometimes offered by seedsmen. Seeds are sown in early spring in sunny situations, where the plants are to grow. The name means crown of the field, from *agros*, field, and *stemma*, a crown.

Selected seed strains of Agrostemma Githago, the Corn Cockle, are valuable for garden display and cutting.

The popular hardy perennial Rose Campion, previously called Agrostemma coronaria, and Jove's-flower (A. flos-Jovis), now go under the name of Lychnis, which see.

AGROSTIS—*Bent Grass* (Agros'tis). A few kinds are used for garden ornament; a number are important lawn and golf-course grasses. The name is an ancient Greek one for a kind of grass.

The principal ornamental kinds are: A. nebulosa, Cloud Grass, 12-15 in. tall and grown for its graceful flower spikes; and A. retrofracta, which has 12-in.-long panicles on stems 2 ft. tall. Both are hardy annuals that grow and flourish in any well-drained garden soil, in a sunny location. Seeds are sown outdoors in spring where the plants are to remain, or they can be sown elsewhere and transplanted. The seeds are best sown in small groups at 6-in. intervals. The resulting plants grow better from seeds so sown, and transplanting, if planned, is more easily accomplished. A. hiemalis (A. laxiflora), Hair Grass or Silk Grass, is a 2-ft.-tall nial. It, too, can be raised from spring-sown seed.

In addition to their value for garden decoration, these grasses are useful as cut material to be dried for indoor use. For the latter purpose, the spikes are cut before the flowers open.

For Lawns and Golf Courses. Several species of Agrostis, and varieties, strains and forms derived from them, constitute an important group of grasses used for lawns and golf courses. They are commonly called Bent Grasses from the habit many kinds have of forming short-jointed stems (stolons) which bend towards the soil and take root. Some few spread by underground stems (rhizomes). This spreading habit results in a dense grass sod. Common names given these Bent Grasses have largely originated among seedsmen. Some are difficult to identify botanically; opinions differ as to the species to which some of the varieties belong.

A. canina, Brown Bent or Velvet Bent, makes an extremely dense growth of fine leaves. It spreads by rhizomes and is much used on putting greens. Very little pure seed of this is available. Attempts are being made to secure greater supplies. In certain old lawns, patches of pure stands exist where the old, mixed South German Bent seed was sown. Such patches are being propagated vegetatively in an attempt to grow stands of seed. Strains have been segregated which show a tendency to spread by stolons as well as by rhizomes.

A. palustris, Creeping Bent, and the plants known as maritima, Seaside Bent, and A. stolonifera var. compacta, are considered to be the same species. Seaside Bent is so named to distinguish it from the inland form of the species. Grown largely on the Pacific Coast, it is also called Cocoos Bent, for Coos County in Oregon, where seed is grown commercially. Of this form, a number of strains exist. Two of these, Metropolitan and Washington (considered by some to be identical), are planted by cutting the stolons into fine pieces. These are then spread over a prepared soil surface in the same manner as seed. They produce a lawn of close and fine texture.

A. tenuis (A. vulgaris) includes a valuable strain that is sold under such names as Colonial Bent, Astoria Bent, New Zealand Bent, and Prince Edward Island Bent. To prevent confusion the United States Department of Agriculture in 1930 decreed that the official name be Colonial Bent. A. alba (Red Top, Fiorin) is used extensively, but mainly as a nurse grass to be sown with more permanent grasses. It is characterized by fast growth, but it makes a poor sod and under average lawn conditions lasts but three years.

AHUWHUETE. A name applied to Taxodium mucronatum.

AICHRYSON (Aichry'son). Tender succulent plants, mostly from the Canary Islands, related to Sedum and Sempervivum. They belong in the Crassula family, Crassulaceae. The name is of classic origin, having been applied by Dioscorides to a species of Aeonium.

Most are short-lived and die after they flower the first time, which may be when they are one, two, or three years old. They require the same culture as Crassula, which see.

A. dichotomum is a pretty species for growing as a biennial in pots. The seeds are sown in June or July and the young plants are grown three together to flower in 4- or 5-in. pots the following May. It is an interesting window plant, with yellow flowers. Other kinds are A. domesticum, A. tortuosum, and A. palmense, all bearing yellow flowers.

AILANTHUS—*Tree of Heaven* (Ailan'thus). Tall, hardy, fast-growing, leaf-losing trees with large pinnate leaves. They are chiefly natives of India and China and belong to the family Simarubaceae. The name is derived from *ailanto*, a word signifying a tree tall enough to reach the skies, hence the common name, Tree of Heaven.

Planting and Making Root Cuttings. These trees thrive in any soil. Planting may be done in fall or spring. They are easily raised from seeds and self-sow abundantly. To prevent this as much as possible, propagate desirable female trees from root cuttings and eliminate all nearby males. An increased stock of favored forms and varieties is obtained easily by root cuttings. In early spring, suitable roots should be dug up, selecting, for preference, pieces the thickness of steel knitting needles and averaging 2-3 in. long. These are placed in a flat of sandy soil in a cold frame kept close, or are dibbled in sandy ground. If the ground beneath Ailanthus trees is forked over, it is usual for suckers to develop from the damaged and broken roots. These can easily be transplanted.

Pruning, when necessary, is best done in winter by removing crowded branches and keeping the leading shoot on each tree clear of other shoots or branches.

The most common kind is Ailanthus altissima, a tree 50-100 ft. high, native of northern China. It has large pinnate leaves 12-30 in. long and 6-12 in. wide, composed of fifteen to thirty leaflets. The male and female flowers are usually produced on separate trees. They are greenish and are borne in terminal panicles, but they have no beauty. The female flowers are followed by clusters of winged, reddish-brown fruits or "keys" (not unlike those of the Ash) which are very showy in autumn. Male trees give off an unpleasant odor when in flower. Never plant them. Female trees produce fruits, but not viable seeds, without being pollinated by a male.

A Good Tree for Town Gardens. Ailanthus is of value for planting in pleasure grounds and parks, and is one of the most tolerant trees for town and city gardens. It is smoke resistant, is remarkably free of pests and diseases, and will even live through occasional inundations of sea water. In some places it has run wild to such an extent that it is a nuisance.

In A. altissima pendulifolia the leaves, but not the branches, are semiweeping or pendulous. A. altissima erythrocarpa has bright red fruits. A. Vilmoriniana is readily distinguished from the common Tree of Heaven by its spiny young shoots.

AIRA—*Hair Grass* (Ai′ra). Hardy perennial ornamental grasses, belonging to the family Gramineae. Aira is derived from *airo,* the Greek name for a kind of grass.

Aira pulchella, the most popular kind, grows only about 9 in. high, and is sometimes used as an edging plant for flower borders. It is easily propagated by lifting the plants in October or March, separating them into rooted pieces, and replanting 8 in. apart. The dried open flowers may be used for winter decoration indoors.

AIR LAYERING: A MEANS OF PROPAGATION
A Simple Way to Raise New Plants from Old Ones

Air layering is a method of vegetative propagation that often may be conveniently used when stems or branches do not lend themselves to ground layering. Circumposition, ringing, mossing, stem layering and Chinese layering all are names that have been used for this form of propagation. In the past, in temperate climates, it was chiefly employed in greenhouses to secure increase of such plants as Ficus, Cordyline, Dracaena and Croton, and proved especially useful when dealing with specimens that had lost their lower leaves and had become leggy.

To accomplish air layering, girdle the stem or branch by removing a narrow strip of bark all around it at a point some 8-12 in. from the top of the shoot; or, at about the same distance from the tip of the shoot, make a cut in the stem about an inch long and extending one third of the way through the shoot. Make this cut upwards, towards the tip of the shoot. Peg the cut open with a thin sliver of wood. Around the incision wrap a largish bundle of moist sphagnum moss and tie it securely in position with string or raffia. Keep the moss always moist (this may be done by wrapping it tightly in polyethylene film) and the roots of the old plant rather dry. Under this treatment new roots will shortly appear at the incision, and will usually soon penetrate the moss ball and show on its outside. The new plant should then be separated from the old one by cutting it off below the moss ball. It should then be lotted. After potting it should be kept in a close, moist atmosphere until it has become re-established.

Another method of air layering is as follows. Take a flowerpot and break away a considerable portion from the rim to about halfway down, on one side. Then fix it to a stick by pushing one end of the latter through the hole in the bottom of the pot. The stick, when fixed in the ground, should be long enough to bring the pot to within about 12 in. of the selected shoot.

One method of air layering is to make a cut in an upward direction and about ⅓ through the stem.

Next, a sliver of wood is pushed into the incision to keep it open.

A mass of moist sphagnum moss is wrapped tightly around the cut area.

When the pot is in position, half fill it with sandy soil. Make a slit upwards halfway through the shoot where it will touch the soil in the pot when the shoot is bent down. The slit must be on the underside of the shoot.

Carefully bring down the shoot until it lies across the broken side of the pot and touches the soil in it. The "tongue" of the slit portion should be pushed carefully into the soil as the shoot is lowered; this will keep the slit part open.

The pot should then be filled with soil, which must be kept moist.

A New Method. In recent years many hardy woody plants have been successfully rooted outdoors by air layering. Leaves are removed from the incision area, a longitudinal cut of about 1½ inches is then made, forming a tongue over which a hormone rooting powder suitable for woody plants is dusted. Moist sphagnum moss is immediately wrapped around the cut and a few

The sphagnum is then encased in polyethylene film and tied top and bottom.

After a few weeks new roots will have penetrated to the outside of the moss. The top of the plant is then removed and planted separately in sandy soil.

The cut-back stem of the Cordyline which was air layered produces new shoots which may also be used for propagation.

shreds are drawn into the incision to keep it open. Around the ball of moss polyethylene plastic film (the type used in deep freezers) is wrapped tightly and is tied firmly at either end so that air cannot penetrate to cause drying. Overlap the film in the way that clapboards and shingles are laid so that water will be shed and there will be no seepage of rain water into the ball of moss, and finish by sealing with Scotch Electric Tape at both ends. This method of propagating woody plants will prove advantageous with plants difficult to root by stem cuttings or other methods, or where suitable propagating facilities are not readily available.

AIR PLANT. See Kalanchoë pinnata; and Aerides.

AIR PLANTS OR EPIPHYTES are plants that grow on other plants, usually trees, but do not derive nourishment directly from them as do parasites and saprophytes. They merely use the plant on which they grow as a support and obtain their nourishment from rotted leaves and other debris that collects in the crotches of branches, etc., from water, and from the air. Many Orchids, Ferns, and Bromeliads are epiphytes; so also are some Cacti, as well as representatives of many other plant groups.

AIR POTATO. See Dioscorea bulbifera.

AJUGA—*Bugleweed* (Aju'ga). Hardy annual or perennial herbaceous plants of creeping habit, 6-12 in. high, which bloom in early summer. The commonly cultivated kinds are all perennials, are of easy cultivation in ordinary garden soil and are suitable for the rock garden, for the front of the herbaceous border, and for ground covers. They are natives of Europe and belong to the Mint family, Labiatae. Ajuga is derived from *a*, not, and *zygon*, a yoke, in reference to the shape of the calyx.

These plants flourish in almost any situation, though those kinds which have variegated leaves color best in a sunny place. They are propagated in fall or spring by lifting the plants, separating them into rooted pieces, and replanting.

A favorite kind is Ajuga reptans atropurpurea, 6-12 in., with dark bronze-purple foliage and spikes of blue (occasionally white or pink) flowers in spring. A. reptans Rainbow has leaves splashed with cream, bronze and pink markings. A. genevensis Brockbankii, 6 in., has showy

spikes of blue flowers in summer, and A. pyramidalis metallica crispa has curiously crinkled metallic-green leaves.

AKEBIA (Ake'bia). Attractive twining shrubs particularly well suited for training over porches, trellises, arbors and wooden fences. The Akebias are ideal climbers for the cool greenhouse. They belong to the family Lardizabalaceae, and grow wild in China, Japan and Korea. The name Akebia is of Japanese origin.

Planting and Pruning. These plants will thrive in ordinary, well-drained, cultivated garden ground, and should be planted in spring; they do better in rather light than in heavy soil. If provided with suitable supports, the Akebias need little training when the long trailing growths are established on a porch, arbor, trellis or fence. From time to time it is necessary to tie in or cut off loose long shoots, and in late autumn or early spring to do a little thinning. Every three or four years it may be necessary to cut down the whole mass of shoots in winter.

Layering and Taking Cuttings. Propagation is by layering, cuttings and seeds. Autumn is the best time to make the layers by fastening the ends of the shoots in the ground with wooden

Akebia quinata is a charming vine of refined appearance. In spring it bears fragrant flowers which are sometimes followed by interesting edible fruits.

pegs. Cuttings can be rooted in pots of sandy soil in a frame kept closed for a few weeks, during July and August, or in sandy soil out of doors if covered with a bell jar or hand light in September. The seeds should be sown as soon as quite ripe in a pot or shallow box filled with sandy soil and placed in a greenhouse or cold frame.

The Chief Kinds. Two Akebias are grown: Akebia trifoliata (lobata), of which the parts of the leaves are in threes, and A. quinata, having leaves composed of five leaflets. A trifoliata is a twining shrub of vigorous growth, leaf-losing in the North but evergreen in mild climates. Male and female flowers are borne in April in the same raceme, the pale purple male flowers being less than half the size of the dark-purple female flowers.

Akebia quinata loses its leaves in cold climates but is evergreen in the South. The flowers, borne in pendant racemes during April, are fragrant, the male blooms pale purple, ¼ in. across, the female blooms 1-1½ in. across, chocolate-purple in color. Both Akebias produce edible sausage-shaped fruits 2½-3 in. long.

ALABAMA, GARDENING IN. See Regional Gardening.

ALABAMA SNOW WREATH. See Neviusia.

ALBIZZIA (Albiz'zia). Acacia-like plants generally suitable for outdoor cultivation in mild districts only, but one is hardy into New England. They belong to the Pea family, Leguminosae, and grow wild in Persia, Japan, and other eastern countries and in Australia.

Potting and Soil Compost. If grown in the greenhouse, the plants should be potted in March, using a soil of loam and leaf mold, with a free scattering of sand; the addition of a little peat moss is beneficial. When the plants need repotting into larger flowerpots the work should be done in March. Albizzias used in summer flower beds are planted out of doors late in May or early in June, after having been hardened off in a cold frame.

Raising Plants from Seeds and Cuttings. Seeds provide the easiest means of obtaining young plants. They are very hard and should be soaked in warm water for twelve hours before sowing in February in a greenhouse having a minimum temperature of 50 degrees. Cuttings 1½-2 in. long, made of the ends of young side shoots, are

Albizzia Julibrissin has fernlike foliage the leaflets of which fold together at night. The flower heads resemble pink powderpuffs.

inserted in sandy soil on a partly shaded border out of doors in summer, and are covered with a bell jar or hand light until rooted—a process which takes four or five weeks. The rooted cuttings are potted singly in small pots and kept in a greenhouse for the winter.

When pruning becomes necessary to keep the plants within limits in a greenhouse, it should be done in early spring; the plants soon grow freely again after very severe pruning.

The hardiest kind is Albizzia Julibrissin variety rosea. A. Julibrissin grows wild from Persia to Japan; it will reach a height of 30-40 ft. It is a favorite street tree in the South, where it is known by the common name Mimosa (this is a common name also applied to Acacia). The pompons of pink flowers are freely produced in summer. A. Julibrissin is hardy in sheltered locations in the vicinity of New York City, its variety rosea as far north as Boston, Massachusetts.

For Summer Flower Beds. Next in point of hardiness is A. lophantha, from southwestern Australia. It will grow 10-12 ft. high, but it can be kept much smaller by annual pruning in early spring before new growth begins, although if this is done the plants do not produce many flowers. The yellow flowers are borne in axillary racemes in early summer. Seeds of this Albizzia are listed in many seed catalogues, and, as they germinate freely, the plants are used in summer flower beds for the sake of their attractive leaves. This species is planted outdoors in mild climates.

Other Kinds. In tropical and subtropical regions other kinds are grown including A. Kalkora, from India and A. Lebbek, the Lebbek Tree or Woman's-tongue Tree, from tropical Asia and Australia.

ALBUCA (Albu'ca). Tender bulbs from South Africa, with yellow or white fragrant flowers on stems 2-3 ft. high, in May and June. They are suitable for cultivation in pots in a frostproof greenhouse, and in sunny borders out of doors in the South. Albuca belongs to the Lily family, Liliaceae. Albuca is derived from *albus,* white.

If grown out of doors, the bulbs should be planted 4 in. deep in spring, in fertile, well-drained soil. If grown in the greenhouse, the bulbs should be potted in March in well-drained, fertile soil, with their tips protruding from the surface. A minimum temperature of 45 degrees is suitable. A. fastigiata, 2-3 ft., has white flowers in June; A. aurea, 12 in., bears yellow flowers in early summer.

ALBUS. Latin for white. A word used in describing many plants with white flowers: for example, Agapanthus africanus albus is a white-flowered variety of the blue African Lily.

ALCHEMILLA—*Lady's Mantle* (Alchemill'a). Hardy annuals and perennials, 6-12 in. high, which have tiny greenish or yellowish flowers in summer. They are not of much value in gardens though the lobed leaves are attractive. They grow wild in the mountain districts of Europe, Asia and America, and other areas, and belong to the Rose family, Rosaceae. Alchemilla is derived from the Arabic name of one of these plants.

All are easily grown in ordinary, well-drained soil; they are suitable for the rock garden and the front of the flower border and are increased by seeds and by division. Seeds are sown in a greenhouse or cold frame in April–May, in light, sandy soil. The seedlings are set 2 in. apart in flats filled with equal parts of sandy loam and rotted leaf mold and grown in a cold frame or in partial shade out of doors during summer; they are planted out of doors 6 in. apart in spring or early autumn. Fully grown plants may be in-

creased by division in March and September.

The chief kinds are: A. alpina, 6 in., gray leaves; A. sericea, 6 in.; and A. vulgaris, 9-12 in. All of these are perennials.

ALDER. See Alnus.

ALDER, BLACK. See Ilex verticillata; and Alnus glutinosa.

ALDER, WHITE. See Clethra and Alnus rhombifolia.

ALETRIS FARINOSA—*Star Grass, Colic Root* (Ale'tris). A hardy perennial of the eastern United States suitable for wild gardens. Its name is derived from *aletron,* meal, and has reference to the mealy flowers. It belongs to the Lily family, Liliaceae.

Aletris farinosa is an acid-soil plant that grows best in rather moist situations in full sun. It bears white flowers in slender spikes in July. Propagation is by seeds sown in peaty soil in a cold frame in fall; and, much more slowly, by division in early spring. Another species, A. aurea, the Yellow Colic Root, native of the southeastern United States, is also worth trying in a wild garden.

ALEURITES—*Tung Oil Tree, China Wood Oil Tree, Japan Wood Oil Tree* (Aleuri'tes). Small trees that are natives of the eastern tropics and are of great commercial importance because of the valuable oils they produce. Aleurites is derived from *aleuron,* floury; the name refers to the mealy appearance of some species.

In the South, A. Fordii is grown for oil production, and, together with some other species, as small shade trees. They thrive best in loamy, somewhat acid soils where drainage is good, and grow rapidly under favorable conditions. They are propagated by seeds sown early in the year, and by budding. Germination of the seeds takes about two months. The young plants are usually set in their permanent positions when about a year old.

Kinds grown include A. Fordii, Tung Oil or China Wood Oil Tree; A. cordata, Japan Wood Oil Tree; A. montana, Mu Oil tree; and A. moluccana, the Candlenut Tree.

ALEXANDRIAN LAUREL. Danaë racemosa, which see. Also sometimes misapplied to Calophyllum inophyllum.

ALFALFA. The common name of Medicago sativa, which, in garden practice, is sometimes used as a cover crop or green manure. In England and some other countries this plant is called Lucerne. See Medicago.

ALGAE. These are lowly nonflowering forms of plant life which inhabit all parts of the world. They have no true stems, roots or leaves. Moisture and food materials are absorbed by all parts of the plant.

Typical forms of Algae are the green slimes on the trunks of trees and on flowerpots, and the green scum on the surface of pond water. Submerged forms may also be found in ponds and streams where their thin, filamentous growths form masses of green slimy material commonly known as Blanket or Flannel Weed, which see. Seaweeds are also Algae.

If scum is troublesome in water tanks or barrels, it can be exterminated by the simple means of excluding the light. Algae are found frequently in tubs containing aquatic plants such as Aponogeton (which see), as well as in aquariums. Their growth may be checked by the introduction of fresh-water snails.

If reservoirs or swimming pools become contaminated with algae a mild solution of copper sulphate crystals may be thrown directly into the water, where they dissolve and kill the algae; or the crystals may be placed in bags which are pulled slowly through the water by rowboats. A weak solution of copper sulphate does not harm fish or animals, nor does it poison drinking water. See also Scum on Ponds.

In moist areas such as those found in the vicinity of streams and ponds, the presence on a lawn of brown, curled-up jelly-like Algae indicates that the drainage is bad, and measures must be adopted to cure this trouble before good turf can be grown.

ALGERIAN IRIS. See Iris unguicularis.

ALGERITA. See Mahonia trifoliolata.

ALISMA—*Water Plantain* (Alis'ma). Hardy aquatic plants belonging to the family Alismaceae. The origin of the name is obscure.

These plants flourish in wet ground by the margin of a pool, or in shallow water. They may be planted in autumn or spring. They are increased by dividing the plants in autumn or spring, or by sowing seed at those same seasons in a flowerpot filled with loamy soil and placed about 10 in. below the surface of the water.

The most ornamental kind is Alisma Plantago-aquatica, 2-3 ft., with small white flowers in June and July.

ALKALINE SOIL PLANTS. This term is used to designate plants that are believed to need an alkaline soil for their successful growth, or at least to tolerate such soils, and that will not prosper in acid soils. For a fuller discussion of this matter see Acid Soil Plants.

ALKANET. See Anchusa.

ALKEKENGI. See Physalis Alkekengi.

ALLAMANDA (Allaman'da). Handsome tropical evergreen, mostly climbing plants which bear large, yellow or rosy-lavender trumpet-shaped flowers freely in summer. They grow wild in tropical America. Allamanda belongs to the Dogbane family, Apocynaceae. The name commemorates Dr. Allamand.

The vines have long trailing shoots which scramble over any available support; they are generally trained on wires. In the North, a greenhouse having a winter night temperature of not less than 55 degrees F. is required for their cultivation. In the far South, they are popular plants for outdoor cultivation and thrive in ordinary soils in full sun or in light shade provided they are sheltered from cold winds.

The bush Allamanda, A. neriifolia, has yellow flowers and spiny seed pods.

Greenhouse Management. These vigorous

plants should be set out in autumn or spring in well-drained 16-in. wooden tubs, or in a prepared bed of soil; a suitable compost consists of loam two parts, leaf mold one part, and decayed manure one part. As the shoots develop they are trained on wires attached to the sides or roof of the greenhouse. Very little water is required during the winter, but throughout the summer the soil must be kept moist. If grown in large tubs the plants must be top-dressed in spring with the compost described above after some of the old surface soil has been taken off.

Pruning and Taking Cuttings. Pruning is done by cutting back the side shoots of the past summer's growth to one or two buds in February. Propagation is by cuttings of young shoots 3 in. long in March, which form roots quickly in a propagating case in a hothouse; when rooted they are potted in 3-in. pots, and two or three weeks later the tips of the shoots are pinched off to induce several shoots to form. They are next repotted in 5-in. pots and, when established in these, are ready for planting out or for setting in tubs.

The best kinds are A. cathartica and its varieties Hendersonii, nobilis, Williamsii and Schottii, all of which have yellow flowers. A. violacea, a slender climber with red-purple flowers, is most successful when grafted on rooted cuttings of A. catharctica Hendersonii or A. catharctica Schottii. A. neriifolia is a low- to medium-sized shrub with deeper yellow and smaller flowers than the climbing kinds.

ALL-AMERICA SELECTIONS. This is a nonprofit, educational corporation, founded in 1932. It provides for the coordination of horticultural variety research, the assembling, testing and screening of proposed new varieties in North America, and for publicizing the award winners.

New varieties found to be sufficiently different and superior to others of their kinds, or answering especially desirable purposes, are considered for general awards or regional recommendations, according to their merits, usefulness, and adaptation.

There are from 20 to 25 judges with trial grounds for each general class of horticultural material such as, for example, for vegetables and for flowers commonly reproduced by seeds. Similar testing and screening in the United States for

new varieties of Roses is conducted by All-America Rose Selections, organized in 1939.

Pre-introductory testing and screening, requiring separate trials with responsible resident judges, is now operating for Camellias, Gladioli, and Chrysanthemums.

Trial grounds for new seed varieties are located at many places from the Atlantic to the Pacific coastal areas and from southern Canada to southern Florida in all climatic zones. They represent sea-level to mile-high elevations; range from sandy to clay soils; and vary from about 10 to over 70 in. average annual rainfall. Each qualified resident judge reports on comparisons with similar varieties, and rates the trial entries according to their all-season behavior at his trial location only. Entries are open to any person, firm or institution. A nominal entry fee is charged.

All varieties expected to be introduced should be entered in the All-America trials at least two years before any distribution is made to the public. Only undisseminated varieties are eligible for award.

ALLEGHENY SPURGE. See Pachysandra procumbens.

ALLEGHENY VINE. See Adlumia fungosa.

ALLEY. A path between hedges or other enclosures, or beneath a leafy covering. The pleached alley, to be seen in some old English gardens, is one that runs beneath trees the branches of which are pleached or interwoven. A good example of a pleached alley exists in the garden of the Governor's Palace at Colonial Williamsburg in Virginia.

ALLHEAL. Valeriana officinalis, which see.

ALLIGATOR APPLE. See Annona.

ALLIGATOR PEAR. Another name for the Avocado Pear, a fruit which is the product of a tropical American tree (Persea gratissima). See Persea.

ALLIUM—*Flowering Onion* (Al'lium). Hardy bulbs which grow wild in many parts of the world; among them are the Onion, Leek and Chives, as well as many kinds grown for the decorative value of their flowers. They belong to the Lily family, Liliaceae. Allium is a Latin word for Garlic. For kinds used as vegetables see Chives, Garlic, Leek, Onion and Shallot.

These bulbs are mostly easily managed in

ordinary garden soil and are useful for planting in the wild garden or among hardy ferns, where their umbels or flower clusters, bearing blooms of various colors, are attractive in spring and summer. Some of the smaller kinds are admirable for the rock garden and some are useful in the flower border. A. neopolitanum is excellent for cultivating in pots in a cool, sunny greenhouse.

A Flowering Onion, Allium tuberosum, bears fragrant white flowers in great profusion in summer.

Allium neapolitanum is a splendid kind for growing in a cool greenhouse. Its flowers are good for cutting.

When to Plant. The bulbs are set out in fall or early spring and need a sunny position. Most should be covered with about 3 in. of soil, though the smaller kinds need not be set more than 2 in. deep. They may be left undisturbed for several years until, in fact, they become overcrowded. They should then be lifted, separated and replanted as soon as the leaves have died down. A fresh supply can be raised from seeds sown out of doors in a bed of fine soil in late summer or spring, or by separating the offset bulbs that many kinds produce freely.

The Chief Kinds. Two of the most useful kinds are: A. Moly (Golden Garlic), 12 in., with yellow flowers, and A. neapolitanum, 15 in., which bears white blooms; both are at their best in May. Allium Rosenbachianum is one of the most handsome; it bears rose-purple flowers on stems 2½-3 ft. high in July. A. albo-pilosum, 2 ft., has immense heads of silvery lilac flowers in June; A. senescens glaucum, 1 ft., lilac, is a popular rock garden plant, flowering in July. Others are A. caeruleum, 15-24 in., blue, July; A. cyaneum, 6 in., blue; A. karataviense, 6 in., reddish-lilac, June (its gray-green leaves are unusually

large); A. Ostrowskianum, rose-purple, 9 in.; A. narcissiflorum, mauve, 1 ft.; A. triquetrum, 12 in., green and white, June; A. zebdanense, 1-2 ft., white, May; and A. tuberosum, 3 ft., fragrant, white, July–August.

ALLOPHYTON MEXICANUM (Allophy'-ton). A small plant from Mexico and Guatemala sometimes called Tetranema mexicana and well

Allium albo-pilosum has attractive large heads of silvery-lilac flowers in early summer.

adapted for growing in greenhouses, in terrariums, and as a window plant. It belongs in the Figwort family, the Scrophulariaceae. Its name comes from *allos,* diverse, and *phyton,* a plant.

It is easily raised from seeds sown in woodsy soil at any time. The plants should be grown singly or several together in well-drained pans of rich, humus-rich soil that is kept always fairly moist. Shade from strong sun is desirable. Plants bloom in less than a year from seeds sown in spring. The flowers are violet or purple. A temperature of 55-60 degrees suits this species.

ALLOPLECTUS (Alloplec'tus). Tropical American shrubby or climbing plants that are often more or less epiphytic. They belong to the Gesneria family, Gesneriaceae, and are suitable for growing in warm greenhouses. The name is from *allos,* diverse, and *pleco,* to plait; the calyx looks as though it were plaited.

Alloplectus vittatus is attractive both in foliage and flower.

Culture. They need a loose, coarse, humus-rich soil that is kept moderately moist at all times but somewhat drier in winter than at other times of the year. Shade from bright sun is necessary and a temperature between 60 and 70 degrees. The atmosphere should be humid. Repot old plants in spring.

Propagate by cuttings inserted in a mixture of peat moss and sand in a propagating case in a greenhouse in spring, or by seeds sown under similar conditions in late winter or spring. The seeds are very fine and need little or no soil covering. Kinds sometimes grown are: A. Schlimii, flowers red and yellow; A. bicolor, yellow and purple; A. vittatus, flowers yellow, foliage green and gray; and A. repens, yellow.

ALLSPICE. The dried unripe fruits of Pimenta officinalis, see Pimenta. The name Carolina Allspice is applied to the North American shrubs named Calycanthus, which see.

ALLWOODII PINK. The name of a race of hardy garden Pinks obtained by crossbreeding between the Pink and the perpetual flowering Carnation. They are described under their botanical name, Dianthus.

ALMOND. A name given to the tree and fruit of Prunus Amygdalis, which belongs to the Rose family, Rosaceae. It is thought to be a native of western Asia. There are both bitter and sweet races of Almonds. The former are grown mostly in Mediterranean countries. The sweet or edible types include both hard-shelled and soft-shelled varieties. The soft-shelled kinds produce the edible "nuts" of commerce. In the United States commercial Almond growing is largely located in California, where the trees are usually cultivated on the drier lands of the valleys, because of their intolerance of wet soils. They withstand more drought than most fruit trees.

Almonds flower early and the buds are susceptible to being killed by late frosts. For this reason they are unsuited to northern conditions although the tree itself is hardy as far north as New England. Named varieties of Almonds are propagated by budding them on to seedlings of sweet or bitter Almonds or of the Peach.

Pruning and Cultivation. Almonds are usually pruned back severely at planting time. Pruning during the next two seasons is aimed at establishing a well-spaced framework of branches. Later pruning consists of judicious thinning out of crowded branches. Trees normally fruit 3-4 years after planting. Cultivation sufficient to keep down weeds and conserve soil moisture is desirable.

ALMOND, EARTH. See Cyperus esculentus.

ALMOND, FLOWERING. See Prunus.

ALMOND, INDIAN. See Terminalia Catappa.

ALMOND, TROPICAL. See Terminalia Catappa.

ALNUS—*Alder* (Al'nus). Hardy, leaf-losing trees which reach a height of 50 ft. and flourish in wet or boggy land. They are natives of Europe, Asia and North America, and belong to the Birch family, Betulaceae. In North America they are adaptable to the cooler parts only. The botanical name, Alnus, was taken from the Latin.

The Black Alder, Alnus glutinosa.

Two Kinds of Flowers. The Alders bear two kinds of inflorescences (catkins). The yellow or reddish-yellow male flowers are in drooping catkins of varying length; the female flowers are reddish, not very conspicuous, and are borne in short, conelike structures. They are usually pro-

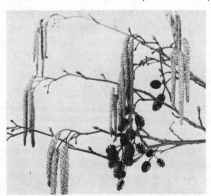

Alders bear two kinds of flowers. The male flowers are in pendulous catkins, the females in short, conelike bodies.

duced during late winter and early spring, well in advance of the leaves, and are followed by ovoid or ellipsoid conelike fruits which ripen in autumn, when they open and release the numer-

ous seeds during winter. The seeds are readily distributed by wind.

Raising Trees from Seeds. The Alders are best raised from seeds, although one kind, Alnus viridis, can be increased by detaching suckers and planting them. Seeds should be sown in a bed of fine-broken soil out of doors in March or April, or in pots or flats of sandy soil in a greenhouse or frame from January onwards. The young trees must be set out in lines 6 in. apart when large enough to handle, and be transplanted biennally until put in their permanent places. If they are to be planted under forest conditions, trees 2 ft. high may be used, but when grown as ornamental specimens they can be transplanted when much larger.

How to Prune. Trees should be restricted to a central stem and side shoots must be shortened. As the trees increase in height, the lower branches should be gradually removed until the desired height of clear trunk is obtained. All such pruning may be done in summer, after the leaves are fully developed.

For Wet Land. Alders are useful trees for planting in wet ground, for they thrive under such wet conditions as would be fatal to most trees. They also succeed in a great variety of soils, even on heavy clay. Planting may be carried out in fall or spring.

The Chief Kinds. Alnus cordata, Italian Alder, makes a handsome specimen tree of rounded form with glossy leaves; it is hardy in southern New England. A. glutinosa, Black Alder, is a hardy shapely tree that holds its leaves green until late in the fall; it has many variations, of which the variety laciniata, with deeply lobed leaves, and variety pyramidalis, of narrow upright form, are outstanding. A. hirsuta, Manchurian Alder, soon grows into a handsome pyramidal specimen and is hardy to northern New England. A. incana, the Speckled Alder, is the hardiest kind, and varies from shrub to tree form, depending on the geographical location. Of the several varieties of A. incana, pendula is notable for its weeping habit. A. japonica, Japanese Alder, grows into a handsome pyramidal tree with dark green foliage; it is hardy to southern New England. A. maritima, Seaside Alder, is a large shrub or small tree, conspicuous in fall with its dark green foliage. A. rubra, Red Alder, is an outstanding tree of the northwestern United States, with light gray bark, dark red branchlets, and leaves that are whitish beneath. A. rhombifolia, White Alder, is the largest, growing up to 100 ft. in its native California. It is conspicuous with silvery bark and leaves that are yellowish-green beneath.

Economic Uses. Alder wood is light in weight but firm. It decays quickly in contact with the ground. That of the Red Alder (A. rubra) is used in the Pacific Northwest for furniture, millwork and handles. It is frequently stained to imitate mahogany and walnut.

ALOCASIA (Alocas'ia). Tropical plants from Borneo, Ceylon and other warm parts of Asia, grown for their very large and beautifully colored leaves. They belong to the family Araceae. The botanical name is a corruption of Colocasia, which is a nearly related plant.

Alocasias are among the most handsome of tropical foliage plants. This is A. amazonica.

Details of Cultivation. They must be grown in a greenhouse having a minimum temperature of 60 degrees; or outdoors, in climates similar to that of southern Florida. In the North they may be planted or plunged outdoors during the hot summer months to provide tropical effects. The thick rootstocks are potted in March in a compost of equal parts of peat, sphagnum moss and

loam with sand and crushed charcoal added. The top of the rhizome should not be below the rim of the pot or the leaves may decay at the base. Warm moist shady conditions are needed during the summer months and the plants need a good deal of water when in full growth. Then the leaves fade in autumn, less water is given and finally, when the leaves have died down, the soil is only moistened occasionally.

Propagation is accomplished in March by inserting pieces of the rhizome or rootstock in small pots filled with peat and sand; these are set in a propagating case in the hothouse. When rooted they are potted separately in small pots and are gradually transferred to larger ones as they develop. In winter the temperature ought not to fall below 60 degrees. The roots remain in the pots of soil until March, when they are taken out and repotted.

Colorful kinds are Alocasia indica varieties metallica, purple leaves with a metallic sheen, and variegata, deep green, gray beneath; A. Lowii, olive-green, deep purple beneath, and variety Veitchii, with whitish veins; A. macrorhiza, green with wavy margins, and its variety variegata with white blotches on its leaves; A. cuprea, leaves dark, metallic purple-green, red beneath; A. longiloba, arrow-shaped, veined and margined white; A. Sanderiana, arrow-shaped, with lobed margins and white veins and margins; A. Watsoniana, puckered blue-green leaves with white veins; and A. zebrina, with zigzag bands on the leafstalks.

ALOE (Al'oe). Tender succulent plants, native chiefly to South Africa, where they grow in poor, sandy or stony soil. They have thick, succulent or fleshy leaves which store large quantities of water during the rainy periods and are thus able to withstand long periods of drought. They belong to the Lily family, Liliaceae. Aloe is derived from the Arabic name for these plants.

Some of the Aloes become treelike, with stout woody stems about 5 ft. in height, while others form dwarf clumps with clusters of leaves arising from the base. Many kinds have attractive spikes of flowers. A sunny greenhouse with a minimum winter temperature of 45 degrees or even slightly less suits them. The smaller-growing kinds are excellent window plants. In frostless and nearly frostless climates, particularly those that are dry such as that of southern California, they thrive outdoors, requiring essentially the same conditions as Cacti and other desert plants.

Summer and Winter Treatment Indoors. The pots are a quarter filled with drainage and the best compost consisting of two parts loam and one part coarse sand, broken brick and crushed

Aloe ecklonis is an attractive plant that bears greenish-yellow flowers.

limestone with a little bone meal added. They should be potted in spring and watered sparingly until established. During the summer, water must be given as soon as the soil becomes fairly dry, but from September to March very little water is required, merely sufficient to prevent shriveling of the leaves.

Overwatering in winter is one of the chief causes of failure in the management of Aloes. At that season the soil ought not to be watered until it is decidedly dry; it should then be moistened thoroughly and allowed to get dry again. Well-rooted specimens benefit from occasional applications of dilute liquid fertilizer in summer.

Aloes require repotting at long intervals only; plants in large pots thrive for years without this attention. Such large specimens do, however, benefit from top-dressing occasionally, and so, each spring, they should be examined and have any loose soil or soil unfilled with roots removed with a pointed stick, and this replaced with new earth of suitable type. At the same time the

drainage hole or holes in the bottom of the container should be examined to make sure that they have not become plugged with soil so that the free escape of water is impeded. Large specimens of these plants may be grown in either pots or wooden tubs; where space in a greenhouse or conservatory is sufficient, they may be planted out directly into well-drained beds of very porous soil.

When grown indoors or in greenhouses, Aloes stand a wide range of temperature variation. Night temperatures of 50-60 degrees with an increase of 5-15 degrees in the daytime are satisfactory; thus, they can be grown in most sunrooms and living rooms provided they receive ample sunlight.

The atmosphere in homes, schoolrooms, offices, etc., is normally quite dry enough for Aloes; in greenhouses, care should be taken to avoid excessive atmospheric humidity, especially in winter.

It is quite practicable to grow Aloes in pots or tubs for use outdoors on terraces and similar situations in summer, and to winter the plants in a fairly cool, frost-free, light place such as a cellar, returning them to the outdoors when the weather is warm and settled.

Outdoor Culture and Uses. Aloes thrive outdoors in warm, dry climates such as those of the Mediterranean region, South Africa and southwestern United States. They withstand only a slight amount of frost and are impatient of wet soils. For their ideal development they need an abundance of sunshine and a well-drained, porous earth; one that is not very rich in nitrogen suits them admirably.

In landscape planting, Aloes may be associated with buildings and other architectural features, with excellent results. They are also admirable for use in rock gardens in dry-climate regions and for planting with other succulent plants such as Cacti, Agaves and Euphorbias.

Propagation by seeds affords a ready means of securing new stock of many kinds of Aloes. They may be sown in late winter or spring in a well-drained pot or pan containing a very sandy soil mixture. Both seeds and tiny plants require soil that is kept always just moist (but not constantly wet). Complete or excessive dryness is harmful to seeds that are germinating and to young plants that have not yet developed sufficient fleshy leaf tissue to serve as storage for very much moisture.

Tiny Aloe plants benefit, too, with a little light shade from very bright sunshine.

Taking Cuttings. The simplest method of propagating the low-growing kinds is by detaching the suckers (small shoots which develop at the base of the plants) in summer, and inserting them as cuttings in pots of sandy, loamy soil.

Aloes which have upright, treelike stems can be propagated from cuttings which are prepared by severing the stems just beneath a joint. They are laid on a shelf or bench for several hours to allow a corky skin to form over the cut surface. This discourages decay. The prepared cuttings, 6-8 in. long, are then inserted in pots of sand or sandy soil. No covering with glass is required, as the leaves do not droop. Water must be applied sparingly for a month or so until roots have formed.

Aloe striata and its varieties have open-branched heads of drooping flowers. Their leaves are thick and fleshy.

The most popular of the dwarf kinds is the Partridge Breast Aloe, A. variegata; it is commonly grown as a window plant; the green and white leaves are very ornamental. Others of this

type which can be grown in a sunny window are A. humilis, of which there are many varieties, A. Ecklonis and A. striata. The chief arborescent or treelike Aloes are A. arborescens, A. ferox and A. Johnstonii. Many others are grown by collectors of succulents.

Economic Uses. The dried juice of the leaves of several Aloes, but chiefly of A. vera, is used in medicine, chiefly for its purgative properties. The leaves are broken and the exuding juice collected in vessels and evaporated by artificial heat until the requisite amount of moisture has been driven off. The residue from leaves of A. vera is known as Barbados Aloes and Curaçao Aloes. A. spicata, A. ferox and A. africana yield Cape or South African Aloes.

ALONSOA—*Mask Flower* (Alonso'a). Tender evergreen perennials usually grown as annuals. They are 9-24 in. high, of erect, branching growth with wiry stems, and bear small, flat, 2-lipped blooms in summer and autumn. They can be grown out of doors during the summer months; at other times they must be kept in a greenhouse, having a minimum temperature of 45-50 degrees. All are natives of Peru and other parts of South America, and belong to the Figwort family, Scrophulariaceae. Alonsoa is derived from Alonzo Zanoni, a Spanish diplomat.

When to Sow Seeds. Alonsoas are raised either from seeds or cuttings. Seeds are sown in a greenhouse in February–March, temperature 50-60 degrees, in a light sandy soil; the seeds are covered with a mere sprinkling of soil. When an inch or two high the seedlings are potted singly in small pots—2½-3 in. in diameter—filled with equal parts of loam and leaf mold and a little sand, or set 2-3 in. apart in flats filled with similar soil. They are grown in a cool greenhouse or frame until May and then are planted out of doors 6-9 in. apart or repotted in 5-in. pots to flower in the greenhouse. Young plants should be pinched to encourage bushiness.

When to Take Cuttings. Cuttings made from shoots of the current year's growth are taken in August–September, or from the young shoots on old plants in March. If inserted firmly an inch apart in sand and covered with a hand light or bell jar, they form roots in 4-6 weeks and should then be potted separately in small pots and finally in 5-in. pots.

The favorite kind is Alonsoa Warscewiczii, a Peruvian plant, 18-24 in. high, with semiwoody stems and small scarlet flowers in July and August. Others are A. incisifolia, 24 in., scarlet and black; A. miniata, 12 in., scarlet; and A. Mutisii, 12 in., pink with crimson center.

ALOYSIA. See Lippia.

ALPINE. A term loosely applied to plants found in mountainous regions and grown in rock gardens, but which correctly denotes those that occur above the tree line.

ALPINE GARDEN. A garden for the cultivation of alpine or mountain plants.

ALPINE HOUSE. This is an unheated greenhouse devoted to the cultivation of alpine or mountain plants grown in flowerpots or shallow pans. There the plants bloom earlier than they would do out of doors and the flowers, protected from wind and rain, open perfectly and display their full beauty. The alpine house also affords an opportunity for cultivating rare alpine plants and others which are difficult to manage out of doors. Alpine houses are common in Great Britain but little known in the United States.

ALPINE ROSE (Alpen Rose). A name given to two Rhododendrons, R. ferrugineum and R. hirsutum, dwarf, red-flowered kinds found wild in the European Alps. For particulars of these shrubs see Rhododendron. The term Alpine Rose is also applied to Rosa pendulina, a native of Europe.

ALPINE STRAWBERRY. The Alpine Strawberries are smaller and less acid than the popular large varieties, and the plants provide a succession of fruit from June until autumn. See Strawberry.

ALPINIA (Alpin'ia). Tropical plants from India, China and the East Indies having thick aromatic rhizomes or rootstocks, from which fresh shoots develop annually in spring in the same manner as in Solomon's Seal; they grow 3-6 ft. high. The flower spike which terminates the leafy stem bears blooms of red, pink or white. These plants belong to the Ginger family, Zingiberaceae. The name Alpinia commemorates an Italian botanist, Prospero Alpino.

Summer and Winter Treatment. When the plants are grown in greenhouses, a minimum temperature of 55 degrees in winter is required. Repotting is carried out in March; a fertile

Visitors to Hawaii and other tropical places soon become familiar with Alpinia speciosa, the Shell Ginger.

soil of equal parts of loam, leaf mold and well-decayed manure is suitable. The plants may be divided annually and kept in 6-in. pots, or they can be "grown on" to fill large tubs. Only a moderate amount of drainage is required, for they are moisture-loving plants. The rhizome should be placed about an inch below the surface when potting. During the summer the soil must be kept constantly moist, and the atmosphere humid by syringing the leaves, floor and benches of the hothouse. Shade should be provided from strong sun. After flowering, the plants are allowed to rest; they must be watered sparingly during the winter, just enough to prevent the soil from becoming thoroughly dry.

In the far South, Alpinias may be grown outdoors in rich soil in partial shade. The best method of propagation is to divide the rhizomes or rootstocks into the required number of pieces in March; these are potted separately in small pots and subsequently in the larger ones. They may also be raised from seeds.

Kinds most frequently grown are: the Shell Flower, A. speciosa, white, tinged purple, fragrant, May; A. Sanderae, leaves striped white and green, rarely blooms; and A. calcarata, green, red, and yellow, the flowers followed by handsome orange fruits; all about 5 ft. tall.

ALPINUS. Native of the Alps or high mountains, as, for instance, Anemone alpina, Dianthus alpinus.

ALSOPHILA—*Tree Fern* (Alsoph'ila). Handsome Tree Ferns with stems 15-20 ft. high, covered with the stumps of dead leafstalks and surmounted by large, spreading tufts of feathery fronds. They are natives of tropical Asia, Tasmania and Australia, and belong to the Cyathea family, Cyatheaceae. Alsophila is derived from the Greek word *alsos,* grove and *phileo,* to love. These Tree Ferns may be cultivated in a lofty greenhouse or conservatory having a minimum temperature of 45 degrees in winter, and out of doors in the moister localities of the far South.

Cultivation in Tubs. The tubs in which they are planted must be drained; the best compost consists of equal parts loam, peat and leaf mold, with a sprinkling of sand and crushed charcoal. The Ferns must be shaded from strong sunlight in summer, and the stems syringed every day in hot weather. The air of the greenhouse must be kept moist. The plants can remain in the same tub for many years. When they become too high for the greenhouse they may be sawed off just above the soil and replanted. If the stem is kept constantly moist, new roots will develop.

Propagation is effected by sowing ripe spores, found on the back of the fronds, on the surface of pots of sterilized soil. It is, however, a very slow and tedious process. The chief kind is Alsophila australis.

ALSTROEMERIA—*Peruvian Lily* (Alstroemer'ia). Tuberous rooted plants, 1-3½ ft. high, with lily-like flowers in June to August chiefly.

Alstroemeria pulchella is a dainty South American relative of the Amaryllis.

ALSTONIA SCHOLARIS (Alston'ia). Evergreen trees and shrubs of the Dogbane family, Apocynaceae, natives of tropical Asia and Pacific Islands. The name commemorates Dr. Alston, a professor of Botany at Edinburgh, Scotland.

Alstonias are planted in southern Florida and in southern California. Most common is A. scholaris, the Scholar Tree or Devil Tree, which grows up to 60 ft. tall, has narrow oblong or oblanceolate leaves, terminal cymes of small white flowers and long, slender seed pods. These trees grow in any ordinary soil. They are propagated by seeds and cuttings.

Most are natives of South America. None are hardy in the North although A. aurantiaca, the hardiest, will live outdoors over winter at Washington, D.C., if well protected, and perhaps somewhat further north. Except in the South, most must be grown in a greenhouse or must be wintered indoors and planted outdoors in rich, moist soil in light shade in spring. Plenty of moisture throughout the growing season is essential. They belong to the Amaryllis family, Amaryllidaceae. Alstroemeria is named after Baron Alstroemer, a Swedish botanist.

When to Plant. If planted in the open, in mild climates, in fall or spring, 6-9 in. deep, in well-drained, rather light ground enriched with decayed manure or compost, they will flourish and increase rapidly. In colder gardens, where they are on the borderline for hardiness, they should be planted at the foot of a sunny wall and covered with straw, salt hay or other suitable protection during winter. They may also be grown in cold frames where winters are not too severe. As these plants take two or three years to become established, they should be planted where they will be undisturbed. All are lovely for cutting.

The easiest method of propagation is by root division. The plants are lifted when the tops have died down, or in March, separated, and replanted at once; the roots are very brittle and easily injured. Seeds may be sown, as soon as ripe, in early autumn, in pots of light sandy soil in a greenhouse temperature of 55 degrees. The seedlings are transplanted 2 in. apart, in flats filled with leaf mold and sandy loam, kept under glass safe from frost and planted out of doors 12 in. apart in May. Seedlings will flower the second year after germinating.

The Hardiest Kinds. There are many beautiful kinds, most of which are natives of Chile and Peru. The hardiest and best for general planting is Alstroemeria aurantiaca, 2-3 ft., with orange-red flowers. Especially showy varieties of this are Orange King, deep orange, Dover Orange, rich copper-orange, and lutea, yellow. The flowers of the Chilean Lily, A. chilensis, 2 ft., vary from orange to deep red, and those of the Parrot Lily, A. pulchella (psittacina), 2-3 ft., are greenish red, with purple spots.

Two very beautiful kinds are A. haemantha, blood-red, orange-throated flowers in large heads; and A. Ligtu, of which many beautiful color forms have been raised, in pastel shades of pink, yellow, orange and red.

The greenhouse kinds are potted in September–October, separately, in 8-in. or 9-in. pots, filled with equal parts of loam and leaf mold with a scattering of sand, and placed in a temperature of 50-60 degrees. When the leaves begin to change color after the flowers are over, watering must be discontinued gradually; in winter, when the plants are dormant, the soil must still be watered occasionally to prevent its becoming dust-dry. The favorite is the Chilean Alstroemeria Pelegrina, commonly called the Lily of the Incas, which bears purplish flowers on stems 1 ft. high; there are rose- and white-flowered varieties of this plant.

ALTERNANTHERA (Alternan'thera). Very dwarf, tender plants, with colored leaves, which are principally used for carpet bedding and for edging flower beds. Most are natives of South

ALPINUS. Native of the Alps or high moun-

family, Amaranthaceae. The name Alternanthera refers to the alternate barren and fertile anthers of most kinds.

Propagation. They are grown from tips of the shoots, 1-2 in. in length, inserted in sand or sandy soil in February–March, in a greenhouse temperature of about 65 degrees. Roots will form very quickly if the pots are placed in a propagating case. When rooted they are set about 1 in. apart in shallow flats filled with light sandy soil and are gradually hardened off for bedding out after warm, settled weather has arrived. They are also increased by dividing, in early spring, old plants lifted in the fall and wintered indoors. As the leaves are small and the growth compact, these plants can be used to make various designs in summer bedding schemes. During the summer the points of the shoots must be pinched out or the plants must be sheared to keep them compact. Before fall frost, sufficient plants are potted in loam, leaf mold and sand to keep in the greenhouse during the winter to provide cuttings in spring.

The chief kinds are A. Bettzickiana, a species that is creamy yellow and red and that comes in many varieties, variously colored; A. amoena, green with red and orange blotches; and A. versicolor, in which the leaves are crimson or coppery. These plants are sometimes named Telanthera and sometimes Achyranthes.

ALTERNATE. A botanical term used to describe the arrangement of the leaves on a stem; they are said to be alternate when they occur singly at different heights on a stem, not opposite to each other.

ALTHAEA or HOLLYHOCK
A Stately Summer Flower of Old-World Charm

ALTHAEA (Althae'a). Hardy annuals, biennials and perennials chiefly represented in gardens by the Hollyhock, A. rosea. Althaea belongs in the Mallow family, the Malvaceae. Its name is derived from *altheo,* to cure; some of the species possess medicinal properties.

The Hollyhock is a hardy perennial plant, 6-10 ft. high, native of China. Its stem is fur-

nished with large, rough leaves, and erect, terminal racemes of very handsome flowers which are in full beauty June–August.

When to Plant. The Hollyhock thrives best in deeply dug fertile soil. The best times to plant are early fall or early spring. On heavy, clayey land that becomes very wet in winter, spring planting is preferred. Although hardy perennials

Hollyhocks are stately plants that bloom freely in summer.

on well-drained land the finest Hollyhocks are obtained by treating the plants as biennials, especially when the rust disease is troublesome. The tall stems need support by stakes to prevent them from being damaged in windy weather.

When to Sow. Seeds may be sown out of doors in a nursery border of finely broken soil in May, or in flats of sifted sandy soil placed in a frame at that time. The seedlings should be transplanted when they are large enough to be moved, set 10 in. apart in a nursery border in ordinary soil, and left there until the fall or following spring, when they should be set in their flowering locations. Seedlings raised in a greenhouse, temperature 60-65 degrees, in January, will be large enough to plant out in May and will begin to bloom in August; they must be hardened off in a cold frame before being set outdoors.

Although at one time fine named varieties of Hollyhocks could be purchased, it is now usual for ordinary garden display to buy packets of seed, either in mixture or in separate colors, and of double or single varieties as may be preferred. Most of the seedlings of both single and double varieties come true to color and to type. The common Hollyhock is Althaea rosea; there are double and single varieties with flowers in white, rose, crimson, yellow, cream and other shades.

Single-flowered Althaeas are more graceful in appearance than the double kinds.

The fig-leaved Hollyhock (Althaea ficifolia), a Siberian plant, has deeply lobed, ornamental leaves and pale yellow flowers on stems 4-5 ft. high. Seedsmen have raised varieties of this kind and seeds can be purchased which will provide flowers of several distinct colors.

There is an annual Hollyhock which will begin to bloom in July–August from seeds sown out of doors in April; the plants reach a height of about 4 ft. and the single flowers are of various colors.

ALTHAEA, SHRUB. See Hibiscus syriacus.

ALUMINUM PLANT. See Pilea Cadieri.

ALUMINUM SULPHATE. A chemical used to acidify soil. The amount needed to change the pH value by a specific amount varies with the type of soil. As little as $\frac{1}{2}$ lb. applied to each 10 sq. ft. will reduce the pH of a sandy soil from 6 to 5, but 3 lb. or more may be needed to effect the same change in a heavy clay soil. From 1 to $1\frac{1}{4}$ lb. will change a medium loam soil from pH 6 to pH 5. Harm to plants may result from applying aluminium sulphate to soils deficient in phosphorus.

ALUM ROOT. See Heuchera.

ALYSSUM (Alyss'um). Low-growing, hardy plants which bear white, yellow or pinkish flowers in spring. They belong to the Mustard family, Cruciferae, and grow wild chiefly in middle Europe, the Mediterranean region, and the Caucasus. The word Alyssum is derived from *a*, not, and *lyssa*, rage, a reference to its supposed virtue in mitigating rage (hence the popular name Madwort).

Planting and Taking Cuttings. The Alyssums are valuable rock garden plants and some are used for edging flower beds. The perennial kinds should be planted in a sunny situation in well-drained soil; there they will live for several years. They are not a success in heavy or poorly

A mass of golden flowers in spring, Alyssum saxatile thrives with little care in full sun.

[1–12]
Hollyhocks (Althaea rosea)

[1–13]
Amaranthus tricolor with Zinnias in front

[1–13a]
Basket of Gold (Alyssum saxatile)

[1–13b]
Tung Oil Tree (Aleurites Fordii)

[1–13c]
Coral Vine (Antigonon leptopus)

drained land; this, however, can be made suitable by adding compost, sand, and grit. After a few years the plants become rather bare-stemmed and straggling, but fresh stock is easily raised by taking cuttings, made from the young shoots in June. These are inserted in a cold frame which must be kept close for a few weeks until the cuttings have become rooted. Alyssum can also be raised from seeds sown in fine soil in a frame or greenhouse early in the year, or out of doors in May. The seedlings will bloom the following year.

The favorite kind is Alyssum saxatile, familiarly known as Gold Dust, Golden Tuft and Basket of Gold. It grows 9-12 in. high, has gray leaves and bears golden-yellow flowers. Four varieties are noteworthy—citrinum, also known as Silver Queen, with sulphur-colored flowers; compactum, a diminutive plant; variegatum, which has variegated leaves; and plenum, with double blooms. Except citrinum, these varieties must be increased by cuttings.

A. alpestre, 3 in., has rough, hoary leaves and golden-yellow flowers in spring; A. argenteum, 12 in., bears yellow flowers in late spring; A. montanum, 3 in., has fragrant yellow blooms in spring; A. Moellendorfianum is similar; A. pyrenaicum, 3-4 in., bears white fragrant flowers. For A. spinosum see Ptilotrichum.

Sweet Alyssum, the charming little hardy annual so long cultivated by gardeners under the name of Alyssum maritimum, is now classified by botanists as Lobularia, which see.

AMACRINUM HOWARDII (Amacri'num). The name commonly given in America to a hybrid produced in California between Amaryllis Belladonna and Crinum Moorei. The same hybrid, produced simultaneously in Italy, was described and named earlier as Crinodonna Corsii. See Crinodonna.

AMARANTH, GLOBE. See Gomphrena.

AMARANTHUS — *Love - Lies - Bleeding, Prince's-Feather, Joseph's-Coat* (Amaran'thus). Tender annuals which bear spikes of showy flowers or have highly colored leaves, and are used for sunny summer beds. They are natives of India, the Philippines and other warm countries. The long-lasting character of the flowers is indicated in the botanical name, which is derived from *a,* not, and *mairaino,* to wither. These plants belong to the family Amaranthaceae.

When to Sow Seeds. The plants are raised from seeds sown in a heated greenhouse, temperature 60 degrees, in March or early April, in pots or flats filled with a finely sifted compost of two thirds sandy loam and one third leaf mold. When an inch or so high, the seedlings are placed separately in 3-in. pots, using similar compost passed through a coarse sieve. They are planted out of doors 18-20 in. apart in late

Love-Lies-Bleeding, Amaranthus caudatus, bears drooping tails of red-purple flowers.

May or early June. Alternatively, seeds may be sown directly out of doors as soon as it is warm enough to sow Beans, and the plants thinned to stand the required distance apart.

Love-Lies-Bleeding, or Tassel Flower, Amaranthus caudatus, 2 ft., has drooping flower stems bearing dark reddish-purple blooms. Prince's Feather, A. hybridus variety hypochondriacus, 3-4 ft., bears deep red flowers on erect stems.

The following varieties of A. gangeticus (melancholicus), are grown for their highly colored leaves; Joseph's-Coat (tricolor) has red, yellow and green leaves; those of tricolor splendens are even more brilliantly colored; ruber, 12 in., has red leaves, Molten Fire, brilliant carmine leaves, and Fire King, dark red and scarlet. In A.

salicifolius, 3 ft., the long, narrow leaves are orange, carmine and other shades.

AMARYLLIS (Amaryll'is). The favorite greenhouse spring-flowering bulb, which bears handsome, trumpet-shaped blooms on stems 18-24 in. high, is correctly named Hippeastrum, which see. For the genus Amaryllis of botanists see Amaryllis Belladonna.

AMARYLLIS BELLADONNA—*Belladonna Lily* (Amaryll'is). A handsome bulbous plant, from the Cape of Good Hope, with long, narrow leaves and large, funnel-shaped flowers, rose, blush or white, on stems about 18 in. high, in

Amaryllis Belladonna, Belladonna Lily, a beautiful bulbous plant, bears its large, fragrant rose-pink flowers in September, after the leaves have died down.

full beauty in September, when the plants are leafless. This plant flourishes in California but does not take kindly to eastern American conditions. The bulbs should be planted in June or July. Poor soil should be excavated to a depth of 2 ft. and replaced by a mixture of loamy soil, two thirds, and compost and decayed manure, one third; sand should also be added freely. Soil of moderate fertility should be improved by forking in compost and bone meal.

How Deep to Plant. The bulbs must be covered with 5 in. of soil, and set about 12 in. apart. The plant must be left undisturbed as long as it continues to bloom satisfactorily. If it becomes necessary to lift and replant the bulbs, the work should be done in June. There are several varieties with flowers of rose, blush or

white, e.g., purpurea, blanda, and major. The Belladonna Lily belongs to the family Amaryllidaceae. The botanical name commemorates the Amaryllis of Virgil.

AMARYLLIS, BLUE. See Griffinia.

AMATEUR. An amateur gardener is one who engages in the occupation of gardening as a hobby rather than as a business venture; he is a gardener who does not ordinarily sell the results of his efforts or his labor, advice or services in matters horticultural. Amateur is in contradistinction to professional. A professional gardener either sells his services or the products of his horticultural efforts.

AMAZON LILY. See Eucharis amazonica.

AMELANCHIER—*Snowy Mespilus, Serviceberry, Juneberry, Shadbush* (Amelan'chier). Beautiful hardy spring-flowering trees and shrubs, chiefly of North America, which belong to the Rose family, Rosaceae. *Amélanchier* is of French derivation.

Planting and Pruning. All thrive in ordinary garden soil, and need a sunny or lightly shaded position. They should be planted in fall preferably, but may be set in early spring. Little pruning is necessary.

Propagation. The usual method of propagation is by sowing seeds out of doors in October;

The Amelanchiers are leaf-losing hardy shrubs and small trees chiefly natives of North America. A most attractive kind is A. grandiflora, a hybrid between two native American kinds, the Juneberry, A. canadensis and A. laevis. It bears large white flowers.

but one kind, Amelanchier oblongifolia, can be increased by lifting and dividing the clumps in autumn when the leaves have fallen.

The fruits of the Amelanchiers are reddish-purple or sometimes almost black, sweet but insipid, and edible. They were a source of food for various American Indians and are sometimes used for making jellies. They are known as June-berries, Serviceberries, and May Cherries.

The most beautiful is Amelanchier canadensis (Juneberry), 20-30 ft., which bears small white flowers and is the earliest to bloom; others are A. oblongifolia, 5-6 ft.; A. laevis, 30-40 ft.; A. asiatica, 30-40 ft.; A. ovalis, 6-9 ft.; and A. alni-folia, 20 ft., all of which have white flowers. Of the above, all are natives of North America except A. ovalis, which is European, and A. asiat-ica, which has its home in Japan and Korea. A. grandiflora is a good hybrid kind.

AMERICAN ALOE. See Agave americana.

AMERICAN ELM. Ulmus americana, which see.

AMERICAN SPIKENARD. See Aralia race-mosa.

AMIANTHIUM MUSCAETOXICUM—*Fly Poison* (Amian'thium). A hardy bulbous peren-nial, native to eastern North America, that is suitable for growing in light sandy soil in open

Amianthium muscaetoxicum, Fly Poison, is suitable for planting in wild gardens.

places in the wild garden. A member of the Lily family, Liliaceae, its name is derived from *amiatos*, unspotted, and *anthos*, a flower, and alludes to its glandless perianth.

Amianthium is propagated by division in early spring and by seeds sown, as soon as they are

ripe, in a cold frame. All parts of the plant are poisonous if eaten. Its flowers are white.

AMMOBIUM ALATUM—*Winged Everlast-ing Flower* (Ammo'bium). A plant from Australia which belongs to the Daisy family, Compositae, grows about 24 in. high and, in summer, bears large white flowers which are useful to cut and dry for indoor vases in winter. It is treated as an annual. The word ammobium, from *ammos*, sand, and *bios*, life, refers to the sandy soil in which the plant grows wild.

Culture. Seeds are sown in spring in a green-house having a temperature of 55-60 degrees, in pots of sifted sandy soil. The seedlings are trans-planted 2 in. apart in flats of loam, leaf mold, and sand, and are planted out of doors, when all danger of frost is past, 15 in. apart. Seeds may be sown directly out of doors as soon as the ground is fit to work in spring, and the seedlings later thinned to 10-12 in. apart. In mild climates a sowing may be made out of doors in fall. Cut the flowers before they mature and hang them upside down in a cool, dry, shady place to dry.

AMMONIA. Salts of ammonia, i.e., sulphate of ammonia, are a valuable source of nitrogen, an essential plant food, but before they can be taken up by roots they must be converted by bacterial action into nitrates (see Fertilizers, Ni-trification). A high concentration of ammonia gas, caused, for instance, when lime is placed in direct contact with fresh manure or ammonia fertilizers, is harmful to plants.

AMMOPHILA—*Beach Grass* (Ammo'phila). Hardy perennial grasses with underground creeping rootstocks. They are invaluable for planting on dunes and in other places to stabilize moving sands, especially near the seashore. The name is derived from *ammos*, sand, and *philos*, loving.

The native American species is A. brevigu-lata. The European species or Marram Grass is A. arenaria. Both are propagated by division of the rootstocks.

AMOMUM CARDAMON (Amo'mum). A herbaceous plant that is a native of the East In-dies and is grown outdoors in tropical and sub-tropical regions and sometimes elsewhere as a decorative pot plant. It belongs to the Ginger family, Zingiberaceae. Its name is probably de-rived from the Arabic.

Amomum succeeds best in rich soil that contains an abundance of organic matter and that is always fairly moist. It stands shade well, and is easily increased by division.

AMORPHA CANESCENS — *False Indigo, Lead Plant* (Amor'pha). Hardy ornamental shrubs which are natives of North America and belong to the Pea family, Leguminosae. They have pinnate (feather-like) leaves and small purplish flowers borne at the ends of the shoots in July and August. The word amorpha refers to the formation of the flowers: it is derived from *a*, not, and *morphe*, form.

The false Indigo, Amorpha fruticosa, is a good hardy shrub for sunny locations and well-drained soils.

Planting and Pruning. These shrubs thrive in well-drained, ordinary soil; they need a sunny position and may be planted in fall or spring. As the ends of the branches die after flowering it is advisable to cut back the previous year's shoots to within a few buds of the base, before new growth starts in spring. Propagation is best carried out by means of seeds sown in spring in sandy soil in a greenhouse or frame.

Amorpha canescens, the Lead Plant of the southern United States, is the most attractive kind; it has small gray, pinnate leaves, and purple flowers with yellow stamens; by annual pruning in spring it can be kept to a height of about 3 ft. A. fruticosa, False Indigo, is a more vigorous plant, 5 or 6 ft. high, but less effective.

AMORPHOPHALLUS (Amorphophal'lus). Tropical plants which belong to the Arum family, Araceae, and are natives of the warm regions of Asia and Africa. The word Amorphophallus is

The Krubi, Amorphophallus titanum. This immense inflorescence was produced for the first time at The New York Botanical Garden in 1937. The plant is a native of Sumatra.

derived from *amorphos*, deformed, and *phallus*, mace, and refers to the structure of the flowers

The flowers or, more correctly, inflorescences, which appear before the leaves, resemble the Arum Lily in shape. They are chiefly reddish-purple, and vary in size from a few inches to 4 ft. or more in diameter. After the inflorescence dies, the ornamental leaves develop.

Hints on Management. The corms or bulbs are potted in March in a humus-rich soil and are placed in a greenhouse with a minimum temperature of 55 degrees. Little water is given until the flower spike has withered and the new leaves are seen. The soil is then regularly moistened until growth ceases in the autumn, when watering is gradually discontinued, and finally the soil is left dry for the winter. Small corms develop on the older ones and these in most cases, if potted in spring, will flower in a few years.

The chief kinds are A. bulbifer, green and red spathe, and with small tubers produced on veins of leaves; A. campanulatus, spathe, pink or purplish; A. giganteus, deep red spathe; and A. titanum, the largest of all, the reddish-purple spathe measuring 3-4 ft. in diameter and the spadix standing 6-8 ft. tall. This remarkable

Amorphophallus campanulatus when in bloom is not more than 18 in. tall. The spathe is pink or purplish, the stem handsomely spotted.

aroid, known as the Krubi, bloomed for the first time in the Americas at The New York Botanical Garden in 1937. It has bloomed twice there since. A. titanum is a native of Sumatra. The plant called A. Rivieri is Hydrosme Rivieri, which see.

AMPELOPSIS (Ampelop'sis). At one time this group of leaf-losing, climbing woody plants was included with the Grape vines in the genus Vitis, but it is now separated from that, as is also the related genus Parthenocissus, the latter including the popular Virginia Creeper. The genus Ampelopsis belongs to the Vine family, Vitaceae, and the name is from *ampelos,* vine, and *opsis,* likeness.

Ampelopsis are grown chiefly for their foliage, and the ripe fruits of some add to their attractiveness. They thrive in any average garden soil and are useful for covering arbors, or for clambering over old trees and large bushes. They can be increased by cuttings of soft shoots inserted in sandy soil in a closed frame in summer, or by cuttings of ripened growth inserted in a sheltered border outdoors in autumn.

The Pepper Vine, Ampelopsis arborea, from the southern United States, is of slender growth, with doubly pinnate leaves and small, dark-purple fruits. A. humulifolia, from northern China, produces a mass of slender, tangled growths, 12-15 ft. high, and has small blue or yellow fruits, while A. Bodinieri (micans), also from China, 20 ft. high, has handsome, deeply lobed leaves and blue fruits.

The most striking of all is A. megalophylla, a vigorous Chinese climber, up to 30 ft. high, but unsuitable for cold climates. Its vigorous shoots bear doubly pinnate leaves up to 3 ft. long and almost as wide. A. brevipedunculata, native of northeastern Asia, is another vigorous species, with three-lobed leaves which color well in autumn, and small blue fruits. A. brevipedunculata variety elegans has leaves variegated with creamy white and pink.

AMPHICOME (Amphic'ome). Herbaceous plants suitable for cultivation in a greenhouse having a minimum winter temperature of 40-45 degrees. In summer they bear large funnel-shaped flowers which resemble those of Incarvillea (which see). They belong to the Bignonia family, Bignoniaceae, and grow wild in the Himalayas. The word Amphicome is from *amphi,* around, and *kome,* hair, and refers to the tufted seeds.

These plants thrive in a compost of equal parts of loam and leaf mold, with the addition of some decayed manure and sand, and should be re-potted annually in March. No pinching or pruning is required. During summer the pots should be sunk to their rims outdoors in a bed of sand or ashes in a cool, lightly shaded place.

When to Sow Seeds. Propagation is by seeds sown in March in well-drained flower pans filled with equal parts loam and sand, and placed in a greenhouse with a minimum temperature of 45 degrees. When the seedlings have formed two leaves, they are transplanted into other flower pans 2 in. apart, and, later, are potted separately in 3-in. pots. Cuttings of side shoots, as well as the sucker-like side growths, may also be inserted in March in a propagating case in the greenhouse.

The chief kinds are Amphicome Emodi, 18 in., having rose-colored flowers with orange throat in September; and A. arguta, 3 ft., which bears rose-colored blooms in August.

AMPLEXICAULIS. A botanical term meaning stem clasping. Calceolaria amplexicaulis is a

Calceolaria having leaves which clasp or embrace the stem.

AMSONIA (Amson'ia). Hardy, herbaceous perennial plants of the Milkweed family, Apocynaceae. They occur wild in North America and eastern Asia. The American species only are in cultivation. They bear terminal clusters of bluish flowers, followed by slender pods. The name commemorates Charles Amson, an American physician of the 18th century.

Culture. Amsonias thrive in ordinary garden soil, in partial shade or, provided the soil is not too dry, in full sun. They bloom in summer and are suitable for planting in the wild garden and in the perennial border. Propagation is easily effected by division in spring or early fall or by seeds sown in a cold frame or an outdoor seed bed as soon as they are ripe.

Kinds. The most popular kinds are: A. ciliata, 2-4 ft., flowers bluish purple; and A. Tabernaemontana, 2-3½ ft., flowers pale blue.

AMYGDALUS (Amyg'dalus). This was formerly the botanical name of the Almond, which is now classified under Prunus, a group or genus which includes not only the Almond, Prunus Amygdalus (P. communis), but the Peach, Prunus Persica, and several other fruiting and ornamental trees. The ornamental flowering kinds are described under Prunus, which see. See also Almond.

ANACAMPSEROS (Anacamp'seros). Slow-growing succulent plants, from the Cape of Good Hope, which need the same treatment as tender Cacti. The flowers are large, soon fade, and open fully only in sunny weather. They belong to the family Portulacaceae. The word

This interesting succulent is Anacampseros arachnoides.

Anacampseros, from *anakampto,* to induce to return, and *eros,* love, refers to a supposed quality of restoring love.

Summer and Winter Treatment. The plants should be potted in March in well-drained pots in a compost of one part sandy loam and one part equal proportions of crushed limestone, finely broken brick and sand. During the summer, water should be applied as soon as the soil becomes dry, but throughout the winter very little is required. The plants must have a light, airy position, full exposure to sunlight, and a winter night temperature of 45-50 degrees.

Propagation is effected by sowing seeds in finely sifted sandy soil in March.

The chief kinds are A. arachnoides and A. filamentosa, both of which grow about 9 in. high and bear pink flowers in summer.

ANACARDIUM OCCIDENTALE—*Cashew Nut* (Anacar'dium). A tropical tree from the West Indies which belongs to the Cashew family, Anacardiaceae, and is only suitable for cultivation in frostless regions. It has large, oval leaves and the young shoots are terminated by clusters of small, rosy-tinted flowers. The fruit consists of a small, edible nut, produced on top of a fleshy berry. The nuts cause a skin irritation, similar to that produced by Poison Ivy, before they are roasted. The word Anacardium refers to the heart-shaped nuts.

The Cashew Nut usually grows only to shrub-size in Florida. Another species, A. excelsum, becomes a strong semideciduous tree, but is somewhat subject to damage by wind scald. Both kinds thrive in dry soils. See also Cashew Nut.

ANACHARIS (Ana'charis). Submerged aquatic perennials that are grown in aquariums. They belong to the Frog's-Bit family, the Hydrocharitaceae. The name is of doubtful origin.

They are propagated by cuttings, and sometimes by winter buds, and grow without trouble in any ordinary soil beneath a foot or so of water. In outdoor ponds they may become troublesome weeds. These plants are sometimes known by the name Elodea. The commonest kind is A. canadensis, the Water Weed, native from Quebec to the south and west. A. densa is a South American species that is of stouter growth.

ANACYCLUS DEPRESSUS (Anacy'clus). A prostrate alpine plant from Mount Atlas, with gray fernlike leaves and white, crimson-tipped daisy-like flowers that are about 1 in. in diameter. It requires well-drained gritty soil. Propagation is by cuttings of young shoots, inserted in sandy soil in a cold frame in late spring, and by seeds. The name Anacyclus is derived from the Greek *ana,* like, and *kyklos,* circle, and refers to circles of ovaries around the disc of the flower. It belongs to the Daisy family, Compositae.

ANAGALLIS—*Pimpernel* (Anagal'lis). Low, hardy annual or perennial plants, 6 to 9 in. high, with flowers of various colors in summer. They are easily grown out of doors in well-drained or rather light soil, and are suitable for planting near the edge of the flower border or in the rock garden. They belong to the Primrose family, Primulaceae, and grow wild in various parts of Europe, northern Africa and India. Anagallis is said to be derived from the Greek word *anagelao,* to delight.

Good strains of the blue form of the common annual Pimpernel, Anagallis arvensis, are offered by seedsmen for sowing in sunny locations.

When to Sow Seeds. The varieties listed by seedsmen have chiefly originated from two species, the Scarlet Pimpernel or Poor-Man's-Weatherglass, Anagallis arvensis; and A. linifolia, blue

and red flowers, native of the western Mediterranean region. The blue form of the Pimpernel (caerulea) is popular. Although A. linifolia is perennial, under garden cultivation it is best treated as an annual, seeds being sown in early spring where the plants are to grow, or earlier under glass if an earlier display is desired. Favorite varieties of A. linifolia include Monellii, blue and red; Breweri, red; lilacina, lilac; and Parksii, red. As the Pimpernels open and close their flowers with the sun, they should be grown in sunny positions.

The Bog Pimpernel (A. tenella), is a trailing perennial, native to Europe, with rose-pink flowers; it is suitable for the bog garden or for a moist place, in leaf mold and loam, in the rock garden. This plant can be increased by division in March, the rooted pieces being replanted where they are to remain.

ANANAS COMOSUS. The botanical name of Pineapple, which see.

ANAPHALIS—*Pearly Everlasting* (Anaph'-alis). The only kind commonly grown is Anaphalis margaritacea, a hardy herbaceous perennial of North America, Europe and northern Asia, 2 ft. high, which bears white daisy-like flowers in summer. It belongs to the Daisy family, Compositae. Anaphalis is the Greek name for a similar plant.

This plant thrives best in well-drained or rather light soil and must be planted in a sunny place, in autumn or spring. It can be increased by lifting the plants in early spring and separating them into pieces for replanting, or by sowing seeds in sandy soil in a cold frame in April to produce flowering plants the following year.

Other kinds suitable for sunny, well-drained positions in the garden are A. yedoensis and A. triplinervis, both with white flowers and 2-3 ft. high.

The flowers of Anaphalis are grown for sale by florists; they are dyed in several colors and are used for winter decoration indoors under the name of Immortelle.

ANASTATICA—*Resurrection Plant, Rose of Jericho* (Anastat'ica). This plant, which is a native of the eastern Mediterranean region, is commonly called the Resurrection Plant, a name also applied to Selaginella lepidophylla (which see). It returns to obvious life after having been

One of the most beautiful hardy perennials is the blue-flowered Anchusa azurea.

dried and apparently dead for long periods. It belongs to the Mustard family, Cruciferae. The word is derived from *anastasis*, resurrection. In the sandy deserts where it grows wild it is green and flourishing during the rainy periods, but loses its leaves after flowering. The roots and shoots curl into a ball, which is blown about over the surface of the desert; as soon as it comes into contact with moisture, the leaves open out and it assumes the green appearance of a growing plant.

When to Sow Seeds. The flowers of this plant are insignificant, and the plants are cultivated only for their curious appearance and their habit of reviving when placed in water. They are propagated by seeds sown in pots of light sandy soil in a heated greenhouse in March. The seedlings are transplanted in flats filled with loam, leaf mold and sand, and planted in a sunny border in May. The full botanical name is Anastatica hierochuntica.

ANCHOR PLANT. See Colletia cruciata.

ANCHUSA—THE BLUE ALKANET
One of the Showiest Hardy Perennial Flowers of Early Summer

(Anchu'sa). Anchusas are hardy perennial and annual plants, 1½-5 ft. high, that produce flowers in spring and early summer. They are natives chiefly of European countries and of Africa and belong to the Borage family, Boraginaceae. The flowers have a great attraction for bees. The word Anchusa is said to be derived from a word meaning paint for the skin, and refers to the use of some kinds for that purpose.

When to Plant. Anchusas flourish in ordinary garden soil, preferring that which is well-drained, and they need a sunny position. Planting of the perennial kinds may be done in early fall or in spring.

They are admirable plants for the herbaceous border, where they provide a delightful show of blue flowers.

In well-drained soil the perennial Anchusas live for several years, but in heavy land they often die in winter, and it is wise, therefore, to raise fresh plants annually from root cuttings or by sowing seeds. In all gardens it is worth while to raise a fresh supply every year or two to maintain a stock of vigorous healthy plants.

When to Sow Seeds. Seeds are sown in a greenhouse or frame in March in flats filled with a sifted compost of two thirds loam and one third leaf mold with sand added, or in a finely pre-

Anchusa capensis Bluebird. Although actually a biennial, it can be grown as an annual by starting it in a greenhouse.

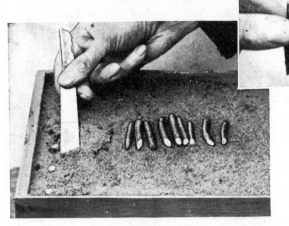

A prepared root cutting of Anchusa. The bottom end is cut slanting.

Left. Inserting the root cuttings of Anchusa in a box of sandy soil.

pared seedbed outdoors as soon as the soil is fit for seed sowing in spring.

When the seedlings are an inch or so high they should be set 3 in. apart in flats filled with similar soil. They are grown in a cold frame until large enough to plant out of doors. As soon as the seedlings raised from outdoor sowings are an inch or two high they should be set 9 in. apart in rows and planted finally in autumn or spring 2½ ft. apart.

How to Take Root Cuttings. Root cuttings are taken at planting time in autumn or early spring. They are pieces of root 2 in. or so long, placed end upwards (that part of the root which was nearest the stem being uppermost), 2 in. apart in boxes of soil and placed in a greenhouse, temperature 50 degrees. When roots and leaves develop, they should be potted singly in 3-in. pots, kept in a cold frame for the winter, and planted out of doors in spring.

The favorite perennial kind is Anchusa azurea (italica), a handsome plant, 4-5 ft. high, with a profusion of blue flowers during June–July. There are several popular varieties, notably Pride of Dover, deep blue; Opal, light blue; and Loddon Royalist, blue-purple. A. Barrelieri grows 1-2 ft. tall, has a profusion of blue flowers in spring. It is a very fine plant. A caespitosa is a hardy perennial of recent introduction; it grows to a height of 18 in., and forms a compact plant smothered with gentian-blue flowers from May to July. The Forget-me-not Anchusa, A. myosotidiflora, is correctly

named Brunnera macrophylla, which see.

The annual Anchusa, A. capensis, has bright-blue flowers on stems 1½ ft. high. A popular variety is Blue Bird; variety alba has white flowers. For early flowering, sow seeds in a 50-55 degree greenhouse six weeks before the plants are to be set in the garden. Make outdoor sowings in early spring where the plants are to flower. For winter and spring bloom in the cool (45-50 degree night temperature), sunny greenhouse, sow seeds from July to October.

ANCISTROCACTUS (Ancistrocac'tus). Previously included in the genus Echinocactus, these Cacti (family Cactaceae) are natives of Texas and Mexico and are small, very spiny, slightly ribbed, cylindrical or round plants, with small flowers produced at the top. They are pale-yellow in A. megarhizus, and greenish-yellow in A. Scheeri. The generic name refers to the hooked species from *ancistros,* a small hook. For cultivation, see Cacti.

ANCISTROCHILUS (Ancistroch'ilus). Orchids from West Africa which must be grown in a hothouse having a minimum night temperature of 60 degrees in winter and of 65-70 degrees in spring and summer. They belong to the family Orchidaceae. The botanical name is derived from *ancistros,* a small hook, and *cheilus,* a lip—the lip having the shape of a small grappling hook.

Treatment. They should be grown in pans rather than pots, for they are usually suspended near the glass, not grown on the greenhouse benches. The pans must be well drained; a good compost consists of half finely cut osmunda fiber but equally good results can by using Fir bark. Repotting should be done every spring, as the plants begin to grow, and the opportunity may then be taken to divide them and place the separated portions in fresh flower pans.

spikes each bearing from two to four flowers, about 3 in. across, white flushed with rose, the lip being greenish brown and purple. A. Thomsonianum, from Old Calabar, has rather smaller flowers, the sepals and petals being white and the lip green marked with purple. It flowers a little earlier than A. Rothschildianus. Both these are sometimes known as Pachystoma.

ANDROMEDA POLIFOLIA—*Bog Rosemary* (Androm'eda). A hardy evergreen shrub which belongs to the Heather family,- Ericaceae. It grows wild in peat bogs in Northern and Arctic regions, rarely exceeds 12 in. in height, and bears pink, drooping, urn-shaped flowers in April and May. Andromeda was the daughter of Cepheus and Cassiope, of Greek mythology.

A dwarf kind of Bog Rosemary, Andromeda polifolia compacta.

Likes Peaty Soil. This shrub should be planted in a sunny or partially shaded position in acid peaty soil or in sandy loam which is free from lime. Planting may be done in fall or in early spring. The soil must be kept always moist.

Propagation is effected by means of seeds sown in sandy peat in a cold frame in April; by cuttings taken from July to September and planted in similar soil in a shaded cold frame; or by lifting and dividing the plants in spring and planting the rooted pieces. Some of the branches may be layered in summer, and left undisturbed for a year.

At various other times hardy flowering shrubs named Pieris and Zenobia (which see) have been confused with Andromeda, but most botanists now limit this genus to two species and recognize only Andromeda polifolia and A. glaucophylla. As a garden plant the former is the more important. The dwarf variety A. polifolia compacta is particularly choice.

ANDROPOGON—*Beard Grass* (Andropo'gon). A group of perennial grasses that belong in the Grass family, Gramineae. They are widely distributed as native plants in both hemispheres but have little or no horticultural importance. A few are grown for forage. The name is derived from *aner,* man, and *pogon,* beard, and alludes to the silky hairs which are part of the flower heads of some species.

ANDROSACE—*Rock Jasmine* (Andro'sace). Alpine plants from the high mountains of Europe, Asia and North America chiefly, which bloom in early spring. They belong to the Primrose family, Primulaceae. The word Androsace is derived from *aner,* a man and *sakos,* buckler, a reference to the shape of the anthers.

Planting and Suitable Soil. The Androsaces are beautiful rock garden plants; some are easily managed, others require special treatment. Their chief needs are well-drained soil of loam, sand, leaf mold and grit; for most kinds, a position not fully exposed to the sun; and frequent watering during dry weather in spring and summer. Some will thrive on level or sloping parts of the rock garden; others should be planted in vertical fissures among the rocks.

Propagation. Androsace is propagated in three ways. As soon as the flowers are over, the old plants may be separated into pieces, repotted singly in small pots of gritty soil, and placed in a shady frame until well rooted.

The choicest Rock Jasmine, Androsace sarmentosa.

Seeds are sown as soon as they are ripe in late summer, in pans of gritty soil kept in a cold, shady frame until germination takes place. When large enough, the seedlings are transplanted 2 in. apart in other flower pans and finally are potted singly in small pots; they are kept in the frame until well rooted and then are planted out of doors.

Cuttings may be inserted in pots of sandy soil in June or July and set in a cold, shady frame kept close for a few weeks.

Most Easily Grown Kinds. A. carnea, from the European Alps, 3 in., has gray leaves and bears rose-colored flowers in May; it should be planted in an open part of the rock garden in 12 in. depth of peat and sandy loam. Two favorite varieties are Halleri and Laggeri.

A. foliosa, from the Himalayas, 6-8 in., bears large heads of lilac-rose blooms; it needs an open sunny place and should be planted in loamy stony soil containing lime.

A. lanuginosa, a Himalayan plant, has gray leaves and small umbels of rose-colored flowers from May onwards; the leaves are covered with silky hairs. This is a beautiful little rock plant which should be so placed that its trailing stems may fall over a rockery ledge. It needs a gritty or stony compost of loam and leaf mold. The variety Leichtlinii has large flowers, white with crimson eye.

The Best of All. A. sarmentosa, from the Himalayas, is considered the best of all. It forms dense rosettes of silvery gray leaves from which develop runners or trailers; the leafy rosettes at the ends of these soon root if pegged down and covered with sandy soil in June–July. The flowers are rose colored. It should be planted in loam, leaf mold and sand or grit. The varieties Chumbyi and Watkinsii have flowers of deeper coloring, and are more compact. A. primuloides, as grown in gardens, is similar.

A. lactiflora, from Siberia, is a pretty little annual with white flowers on stems 6 in. high, from April to June. It seeds freely; sufficient seedlings invariably develop to replace the old plants the following year.

More Difficult to Manage. The following are more difficult to manage and need special treatment. They are suitable for planting in a moraine as well as in the positions described. A. ciliata, a Pyrenean plant, 2-3 in. high, bears carmine-red flowers in June; it should be planted in a partially shaded vertical rock crevice in very gritty soil. A. helvetica, from the Swiss Alps, is a diminutive plant, about 1 in. high, with white, yellow-eyed flowers. It needs very gritty soil.

A. glacialis grows wild on the European Alps. It should be planted, in spring, in a moraine (which see) or in the rock garden in a gritty compost of stone chips and sandy loamy soil. The rose-colored flowers open in April and May.

A. imbricata (argentea), from the high Alps of southern Tyrol, 3 in. high, bears white or pink flowers in June. It should be planted in a rock fissure in very gritty soil. A. pyrenaica, from the Pyrenees, is a very dwarf plant with white, yellow-centered flowers in May. It is best grown in a rock fissure in sandy loam and peat. A. villosa, from the European Alps, is 2-4 in. high, and has rose or white, honey-scented flowers in May and June. It is grown in stony, loamy, gritty soil in a sunny place.

ANEIMIA (Anei'mia). Ferns, from tropical America, which are grown in a greenhouse having a minimum winter temperature of 50 degrees. They belong to the Schizaeae family of Ferns. The name is derived from *aneimon*, naked, and refers to the spore cases.

Aneimia phyllitidis, a Fern that is native of tropical America.

When to Repot. Repotting is done as soon as new growth commences in spring. As these Ferns do best in small pots, only a slightly larger pot is needed each year. The compost should consist of equal parts of loam, leaf mold and peat, with the addition of crushed charcoal and coarse sand. When established, the Ferns must be watered freely during the summer. They should be shaded from bright sunlight and the atmosphere must be kept moist. Less water is needed in winter, but the compost should not be allowed to remain dry for long.

Propagation is effected by division and by sowing spores. The plants are divided in February–March. The old soil is taken off the roots, the plants are separated and the pieces repotted separately in 3-in. pots. Plants can also be raised from spores, as described under Ferns.

The chief kinds are Aneimia adiantifolia, 2 ft., and A. phyllitidis, 12 in., high.

ANEMONE or WINDFLOWER
Delightful Plants for the Rock Garden,
Wild Garden, and Perennial Border

(Anem'one). Charming perennial flowering plants suitable for the herbaceous border, rock garden, and for naturalizing in open spaces among leaf-losing trees. Some are suitable for greenhouse cultivation. They belong to the Buttercup family, Ranunculaceae. The word Anemone is derived from *anemos,* the wind, hence the popular name Windflower. The plants grow wild in many European countries, in Japan and North America. The Anemones have no petals; the showy part of the flower consists of petal-like sepals.

For the hardy flower border and open spaces in the woodland, a favorite kind is the Japanese Anemone, A. hupehensis japonica, a plant 3-4 ft. high which bears flowers of rose, blush or white in September. It thrives in ordinary fertile garden soil in a sunny or shady place; as it dislikes being disturbed, it should not be moved unnecessarily. Planting may be done in early fall or in spring.

Taking Root Cuttings. In addition to division of the crowns, propagation can be carried out by means of root cuttings—pieces of root—taken off in autumn or early spring, and placed in boxes of sandy loam and leaf mold, set in a cold frame or in a cool greenhouse. The cuttings will be sufficiently well rooted to be planted out of doors the following summer. Seeds may be sown in autumn in pots of sandy soil placed in a frame, but the seedlings grow slowly and, if they are of horticultural varieties, do not come true to type.

Beautiful Japanese Anemones. There are many beautiful named varieties of the Japanese

Anemone; some of the best are Alice, pink; alba, white; Queen Charlotte, semidouble, pink; Marie Manchard, semidouble, pink; September Charm, pink-shaded rose, and Whirlwind, double, white. A. hupehensis, the type species of the variety japonica, from which garden varieties of Japanese Anemones are derived, grows 15-18 in. tall, has mauve-rose flowers and begins blooming earlier than japonica varieties. It needs similar care. It is a good plant for the rock garden.

For the Rock Garden. There are two chief sections of rock garden Anemones: those which belong to the Pulsatilla or Pasque flower type and which some botanists separate under the name Pulsatilla; and those of the nemorosa or Wood Anemone type. As the plants in each section need different treatment they must be considered separately. All bloom in spring.

The Pasque Flowers. Of the first section one of the loveliest is the Pasque Flower (Anemone Pulsatilla), which grows wild on chalky downs in Great Britain and other European countries; it has finely cut leaves, grows 10 in. high, and bears large purplish flowers in March. It should be planted in well-drained, limey, loamy soil in a sunny or slightly shaded place. There are several varieties: alba, white; lilacina, pale-lilac; and rubra, brownish-rose.

A. alpina, 18-24 in., from the Swiss Alps, has fernlike leaves and large starry flowers, usually very pale blue outside and white inside, in May. The variety sulphurea has pale-yellow flowers. It thrives in deep, loamy, limey soil.

A. Halleri is the finest and probably the rarest of the Pulsatilla or Pasque flower group. It

Upper left. The Japanese Anemone, A. hupehensis japonica, blooms in early autumn and is good for cutting. It thrives in sun or partial shade.

Upper right. A clump of the purplish Pasque Flower, Anemone Pulsatilla, in full bloom in April. It is a charming plant for the rock garden. It needs a well-drained soil.

Center. The native Anemone canadensis thrives in partially shaded places. It is an attractive plant for naturalizing.

Bottom. The beautiful spring-flowering white Snowdrop Anemone, A. sylvestris.

comes from the Swiss Alps, grows about 9 in. high, and bears large lilac-colored blooms in April. It should be planted in a sunny position in well-drained, loamy, limey soil.

A. vernalis, from the high European Alps, is the smallest of the Pasque flowers; it is about 6 in. high and bears comparatively large, goblet-shaped whitish flowers in March–April. It thrives best in a mixture of loam and peat. A. patens, from northern Europe, northern Asia, and North America from Illinois to British Columbia and also Alaska, is similar to A. Pulsatilla.

The Wood Anemones. There are many beautiful low-growing plants among the Wood Anemones; they are suitable for naturalizing in the open woodland, beneath leaf-losing trees, and in shady places in the rock garden. They flourish in ordinary light garden soil to which leaf mold has been added. Heavy soil can be made suitable by mixing in leaf mold and sand. The somewhat

Anemone blanda is one of the most valuable of the Wood Anemones for naturalizing in semi-shady positions, where it produces masses of flowers in shades of blue in early spring.

sticklike roots should be planted in September, before they have had an opportunity to dry out, about 2 in. deep.

Chief among the plants in this group are the following, all of which flower in early spring: Anemone apennina, the blue Apennine Wind-flower from Italy; A. blanda, from Asia Minor, with flowers of various shades of blue, and variety scythinica, white, tinted blue outside; A. quinquefolia, the American Wood Anemone, similar to A. nemorosa but with more slender stems and smaller flowers; and A. nemorosa, the Wood Anemone of Europe, white or pink-tinged. There are many lovely forms of the last named, notably grandiflora, white; alba plena, double, white; rubra plena, double, flushed red; Robinsoniana, large, lavender-blue; and Allenii, large, soft blue.

Gay Poppy Anemones. These varieties and hybrids of Anemone coronaria, a native of southern Europe, are favorites for providing patches of rich and varied colors in the flower borders, or in beds by themselves in climates that are mild or where adequate winter protection can be provided. They will not stand much frost. They are much grown in greenhouses to supply flowers for cutting, and in the North they succeed well when planted in adequately protected cold frames.

These Anemones thrive best in soil of medium texture, well drained, and enriched with old manure or well-rotted compost. If the soil tends to become waterlogged it is good practice to raise the bed a few inches above the surrounding level. Plant the tubers 2-4 in. deep and about 6 in. apart, in fall. In the greenhouse do not subject them to high temperatures; 40-45 degrees at night with a rise of 5-10 degrees by day is adequate.

The two principal types are the St. Brigid and the De Caen, and both are invaluable for cutting as well as for garden display. The St. Brigids have semidouble flowers in a glorious range of rich colors, and a few named strains are available. In the De Caen or Giant French Anemones the large single flowers are saucer-shaped, and here again a mixture is generally favored, although if separate colors are required they can be obtained as named varieties. Of mixed strains, that called Creagh Castle is especially fine. When the leaves have died down in summer the tubers should be lifted, dried and stored for replanting in autumn. Tubers of Poppy Anemones are offered at reasonable prices in bulb-dealers catalogues. They are easily raised from seeds sown in light, humus-rich soil in May. Seedling plants bloom the following spring.

Anemone fulgens, the Scarlet Windflower of Greece and the Pyrenees, a hybrid of A. hortensis and A. pavonina, is a brilliant spring-flowering plant 9 in. high, suitable for the rock garden. It needs the same treatment as the St. Brigid Anemones previously described.

The easiest method of raising A. fulgens is by sowing seeds out of doors in a cold frame or in a bed of fine soil in a partially shady place as soon as they are ripe in summer. The seeds are covered by raking them in lightly and treading the soil down. The seedlings should be left undisturbed until the leaves have died down the following year.

Other Attractive Anemones. A. sylvestris, the Snowdrop Windflower, 12-18 in., has large, white, sweet-scented flowers; it is a good plant for the shady border or rock garden. A. virginiana, 2-3 ft., grows wild in the woods and meadows of the United States and Canada and has greenish-white flowers. It likes moist soil and a shady place. A. canadensis, 18-24 in., with white flowers, is attractive in wild gardens and shaded borders; A. magellanica, perhaps not true A.

magellanica of botanists, but so known in gardens, is a good creamy-white flowered plant, 18 in. tall, that blooms in late spring and summer in ordinary soil in sun or light shade; A. vitifolia is a Himalayan species, with pink flowers that resemble those of A. hupehensis, and needs the same care. A. ranunculoides, the Yellow Wood Anemone, 8 in., is lovely for naturalizing in woodland. The Hepaticas were previously classed as Anemones, but are now regarded as a distinct genus. See Hepatica.

ANEMONELLA—*Rue Anemone* (Anemonel'la). Belonging to the Buttercup family, Ranunculaceae, and closely related to Anemone, the only kind is Anemonella thalictroides, a hardy, tuberous perennial, native of eastern North America, suitable for naturalizing in the wild garden or open woodland. It bears clusters of white or pink flowers in early spring and has dainty, gray, thalictrum-like foliage. It is best increased by seed or by removing side portions without disturbing the whole plant, in autumn or spring. There is an equally charming double variety, A. thalictroides flore-pleno.

ANEMONOPSIS MACROPHYLLA (Anemonop'sis). A hardy herbaceous perennial which grows 2 ft. high and bears anemone-like flowers of pale-mauve or lilac color in June–July. It belongs to the Buttercup family, Ranunculaceae, and is a native of Japan. The word Anemonopsis means resembling the Anemone. This plant thrives in a slightly shady place in rich, well-tilled garden soil, preferring that which is fairly light and well drained yet reasonably moist. It is planted in autumn or spring and is increased by lifting and separating the plants in spring.

ANEMOPAEGMA CHAMBERLAYNII (Anemopae'gma). A climbing shrub, native to Brazil, that is sometimes grown in greenhouses and is planted out of doors in warm climates. It belongs to the Bignonia family, Bignoniaceae. It has pale-yellow flowers striped with purple or white in their throats, and requires the same culture as Allamanda, which see.

ANETHUM—*Dill* (Ane'thum). An Old World annual or biennial that belongs to the Carrot family, Umbelliferae, and is grown as an herb for its seeds, which are used for flavoring. It thrives in any well-drained soil in a warm, sunny position and is raised from seeds sown out of

doors in early spring where the plants are to remain. The seedlings should be thinned to 8 in. apart. See Dill.

ANGELICA ARCHANGELICA (Angel'ica). A hardy plant which grows wild in eastern Europe; from it is derived the preserved angelica used in confectionery. It belongs to the Carrot family, Umbelliferae, and may be of biennial duration, or it may not flower until 2 or 3 years old, after which it dies and is renewed by seed sown as soon as ripe. It thrives in ordinary garden soil, grows 5 or 6 ft. high and is chiefly remarkable for its large leaves divided into numerous small leaflets and flat umbels of yellowish flowers produced in July.

The roots and leaves have medicinal properties. The candied stems are used in confectionery, the fruits have flavoring properties, and an essential oil of medicinal value is distilled from roots and seeds. A. atropurpurea and A. Curtisii are native American species that have minor value as wild garden plants.

ANGELICA TREE. Japanese and Chinese shrubs or small trees belonging in the genus Aralia. Also the American small tree Zanthoxylum americanum. See Aralia and Zanthoxylum.

ANGELONIA (Angelo'nia). Pretty, tender perennial plants from South America, which some-

This splendid flowering vinelike shrub is Anemopaegma Chamberlaynii.

what resemble Alonsoa, to which they are closely allied; they belong to the Figwort family, the Scrophulariaceae. They have undivided lanceolate leaves and average 2 ft. in height. The inflorescence consists of small, two-lipped blue flowers borne in the axils of the leaves. Angelonia is derived from Angelon, the South American name for the plant.

Angelonia grandiflora, a fragrant summer-flowering plant.

Potting and Pruning. The cool greenhouse kinds require a minimum temperature of 50 degrees and the hothouse kinds a minimum temperature of 60 degrees. The best compost consists of equal parts of loam and leaf mold with sand added freely. In February the shoots are shortened by two thirds, and when the new shoots are ½ in. long the plants are repotted into larger pots. They are watered freely in summer, but during the winter water is given only when the soil becomes quite dry.

Sowing Seeds and Taking Cuttings. Angelonias can be treated as annuals by sowing seeds every year in spring to produce flowering plants in autumn. The seeds are sown in well-drained pans filled with a finely sifted compost of loam, leaf mold and sand. Propagation can also be effected by cuttings. The shoots are taken off in spring when about 2 in. in length, inserted in a bed of sand or of sand and peat moss in a propagating case until rooted. Young plants

should be pinched once or twice to induce bushiness.

Outdoor Culture. In the far South, Angelonias may be grown outdoors as perennials. In the North, plants raised from seeds sown in January or February may be planted out after the weather is warm and settled for summer bloom.

The chief kinds are A. grandiflora, pale-mauve and fragrant, and A. angustifolia, violet, both suitable for the cool greenhouse; and A. salicariaefolia, blue, which must be grown in a hothouse. All may be grown outdoors in summer.

ANGEL'S TEARS. See Narcissus triandrus.

ANGEL'S-TRUMPET. See Datura arborea.

ANGIOPTERIS EVECTA (Angiop'teris). An evergreen fern, 6-10 ft. high, which grows wild in Australia, Japan and Madagascar and is only suitable for large greenhouses or conservatories. It forms immense spreading fronds composed of a large number of leaflets which resemble Ash leaflets in size and shape. The leafstalks average 6 ft. in length and have thick, brown scales at their bases. Angiopteris belongs to the Marrattiaceae family of ferns. The name is derived from *aggeion,* a vessel, and *pteris,* a wing, a reference to the boat-shaped spore cases.

Needs a Warm Greenhouse. A greenhouse with a minimum winter temperature of 55 degrees is required for its cultivation. It must have abundance of water at all seasons of the year. For potting, a compost of two parts loam, one part each of peat and leaf mold and a liberal admixture of sand should be used. When 2 ft. high, this Fern may be set in a tub in which it can be kept for many years with an annual top-dressing of rich soil. It must have a moist, shady place.

To raise an increased stock the fleshy scales at the bases of the leafstalks are removed in spring and laid in pans of sand, which must be kept constantly moist and warm. The dormant buds contained in the scales will eventually grow and form new plants.

ANGRAECUM (Angrae'cum). Mostly hothouse evergreen orchids which with one exception grow wild in Africa and on the island of Madagascar. Curiously enough, one kind, Angraecum falcatum, is found in Japan. They belong to the family Orchidaceae. The name Angraecum is said to be a Latinized form of a Malay word *angrek* or *angurek,* meaning air

[1-14]
Bottle-brush Buckeye (Aesculus parviflora)

[1-14a]
Belladonna Lily (Amaryllis Belladonna)

[1-14b]
Silver King Artemisia (Artemisia albula)

[1-14c]
Artemisia Schmidtiana nana

[1-15]
Aeonium arboreum

[1-15a]
Aglaonema commutatum

[1-15b]
Anthurium Scherzerianum

[1-15c]
Ardisia crispa

plant; it is certainly apt, as all these orchids are epiphytal, i.e., they grow on other trees or plants —not in the soil—and most of them emit long roots which, unable to find attachment, hang in the air. The lip or labellum of the flower is in the form of a long, slender spur which is well shown in the illustration. Pseudobulbs, which are a characteristic feature of most orchids, are absent in Angraecum; the plants produce their flower spikes from the axils of the leaves.

Angraecum sesquipedale, an Orchid of striking appearance because of the long spurs of the ivory-white flowers.

Summer and Winter Management. With the exception of the Japanese Angraecum falcatum, all require tropical heat and a moist atmosphere during the period of growth. In winter a temperature of 60 degrees at night is a safe minimum, but the thermometer should never fall below that, and by day should rise to 65 degrees or 70 degrees. The smaller kinds can be grown in pans or baskets suspended within a foot or 18 in. of the glass roof; baskets are to be preferred for those kinds having strongly developed roots, as the old compost can be replaced by fresh without serious disturbance. The larger kinds must be grown in pots, half-filled with drainage.

Potting Composts. Osmunda fiber forms a satisfactory potting compost for these Orchids; they may also be grown in Fir bark and in other barks suitable for Orchids.

In winter, water must be applied with care; the plants, particularly those with leathery foliage, should be allowed to get fairly dry before the compost is moistened. Hanging flower pans or baskets are useful in this respect as the compost does not retain the water for as long a period as when the plants are in pots.

The most striking kind is Angraecum sesquipedale from Madagascar. Specimen plants exceeding 4 ft. in height have been shown, but a plant 3 ft. high is considered a fine specimen. The stem bears opposite rows of broad strap-shaped leaves 10-15 in. long. The flower spikes appear in winter and early spring, each bearing five or more ivory-white flowers 5-7 in. across; each bloom resembles a six-armed starfish. The spur is sometimes 11 in. long, but it never reached the length designated by the name sesquipedale—1½ ft.

A second kind from Madagascar, A. superbum, bears seven to fifteen greenish-white flowers on each spike in winter. A. eburneum, which has white flowers, is also a native of Madagascar and blooms in the spring. A. Eichlerianum, of West Africa bears green and white flowers in summer.

Climbing Orchids. Quite distinct from the foregoing are two remarkable kinds from the west coast of Africa, A. Eichlerianum and A. infundibulare. Both are of climbing habit, the stems reaching a considerable height and clinging to tree trunks and branches by means of aerial clasping roots; they have greenish-white flowers in summer. They are grown on a long narrow board some 3 in. wide, on which the mixture of osmunda fiber and moss has been firmly secured and one end of the board is placed in a pot or pan filled with similar compost. As the plant grows and extends beyond the board a fresh length of wood and compost are added. The original compost in the flower pan or pot need not be renewed; the plants will support themselves entirely from the moss and fiber on the board if this is renewed from time to time.

The Japanese Angraecum falcatum should be grown in an average temperature of 60 degrees. It seldom exceeds 3 in. in height, and bears white, fragrant flowers. It was first introduced in 1813 and is thus one of the earliest cultivated orchids. A. pertusum is called the Fishbone

Orchid; the flowers are in threes and, as all the segments are very narrow, their appearance is not unlike the spine of a fish.

ANGULOA—*Cradle or Tulip Orchid* (Angulo'a). Orchids which grow wild chiefly in Colombia and Peru, and in North America must be grown in a greenhouse having a minimum winter temperature of 55-60 degrees. The plants belong to the family Orchidaceae. Anguloa was named in honor of Don Francisco de Angulo, a Spanish naturalist.

The pseudobulbs are large, often furrowed and placed close together. The leaves of the most vigorous kinds reach a length of 18-24 in. The somewhat globe-shaped flowers, which bear a resemblance to Tulips, are on erect stems 6-9 in. high. If a flower is moved gently backward and forward the lip rocks to and fro, hence the name Cradle Orchid.

Details of Management. These Orchids are easily grown. In winter they should have a decided rest in a temperature of 55-60 degrees or slightly lower in severe weather. In the spring-to-fall growing season the temperature should not be forced above 65 degrees with artificial heat but may rise considerably higher with sun heat; a moist atmosphere is essential. The flowering season is usually May; as the young growths develop at the same time, repotting should be done as early as possible—at the first sign of fresh growth. Osmunda fiber is a suitable medium in which to pot these Orchids and they can also be successfully grown in Fir bark. Watering must be done carefully after potting, more freely as growth develops and new roots establish themselves.

The most popular kind is Anguloa Clowesii, which has large, fragrant, yellow flowers. A. Ruckeri has slightly smaller flowers, greenish-brown outside, yellow, thickly spotted with red, on the inside. A. uniflora has still smaller flowers, white-spotted and flushed with pink. Peru is the home of the finest of all, Anguloa Cliftonii, which has large flowers, splashed with red on a yellow ground.

ANIGOZANTHUS (Anigozan'thus). Perennial herbs of the Amaryllis family, Amaryllidaceae, from western Australia, suitable for greenhouse cultivation (minimum winter temperature 50 degrees) and for planting outdoors in California and similar mild, dry climates. The long-tubed flowers and stems are curiously downy, borne on tall branching stems above the linear or sword-shaped leaves. The name is derived from *anoigo,* to expand, and *anthos,* flower. In Australia they are called Kangaroo Paws.

Anigozanthus grow best in a mixture of two parts peat moss, one part loam and a sprinkling of sand. Pot or plant them in spring. Give water freely from spring through fall, but comparatively little while the plants are resting in winter. Increase is by dividing the fleshy roots after flowering. In A. Manglesii the 3-ft. stem, bearing greenish flowers, is covered with crimson down. A. flavidus has yellow-green flowers tinted red; those of A. rufus are purple and white.

ANIMATED OATS. See Avena sterilis.

ANISE. A white-flowered annual (Pimpinella anisum) belonging to the Carrot family, Umbelliferae, and growing 12-18 in. high; it is a native of Egypt, southeastern Europe and Asia Minor. Although sometimes grown as a garden annual, its chief use is for the production of seed (aniseed) for the distillation of its oil. Sow outdoors in fertile soil in early spring. Do not transplant, but thin plants to stand 3-4 in. apart in rows 12 in. apart. Star Anise has a very similar odor, but is obtained from the seed of a Chinese shrub, Illicum verum, which see.

ANISE, CHINESE. See Illicium verum.
ANISEED. See Anise and Pimpinella anisum.
ANISEED TREE. See Illicium.
ANISE, STAR. See Illicium verum.
ANNATTO. A dye obtained from the seeds of a tree, Bixa Orellana, family Bixaceae, used for coloring butter, cheese, and, to a limited extent, textiles. B. Orellana is widely planted in tropical countries, particularly in South America and is grown outdoors in southern Florida. See Bixa.

ANNONA CHERIMOLA—*Cherimoya* (Anno'na). A medium-sized tree that is a native of the Peruvian Andes and is suitable for outdoor culture in North America only in southern Florida and southern California. It yields edible fruits. The Annona belongs to the Custard Apple family, the Annonaceae. Its name is derived from *annona,* meaning yearly produce.

The Cherimoya will stand slight frost. It prefers light, well-drained soil. Propagation is by budding selected varieties on seedling stocks.

Other species of Annona that are sometimes grown in southern Florida are A. muricata, the Soursop; A. reticulata, the Custard Apple; A. squamosa, the Sweetsop; and A. glabra, the native Pond Apple or Alligator Apple. The fruit of A. glabra is not very edible but the fruits of the other kinds are much valued for making ice cream, beverages, jams and jellies.

ANNUALS: THEY BLOOM QUICKLY FROM SEEDS
Colorful Plants for the Flower Bed and Border

Annuals are plants which complete their life cycle within one year, that is, they develop from seed, come into flower, ripen fresh seed and die in a single growing season. They include many decorative plants that are suitable for the garden and greenhouse such as Sweet Alyssum, Marigolds, Sweet Peas and Clarkias.

Besides these true annuals, gardeners usually include under the same heading another group of plants which, though grown as annuals, are technically perennials and biennials. Most of these are so sensitive to cold that their term in the garden is ended by low temperature rather than by the natural life span of the plant. Perennials and biennials that are treated as annuals bloom the same year the seed is sown and give a long season of bloom. They form an important part of most annual plantings, and so are rightly considered here. They include Antirrhinum (Snapdragon), Verbena, Petunia, Centaurea Cineraria (Dusty Miller), Nierembergia, Vinca rosea (Periwinkle), Mirabilis Jalapa (Four o'clock), Salvia, Impatiens and many more.

Classifying annuals as hardy, half-hardy and

Annuals remain in bloom for many weeks. This part of a flower border contains tall Ageratums and Snapdragons in the rear and low blue-flowered Lobelia in the front.

tender, as is often done, is somewhat arbitrary. A kind hardy in one region may be tender in another. Even in the North most of the so-called half-hardy annuals can be sown outdoors in spring with excellent results, and so, too, can many of those commonly classified as tender. The practice of sowing these indoors early is usually based upon the desire to have plants in flower as soon as possible after the young plants are set in the open garden.

greenhouse. A number, because of their ability to withstand heat, are suitable for city roof gardens.

Everlasting Flowers. Among annuals are a number of "everlasting flowers." These, when cut and dried, are used for indoor decoration. To retain their natural colors they should be dried rapidly. Some should be cut before the flowers are fully open; in other cases the fully open flowers should be cut. Foliage is removed

French Marigolds are favorite annuals. Their flowers are richly colored and they are easy to grow.

Petunias are great favorites. They are usually raised from seeds sown indoors early.

Uses in the Garden. Because they are adapted to a wide range of soils and conditions, annuals have many uses in ornamental gardening. They can be used effectively in mass bedding schemes to ensure a long season of color. Planted in a mixed border, they help to bridge the gap between the flowering of early and late perennials, and they can be used to fill spaces left after the foliage of early bulbs has gone, if you sow seed directly among the browning foliage. Tall-growing kinds provide temporary screens, and can be used as backgrounds for other flowers. A number of very low-growing kinds are excellent for edging beds, borders and paths, and, not infrequently, for rock garden planting. They are useful in window boxes; some can be grown in the indoor window garden and almost all in the

and the bunches of flowers are hung in a warm but shady place with their heads down. Gomphrena globosa (Globeflower), Limonium sinuatum and L. Suworowii (Statice) should be cut when fully open; Helichrysum bracteatum (Strawflower), Helipterum Manglesii (Swan River Everlasting), Ammobium alatum (Winged Everlasting) and Xeranthemum annuum (Common Immortelle) before they are fully open. Ornamental Grasses used for drying and dyeing for indoor use include Agrostis nebulosa (Cloud Grass), Briza maxima (Quaking Grass), Coix lacryma-jobi (Job's Tears), Hordeum jubatum (Squirrel-Tail Grass), Pennisetum Ruppelii (Fountain Grass), and P. villosum (Plumy Grass).

Annual Vines. Besides being very decorative,

annual vines make fast growth and are useful for covering trellises, fences, arbors and the like. Those most frequently used include Cobaea scandens (Cup and Saucer Vine), Dolichos Lablab (Hyacinth Bean), Cardiospermum Halicacabum (Heartseed), Quamoclit pennata (Cypress Vine), and Q. Sloteri (Cardinal Climber), Tropaeolum majus (Nasturtium), and T. peregrinum (Canary-bird Vine), Thunbergia alata (Black-eyed Susan), and Ipomea (Morning

Annual Scabiosas may be raised from seeds sown indoors early or from seeds sown outdoors. They are splendid flowers for cutting.

Glory) and Calonyction aculeatum (Moonflower). Many of these are tropical. Where the season is short, their seeds are started indoors for early plants.

Growth Habits. There is great variation in the growth habits of annuals. Some are very dwarf, rarely exceeding 3 in.; others are tall, ranging up to 6 ft. or more; still others are creepers or climbers. With a judicious selection of species and varieties it is possible to make a garden completely of annuals. Because they bloom during the year in which their seeds are sown, an annual garden is the quickest to produce results.

Some of the showiest garden flowers are annuals. For this reason, perhaps, more work in selective breeding for improvements and disease-resistance has been done with annuals than with most other kinds of flowering plants. In some instances the size of the flowers has been doubled and trebled (the tetrahybrids of Marigolds for example), while in others the colors have been improved or the habit of growth has been changed. The "Gleam" type of Nasturtium, a dwarf, compact form today, is a far cry from the original trailing species. Resistance to disease has been achieved by breeding work in some species. In former years, growers of Snapdragons were plagued by a rust infection before the season was well advanced, whereas now rust-resistant varieties are accepted as a matter of course. The wilt disease that once affected China Asters is no longer a common hazard.

General Requirements. Coming as they do from many climes, annuals react very markedly to temperatures; indeed, temperature and light, more than other factors, determine the season, as well as the duration of flowering. With some the season of bloom is short; if such kinds as Poppies, Asters, Larkspurs, Clarkias and Godetias are sown early they tend to go to seed well before the summer is over and in any case they fail in very hot weather. Others, especially Calendulas, stop flowering or flower less satisfactorily during the hot period, then flower more profusely toward late summer. In regions of high temperatures and humidity, the California annuals such as Clarkia, Collinsia and Godetia are not successful, nor are Sweet Peas, Stocks and Schizanthus, nor most South African annuals such as Ursinia, Nemesia and Venidium. Under conditions of high temperature and humidity Zinnias, Snow-on-the-Mountain, Amaranthus, Hunnemannia, Torenia and Sunflowers thrive.

Sowing Seeds. The majority of hardy annuals are good-tempered plants and do not require very rich soil. They do respond, however, to good cultivation by giving a much better and longer display than if left to fend for themselves. The ground should, therefore, be broken up well and have a dressing of well-rotted compost and a sprinkling of a general fertilizer mixed with it. It should then be trodden firm and the surface should be raked down to a fine tilth before sowing or planting.

Common faults are sowing the seeds too thickly, and not thinning the seedlings sufficiently to give them room for full development. These

When sowing annuals in flower borders, prepare the soil, then make a criss-cross pattern of shallow drills with the end of a stick.

Next, soak the bottoms of the drills with water so that the seeds will be assured of enough moisture to start them into growth.

faults must be avoided if good results are to be secured. Seeds sown indoors should be transplanted to flats or cold frames promptly, before the young seedlings crowd each other, and every effort should be made to expose them to all the sunlight that is suitable for their kind (which usually means all possible sunlight) and temperatures and other environmental conditions that will ensure sturdy growth.

A few annuals, like Shirley Poppies, Mignonette, Eschscholtzia, Hunnemannia, and other types of Poppies, resent being disturbed and should be sown where they are to grow in the garden. For others, a sunny, well-protected location should be chosen for the outdoor seedbed.

Then scatter the seeds thinly along the drills and cover them with soil.

The soil should be prepared in advance as described. The seed should be sown in straight drills or lines made with the handle of a rake or some other handy tool. These drills should not be more than a half-inch deep for even the largest seeds. Fine seeds should be covered very lightly or not at all. After the seeds are sown, the soil should be raked over lightly to cover them, then tamped down gently to eliminate any air pockets. The ground should be sprinkled lightly, then covered with lath or cloth screens until the seedlings have made their appearance. Care should be taken not to sow the seeds too thickly.

Sowing seeds in the cold frame requires a little more attention to see that adequate ventilation is provided to prevent damping-off. A close, damp atmosphere is ideal to promote germina-

Finally finish off the surface neatly by raking it very lightly, not deep enough to disturb the seeds.

To remove annuals from a flat easily, first tap the end of the flat on the ground so that a space is made between the soil and the upper end of the flat.

tion, but once this has taken place, the atmosphere must be kept fresh and dry at all times. This is accomplished by watering the seedlings early in the morning only on bright, sunny days and by providing plenty of ventilation even on cloudy days. The soil must be moist at all times.

Very fine seeds such as those of Petunias, Lobelias and Snapdragons, or seeds of tender annuals that require a longer season of growth, must be sown earlier and in a warmer temperature. For these, flats or pots often are used. A soil mixture composed of equal parts light loam, coarse sand and pulverized peat is suitable for sowing most annual seeds, although some annuals require a lighter or heavier soil. Increasing the amount of sand and peat in the basic mixture produces a lighter soil, while increasing the proportion of loam gives a heavier soil. Steriliz-

Next insert the hands in this space and lift the mass of roots and soil.

Then break the plants apart, taking care that a good mass of roots with soil attached remains with each.

With a trowel, dig a hole of ample size to take the root ball without crowding.

Set the plant in the hole at such a depth that the upper parts of its roots will be just covered with new soil.

Then make the soil firm about the roots with the fingers.

Finally, water the new plant in thoroughly with a fine spray.

ing the soil before sowing the seeds eliminates damping-off and other fungus troubles. If the annuals are started early in the spring before hot, dry weather commences, and are kept moderately moist in a location where the air can circulate freely, there should not be much loss from damping-off.

As soon as the seedlings have emerged they require more air and light. When they have produced their first set of true leaves they require more room and must be thinned or transplanted. Those that were sown directly into the garden must be thinned. This is done by pulling up the surplus plants. Those that were sown in the greenhouse, nursery row or coldframe must be transplanted. As they grow, most annuals should be pinched back to force them to develop more branches and to become compact and bushy rather than tall and leggy. Pinching back is done simply by cutting off the growing tips when the plants are about four or five inches tall, while they are developing their fourth set of true leaves. One pinching usually is enough, but if the plants continue to grow tall and lanky or they start to bloom too early, they may be pinched back a second time.

Popular Kinds. The following popular kinds can be sown outdoors in spring to flower through the summer. Amaranthus (Joseph's Coat), Abronia, Argemone (Prickly Poppy), Calendula, Celosia (Cockscomb), Cynoglossum amabile (Chinese Forget-me-not), Cleome (Spider Flower), Centaurea americana (Basket Flower), Chrysanthemum carinatum (Annual Chrysanthemum), Emilia sagittata (Tassel Flower), Eschscholtzia californica (California Poppy), Euphorbia marginata (Snow-on-the-Mountain), Gaillardia amblyodon (Annual Gaillardia), Gilia, Gypsophila elegans (Baby's-Breath), Helianthus annuus (Sunflower), Iberis amara (Candytuft), Kochia trichophylla (Summer Cypress), Lobularia maritima (Sweet Alyssum), Phlox Drummondii, Rudbeckia hirta (Annual Black-eyed Susan), Scabiosa (Pincushion Flower, Mourning Bride), Mathiola bicornis (Evening Scented Stock), Nicotiana (Ornamental Tobacco), Reseda (Mignonette).

Some annuals, if sown outdoors in late autumn, will flower the following summer earlier than if sown in spring. These include Larkspur, Coreopsis Drummondii, Cornflower, and annual Poppies.

Kinds to Sow in Late Spring and Early Summer. The late summer and fall garden can be replenished or replanted by using certain annuals which, when sown in early summer, will flower in late summer and autumn. Naturally the length of the flowering season will influence the number of kinds that can be so grown. Most successful are short-season annuals that are natives of the southwestern United States and Mexico. These include Cosmos, Marigold, Phlox Drummondii and Zinnia. From seeds sown the latter part of June to the first week in July, plants begin to bloom in August. Calendula, which hails from southern Europe, also does well when handled in this way and persists longer into the fall than most others. Other kinds successful from mid-to-late June sowings include Torenia, Browallia, Gomphrena, Sweet Alyssum and Sunflowers. Calendula and Zinnia will grow to their full dimensions from these late sowings but the rest, although they flower profusely, will not attain the size of plants of the same kind raised from spring sowings.

In Florida and the Lower South. Annual flowering plants are the backbone of winter gardens in Florida and the lower South. Properly selected, they can be had in bloom from January until spring. Seeds are sown from August to October. The following, sown in August or in early September, flower in January: Sweet Peas, Sweet Alyssum, Baby's Breath, Browallia, Calendula, Cornflower, Petunia, Linaria, Verbena, and Snapdragon. The following flower from February through March and April from seeds sown in September and October: California Poppy (Eschscholtzia), Candytuft, Larkspur, Leptosyne, Lupine, Mignonette, Portulaca, Nicotiana, Phlox Drummondii, Shirley Poppy, Nemophila, and Nasturtium.

Annuals in the Greenhouse. Many annuals are commonly grown in greenhouses to provide cut flowers and pot plants. Some of these are of kinds that are also commonly grown outdoors, such as Sweet Peas, Snapdragons, Stocks, Calendulas, and Clarkias, others such as Cinerarias, Primulas, and Schizanthus, are of kinds that are seldom or never grown outdoors. Some of these so-called greenhouse annuals, Cinerarias and Primulas, for example, are truly perennials but are ordinarily grown as annuals because of the greater convenience of treating them in that way—raising them from seed each year and discarding them after they are through flowering.

ANODA (Ano'da). This is a small group of annuals, or plants grown as annuals, that have mallow-like flowers in summer. The name is from *a*, without, and *nodus*, a joint, and was given because these plants lack nodes on the pedicels. They belong to the Mallow family, Malvaceae, and are of easy culture.

Anodas thrive under the same conditions that suit Lavateras, which see. The most commonly grown is A. lavateroides, with violet, lavender, or white flowers. It is sometimes called Opal Cup.

ANOECTOCHILUS—*Jewel Orchid* (Anoectochil'us). Charming little hothouse Orchids, 2-6 in. high, which have beautifully marked and colored leaves. They are natives chiefly of the Malay Archipelago and belong to the Orchid family, Orchidaceae. Anoectochilus is derived from the Greek *anoiktos*, open, and *cheilos*, a lip, and refers to the shape of the lip.

Special Treatment Needed. They can be grown to perfection only under the shelter of a bell jar, raised slightly for purposes of ventilation; the temperature ought to be maintained at 60-65 degrees in winter and will, of course, rise higher in summer. They must be shaded from strong sunlight and kept free from drafts. A warm moist atmosphere is necessary and the plants must be renewed frequently by propagation. When the jointed side shoots begin to form roots they should be cut through just below the joint from which roots are developing and potted at any time in spring or summer.

These Orchids are grown in small shallow pans, drained and filled with a compost of sphagnum moss and finely cut osmunda fiber, with the addition of a very small quantity of dried oak leaves rubbed to a fine state and some crushed crocks.

One of the most beautiful of all is A. Petola, with olive-green leaves, netted and veined with yellow. A. Sanderianus is a larger plant, the leaves 4 in. by 2 in., dark velvety green, netted with reddish-copper. Others are A. Rollinsonii, bronze-green leaves edged with pale yellow; A. discolor, dark, reddish green leaves with red

veins; A. discolor Dawsonianus, greenish-brown leaves, reddish veins; A. regius, dark velvety green leaves with pale bands; A. regalis, dark green leaves with gold markings; and A. xanthophyllus, dark green leaves banded with yellow and netted with gold.

ANOMATHECA. See Lapeirousia.

ANOPTERUS GLANDULOSUS (Anop'terus). An evergreen tree or large shrub, 20 ft. or more high, native of Tasmania and belonging to the family Saxifragaceae. It bears large, white flowers in early summer and has glossy leaves. It can be successfully cultivated in a frostproof greenhouse, minimum winter temperature 40 degrees, and may be grown in flowerpots in a compost of equal parts loam and peat moss with a scattering of sand. In the South it should prove quite hardy outdoors. By taking cuttings annually a regular supply of plants in small pots is maintained. Cuttings are made from firm, half-woody shoots, 3 in. long, in summer; these are inserted in sandy peat and placed under a bell jar in the greenhouse until well rooted; then they are potted separately. The word Anopterus is from *ano*, upwards, and *pteron*, winged, and refers to the seeds.

ANTARCTIC BEECH. See Nothofagus.

ANTENNARIA—*Cat's-Ear, Pussytoes* (Antenna'ria). Small rock garden and wild garden perennial plants with white, woolly leaves and heads of stiff, dry, gray, white, or pink flowers in summer. They are closely allied to the well-known Edelweiss. Although not showy, they are

Antennarias grow well in poor but well-drained soil and are suitable for rock gardens.

useful for covering bare spaces in the rock garden and for planting between paving stones. They are perfectly hardy, thrive in poor soil, and soon form mats of silvery gray foliage, which is attractive when the rock flowers are over. These plants belong to the Daisy family, Compositae, and grow wild in Europe and North America. The word Antennaria indicates the resemblance of the down on the flowers to the *antennae* of the butterfly.

Propagation is by lifting the plants in September or spring, separating them into rooted pieces, and replanting these. Also by sowing seeds in sandy soil in spring or fall.

The commonest kinds are A. aprica, A. dioica, A. trichophylla, A. neodioica, A. obovata, A. rhodantha, and A. rosea. All are low, creeping plants a foot or less tall.

ANTHEMIS—*Chamomile, Camomile* (Anthe'mis). Hardy perennial plants with aromatic leaves and daisy-like flowers, suitable for the perennial border and the rock garden. They are natives chiefly of eastern Europe and belong to the Daisy family, Compositae. The botanical name indicates the free-blooming character of Anthemis; it is derived from *anthemon,* a flower.

The plant sometimes grown as A. aizoon is Achillea ageratifolia Aizoon, which see.

For the Flower Border. The hardy border kinds are free-growing plants about 2½ ft. tall with attractive ferny foliage. They bloom from July till September. All are excellent for cutting. They thrive in light to medium, well-drained soil

Anthemis Sancti-Johannis, from Bulgaria, has rich orange daisylike flowers produced very freely from July onward, on 2 ft. stems. It likes a sunny location and well-drained soil.

in a sunny position, but are not long-lived in cold, clayey mediums. Propagation is by lifting established plants in March, separating them into small tufts of rooted growths, and replanting them about 12 in. apart. Some support for the flowering stems is desirable, in the form of short, twiggy brushwood inserted among and around them.

The chief kind is Anthemis tinctoria with light-yellow, marguerite-like flowers, but greatly improved garden forms of it are Grallagh Gold, rich golden-yellow; Golden Dawn, double, golden-yellow; Moonlight, pale yellow; Perry's variety, large, bright yellow flowers; and Wargrave variety, sulphur-yellow. A. Sancti-Johannis, from Bulgaria, is another showy kind for well-drained soil in full sun. It is 2-3 ft. tall, with rich orange flowers. It is sometimes not long-lived, possibly because it flowers so freely, but can be perpetuated by potting rooted basal shoots in autumn and wintering these in a cold frame.

Modern varieties of Anthemis tinctoria are showy, free-blooming plants for the perennial border. They grow about 2 ft. tall, and their flower colors range from ivory to rich orange-gold. Though not long-lived in heavy soils, they are easily propagated by division.

Rock Garden Chamomiles. The most ornamental of the dwarf mat-forming kinds, with gray foliage, flowering from spring onwards and suitable for sunny positions in the rock garden, are Anthemis carpatica, white; A. Biebersteiniana, 10 in., with bright yellow daisies in May; and A. montana, 6 in., white or pinkish. They may be planted in autumn or early spring and are increased by separating and replanting rooted portions.

The Herb Chamomile is Anthemis nobilis, of which the double-flowered form is grown extensively for medicinal purposes. In gardens Chamomile is sometimes used for making a fragrant, drought-resisting lawn. For details of cultivation see Chamomile.

ANTHER. That part of the stamen of a flower which bears the pollen.

ANTHERICUM—St.-Bernard's-Lily (Anther'icum). Hardy plants with roots resembling tubers, narrow leaves and erect stems, 1½-3 ft. high, bearing white, starlike flowers during summer. They are natives of Europe, Africa, and Australia, and belong to the Lily family, Liliaceae. The word Anthericum is derived from *anthos,* flower, and *herkos,* hedge.

When to Plant—Suitable Soil. The hardy kinds like a slightly shady place and light loamy soil to which well-rotted manure, compost or peat moss has been added. During dry weather they should be watered freely. Spring is the best time to plant. It is advisable to cover the soil above the roots with litter or other suitable winter covering in the autumn; the covering must be removed when growth begins in spring.

When to Sow Seeds. To provide an increased stock of plants, seeds are sown in September in pots filled with light, sandy soil in a greenhouse, temperature 50-55 degrees. When the seedlings are 1 in. high, they are set 3 in. apart in flats filled with a sandy soil mixture and are grown through the winter in a cool greenhouse or protected cold frame. In spring, they are planted out of doors, or, if required for the greenhouse, are placed in large pots. In autumn or early spring the plants may be lifted and separated into small portions for replanting.

The chief hardy kinds are Anthericum Liliago, 18-24 in., and its variety major, 3 ft.; and A. ramosum, 18 in. All bear white flowers in June–

July. Anthericum Liliastrum, St.-Bruno's-Lily, is now named Paradisia Liliastrum, which see. For other plants commonly called Anthericum. See Chlorophytum.

ANTHOLYZA (Antholy'za). South African corms belonging to the Iris family, Iridaceae, and bearing brilliantly colored flowers in summer. The name Antholyza refers to the supposed resemblance of the flower when it opens, to the mouth of an enraged animal; it is derived from *anthos,* flower, and *lyssa,* rage.

These plants are about as hardy as Gladioli and may be grown in exactly the same way outdoors. After danger of frost is passed, they should be planted 4 in. deep in fertile soil in a sunny location. They may be lifted when the leaves have died down in autumn in the same way as Gladioli, and stored in sand safe from frost in winter. They may also be grown in pots, for early spring bloom, by planting several corms (bulbs) 2 in. apart and 2 in. deep in containers of fertile, well-drained soil in September and growing them in a sunny greenhouse, night temperature 45-50 degrees, day temperature 5-10 degrees higher.

Favorite kinds are Antholyza aethiopica, 2½ ft., red and greenish-yellow, June–July; and A. caffra, 2 ft., scarlet, July. The plant previously known as A. paniculata is now called Curtonus paniculatus. See Curtonus.

ANTHOXANTHUM ODORATUM—*Vernal Grass* (Anthoxan'thum). A hardy perennial European grass which is common in meadows in North America. When drying or ripening, it gives off a pleasant, haylike fragrance. It belongs to the grass family, Gramineae. The name Anthoxanthum is derived from *anthos,* flower, and *xanthus,* yellow. This plant thrives in ordinary soil, may be planted in autumn or spring, grows 12 in. high and blooms in summer. It is best suited to the wild garden.

ANTHRACNOSE. See Pests and Diseases.

ANTHRISCUS—*Chervil* (Anthris'cus). A valuable annual herb, of the family Umbelliferae, found wild in many parts of Europe. Its leaves are used for flavoring and garnishing. For details of cultivation, see Chervil.

ANTHURIUM (Anthur'ium). Hothouse plants, chiefly from tropical America, which belong to the Arum family, Araceae, and are grown for the sake of their brilliantly colored flower spathes in spring and summer, or their ornamental leaves. The word Anthurium refers to the tail-like flower in the center of the spathe and is derived from the Greek *anthos,* a flower, and *oura,* a tail.

Anthuriums have brightly colored and richly marked flower spathes. They are favorites for greenhouse cultivation.

Special Treatment Necessary. Anthuriums are grown in a greenhouse having a minimum temperature of 65 degrees. Potting is done early in the year, as soon as new roots begin to develop from the rootstock. The pots, 6-7 in. in diameter, must be drained and half-filled with crocks; a suitable compost consists of three parts orchid peat, one part leaf mold and one part sphagnum moss, with a scattering of coarse sand, crushed charcoal and broken brick. The roots must be kept high in the pots so that when potting is finished the top of the compost is in the form of a mound above the rim of the pot.

General Management. The plants must be shaded from strong sunlight, the atmosphere kept moist by moistening the floor and benches. The compost must be moist in summer, but in winter, water is applied only when it becomes nearly dry. As the rootstock elongates and produces roots at a higher level each year, the plants eventually become raised high above the rims of

the pots. If a layer of moss is packed around the bare stems, the young roots will penetrate it. Then the plants are cut off just level with the rims of the pots and are repotted in small pots.

Propagation. Anthurium is propagated by dividing the rootstock in February, potting the separate pieces in the way explained, and keeping them in a closed glass case for a few weeks. Seeds may be sown as soon as they have ripened, in shallow earthenware pans filled with chopped sphagnum moss, charcoal and sand. The seeds are scattered among the moss particles; the pan is covered with a piece of glass and placed in a propagating case.

Favorite kinds are Anthurium Andreanum, orange-red spathes, and A. Scherzerianum, scarlet spathes. There are many varieties and hybrids of each, having spathes of different colors. Of the

One of the most magnificent Anthuriums is A. Veitchii. It is sometimes grown in botanical collections.

former, notable variants are album, with white flower spathes; carneum, with pink spathes; and giganteum, with larger spathes. Specially good forms of A. Scherzerianum are atropurpureum, crimson; burfordense, scarlet; maximum album, white; albo-punctatum, red, spotted white; Roth-

Anthurium scandens bearing flowers and fruits.

schildianum, white, spotted red; and atrosangui-neum, with deep red spathes. A. scandens is somewhat climbing plant that has greenish spathes and pearly white, berry-like fruits almost throughout the year.

Two kinds grown for the sake of their decorative foliage are Anthurium crystallinum, leaves green veined with silver, and A. Veitchii, with metallic-green leaves 2-4 ft. long.

ANTHYLLIS MONTANA—*Kidney Vetch, Jupiter's Beard* (Anthyll'is). A dwarf hardy semi-shrubby plant, 6 in. high, with silky, downy, gray leaves and dense clover-like heads of purplish-pink flowers in June. It grows wild in the European Alps and is a very worth-while plant for the rock garden. It belongs to the Pea family, Leguminosae. The botanical name refers to the downy character of the flowers and is derived from *anthos,* flower, and *ioulos,* down.

For Poor Dry Soil. It may be planted in fall or in spring, will thrive in poor dry soil and needs a

sunny situation; crushed limestone mixed with the soil will improve the color of the leaves. Propagation is effected by lifting and dividing the plants and replanting the rooted pieces in September; by sowing seeds in pots of sandy soil in a frame in March; or by cuttings inserted in a cold frame in sand or sandy soil in July–August; or in pots placed out of doors in a shady place and covered with a bell jar.

Three other kinds are sometimes grown in gardens. Anthyllis Vulneraria (Lady's-Fingers or Woundwort), which grows wild in Europe, is only a few inches high and bears yellow flowers in early summer. A Spanish shrub, A. Barba-Jovis, Jupiter's-Beard, grows 4 ft. high and bears light yellow blooms in March–April; it needs well-drained, sandy, loamy soil. A. Hermanniae, a low, dense shrub with orange-yellow flowers, from southern Europe, is suitable for the rock garden. The two last mentioned are hardy in mild climates only.

ANTIGONON (Antig'onon). Tendril-climbing tender vines with showy red, pink, white or yellowish flowers; natives of Mexico and Central America. The name comes from *anti,* against, and *gonia,* an angle, and perhaps refers to the zigzag stems. Antigonon belongs to the Buckwheat or Knotweed family, Polygonaceae. They are grown in warm regions and are of easy cultivation. They prefer a soil that is not too rich and are propagated by seeds and cuttings. A sunny location suits them best.

A. leptopus (Coral Vine, Pink Vine, Corallita, Confederate Vine, Rosa de Montana) is the commonest kind; it climbs to 40 ft. and has flowers of bright pink in racemes 6 to 15 in. long. Its variety album has white flowers. A. macrocarpum differs from A. leptopus only in having thicker and more hairy leaves. It is grown in Florida.

ANTIRRHINUM or SNAPDRAGON
A Favorite for Garden Beds and as a Cut Flower

(Antirrhi'num). Summer-flowering plants which are favorites for garden beds and borders and as cut flowers. Snapdragons are also useful for the decoration of greenhouses and are much grown

under glass by florists for cut flowers. They grow wild in North America and in Europe and belong to the Foxglove family, Scrophulariaceae. Antirrhinum is derived from *anti,* like, and *rhin,*

Antirrhinum seedlings are planted in rich, fertile soil to produce summer blooms.

When cultivated for cut flowers, Antirrhinums are planted in straight rows, and staked to keep the stems straight.

snout or nose, a reference to the form of the flower.

In mild climates, the common Snapdragon, Antirrhinum majus, and its varieties are perennial; they develop into large plants which begin to bloom in late spring and provide a splendid display through the summer. More commonly they are cultivated as annuals.

Sowing Seeds in Early Spring. Snapdragons which are required for flower beds, or for grouping in the mixed border, should be treated as annuals. The plants are usually grown from seeds sown in a greenhouse late in January or in February—temperature 55-60 degrees. Flowerpots or flats are drained and filled with seed soil or with finely screened sphagnum moss or vermiculite. The seeds are scattered thinly and are covered lightly. If glass and brown paper are placed over the seed receptacles and the medium in which they are sown is kept moist, the seeds soon germinate.

Management of Seedlings. When the seedlings are an inch or so high, they should be pricked out,

set 2 in. apart, in other flats containing a well-drained, light, fertile soil, and they should be grown in a temperature of 45-50 degrees. The seedling plants must be hardened off in a cold frame before being planted outdoors after danger from frost is past. Some growers pinch out the tips of the plants when 3 in. high to make them bushy; others prefer to leave them unpruned.

They Love Sun. Antirrhinums must have a sunny position in the garden. The tall or majus varieties should be planted 18 in. apart, the Intermediate 10 in. apart, and Tom Thumb varieties 6 in. apart. The most popular type of Snapdragon is the Intermediate, which grows 12-18 in. high. The majus type, which grows 2-3 ft. high, is the most useful for grouping in the summer border. The Tom Thumb varieties, only 8-9 in. high, are used as edging plants, and the modern Dwarf Bedding Antirrhinums are excellent for small beds. The plant hybridists have also raised a very dwarf type, of almost prostrate habit, in a variety of colors. Aptly named Magic

Carpet, it is ideal for providing splashes of summer color in the rock garden.

Greenhouse Culture. Greenhouse-grown Snapdragons are most useful in winter and early spring as cut flowers. Varieties offered commercially as Greenhouse Forcing or Tall Giant Rust Resisting, are best adapted for this purpose; they may be had in bronze, lavender, red, rose and pink shades, and in white and yellow. Seeds may be sown any time from late May to August.

Dwarf varieties of Antirrhinum grow a foot or less high; they are especially suitable for summer flower beds.

Plants from a June sowing, set in their flowering pots or in greenhouse soil-filled benches in September, should provide good flower spikes in December and on into spring. Sow the seeds as recommended for outdoor plants, placing the container in the coolest part of the greenhouse. Shade heavily until germination begins, after which good light should be provided.

The seedlings should be transplanted 2-3 in. apart into flats or other shallow containers and grown in an airy greenhouse or cold frame. Shade for the first two or three days after transplanting.

When the seedlings have grown large enough to almost touch each other, they should be potted singly in 4-in. pots in a friable potting soil that is rich in humus. A 3-in. potful of superphosphate to each bushel of soil should be mixed in. Continue to grow the plants in a light, airy environment and, about a week after potting,

pinch out the tip of each plant to encourage branching.

When the roots encompass the ball of potting soil, the plants are ready to be moved to their flowering stations. They may be grown individually in 6- or 7-in. pots, but usually space is provided in a 4- to 6-in.-deep bench. There, space them 8-10 in. apart in moderately rich soil; with good drainage they will grow well, provided the

Aotus gracillima, an evergreen shrub for the greenhouse, has yellow and crimson pea-shaped flowers.

house is well ventilated and there is good light, and provided the temperature drops during winter to 45 degrees at night and rises during the day to 58-65 degrees. Overwatering before the plants show signs of good growth is sometimes a cause of partial failure; excessive dryness, which may occur in very porous soils, is equally harmful.

As the plants grow, select 4 or 5 of the strongest growths to be retained, and cut away all side shoots. A light application of a complete fertilizer after the plants are 18-24 in. tall may be watered in once a week. This should stimulate growth; such applications should be discontinued when the flowers begin to show their colors. The plants should be provided with a means of support before they are 15 in. tall.

In a very small greenhouse, or when a variety is not offered commercially but is desirable enough to retain, young plants can be started at any time from cuttings taken from side growths. These root readily in sand. Seedlings, however, are usually more robust and are less subject to attacks from disease.

For the Rock Garden. A few Antirrhinums are

valued as rock garden plants. They are A. Asarina, which has cream-white flowers; A. glutinosum, yellowish-white; A. molle, white with a yellow blotch; and A. sempervirens, pink or white. All are low, trailing plants and bloom in summer. They must be set in well-drained, sandy, loamy soil in a dry, sunny place. Under such conditions all have proved hardy and perennial at New York City.

ANTS. See Pests and Diseases.

AOTUS GRACILLIMA (Ao'tus). An Australian shrub, 3 ft. high, with long, slender branches, small evergreen leaves and attractive pea-shaped, yellow and crimson flowers in April–May. It is excellent for a greenhouse having a minimum winter temperature of 45 degrees and should succeed well out of doors in such climates as that of California. Aotus belongs to the Pea family, Leguminosae. The name is derived from *a*, without, and *ous*, an ear, and refers to the calyx of the flower.

The fragrant-flowered Cape Pondweed, Aponogeton distachyus, is a charming aquatic plant.

Potting and Pruning. Repotting should be in a mixture of equal parts of loam and peat moss with sand added, just after blooming. During summer the plants must be freely exposed to sunlight to ripen the shoots and so induce flower production the next year. Pruning consists of shortening the shoots by about two thirds after flowering. After pruning, the plants should be syringed frequently; and when new growth commences they should be repotted in larger pots.

When to Take Cuttings. Cuttings of short side shoots are removed with a heel, or piece of the old branch, in July or August, and are inserted

in a mixture of peat moss and sand in a cool greenhouse. A bell jar is placed over them and shaded until roots form. The young plants are then potted separately in 3-in. pots and, when established, the tips of the shoots are removed to produce bushy plants.

APHELANDRA (Aphelan'dra). Dwarf evergreen tropical shrubs which are valued for their ornamental leaves and showy flowers in autumn and winter. They grow wild principally in South America and belong to the family Acanthaceae. Aphelandra, from *apheles*, simple, and *aner*, male, alludes to the one-celled anther of the flower. These plants vary in height from 9-24 in. The leaves of some kinds have colored veins and the large terminal spikes of scarlet, yellow, or pink flowers emerge from often brilliantly colored bracts.

Summer and Winter Treatment. Fresh plants are usually raised annually from seeds or cuttings; they are potted first in 3-in. and later in 5-in. pots, using a compost of equal parts loam and peat with sand added freely. The pots must be well-drained. During summer the atmosphere of the greenhouse must be kept moist; a temperature of 65-70 degrees is suitable. The tips of the shoots must not be pinched off as the aim is to produce one stem with one large spike of bloom. The soil should be watered only when it is moderately dry; water must be applied carefully, as sodden or very dry soil will make the leaves fall. After flowering is over, less water is required.

Propagation. In spring, short side shoots are removed with a heel, or piece of the old branch, inserted in sand in a propagating case in the greenhouse. When rooted, they are placed on the open benches for a few days and are then potted as previously advised. Seeds may also be sown in pots of sandy peat and loam in spring in a temperature of about 70 degrees.

Popular kinds are Aphelandra aurantiaca, orange-scarlet flowers; A. aurantiaca var. Roezlii, rich scarlet; A. tetragona (cristata), scarlet; A. nitens, orange-scarlet, with handsome, glossy foliage; A. Sinclairiana with pink flowers and orange-coral bracts; and A. squarrosa, yellow, leaves green, veined white. Garden varieties of A. squarrosa are Leopoldii and Louisae.

APHID. See Pests and Diseases.

APHLEXIS. See Helichrysum.

APHYLLANTHES MONSPELIENSIS (Aphyllan'thes). A dainty little plant from the south of France belonging to the Lily family, Liliaceae. It has rushlike leaves and bears small clear blue flowers on 15-in. stems in late spring or summer. It likes sandy, peaty soil in a warm, sunny, well-drained situation. It has proved hardy in New Jersey. It is a very deep-rooted plant. The name is from *aphyllos,* leafless, and *anthos,* a flower, and refers to the leafless flower stems.

APICRA (Apic'ra). South African succulent plants that belong to the Lily family, Liliaceae. They resemble small Aloes and Haworthias, to which plants they are closely related. Apicra is derived from *a,* not, and *pikros,* bitter, and refers to the fact that, unlike Aloes, the plants are not bitter.

In mild, dry climates such as that of California and Arizona, Apicras are suitable for planting in outdoor rock gardens, but in most sections they are only useful for cultivation in pots in greenhouses or in window gardens and sunrooms.

Culture and Kinds. The plants require the soil and general culture recommended for Aloe and Haworthia, which see. Propagation is by seeds and offsets. The kinds most commonly grown include: A. aspera, 4-6 in., flowers pinkish; A. deltoidea, 6 in., flowers yellow-green; and A. pentagona, 12 in., flowers greenish.

APICULATE. Terminated by a short, but not stiff, point, as for instance the leaves of Saxifraga apiculata.

APIOS AMERICANA—*Potato Bean, Wild Bean* (A'pios). A hardy North American climbing plant, 5-7 ft. high, which bears purplish-brown, fragrant, pea-shaped flowers in summer. It belongs to the Pea family, Leguminosae. The word Apios, from *apion,* pear, refers to the shape of the tuberous roots. This plant was an important food plant of the Indians. It is reasonably attractive and has some value as a wild garden subject. Easily propagated by tubers and seeds, it thrives in sandy soil.

APIUM. The botanical name of a genus of plants which includes the Celery and Celeriac, which see.

APLECTRUM—*Puttyroot* (Aplect'rum). There is only one member, Aplectrum hyemalis, a North American terrestrial Orchid (family Orchidaceae). It is a difficult plant to cultivate but is most likely to succeed in a cool, rather moist, shady spot in loamy soil containing plenty of leaf mold or peat. It produces a single large, ribbed leaf, followed by a spike of yellowish-brown flowers on a stem 1 ft. tall in May–June. It is curious rather than beautiful and when once established should be left well alone. Aplectrum is derived from *a,* without, and *plectron,* a spur, and refers to the structure of the flower.

APOCYNUM—*Dogbane* (Apo'cynum). North American and European herbaceous perennials that belong to the family Apocynaceae. They are grown for medicine and for ornament. The name is derived from *apo,* away, and *kyon,* dog, and was given by Dioscorides because the roots of A. venetum were believed to be poisonous to dogs. The American species have caused the deaths of horses and cattle.

In Gardens. Two or three native species are occasionally grown in gardens. They are of easy culture in open situations and they prefer sandy soils; they stand dry conditions well and are suitable for borders and wild gardens. Propagation is easily carried out by division in spring or fall, and by sowing seeds in a cold frame or in a prepared bed outdoors in spring. Kinds likely to be grown are: A. androsaemifolium, height 4 ft., flowers pinkish; A. cannabinum, height to 8 ft., flowers greenish white; A. pumilum, height 2 ft., flowers rose pink.

APONOGETON—*Cape Pondweed, Water Hawthorn* (Aponoge'ton). Attractive hardy and tender aquatic plants, natives of Africa, Asia, and Australia, belonging to the family Aponogetonaceae. The name is derived from *aponi,* water, and *geiton,* neighbor, with reference to the habitat of the plants.

The hardiest and most popular kind is Aponogeton distachyus, the Cape Pondweed, a quick-spreading plant with submerged tuberous roots and floating leaves, producing in summer two-forked inflorescences, rising clear of the water, of fragrant white flowers. It thrives in water up to 2 ft. deep, the roots being set in pots or baskets of soil and dropped in in April. It spreads very quickly and is not recommended for small pools containing choice Water Lilies. It is hardy in the North if the roots are not permitted to freeze. Distinct varieties of it are aldenhamensis, larger flowers shaded with purple; Lagrangei, violet-tinted flower bracts and leaves; and roseus, pinkish flowers.

The Lattice-Leaf Plant. The only other species of importance is A. fenestralis, the tender Lace-leaf or Lattice-Leaf from Madagascar, previously called Ouvirandra fenestralis. It is a remarkable plant, growing naturally in the mud near the margins of running streams. From its creeping rhizomes it sends up long-stemmed leaves to just below the surface; these leaves are lacelike in appearance because they consist merely of midribs and delicate veins enveloped in cells which perform the normal functions of the leaf. The leaves are pale-yellow at first, becoming olive-green and finally black.

It may be grown in tubs 2 ft. deep in a greenhouse, minimum winter temperature 50 degrees; set the roots in 6 in. of loamy soil placed in the bottom of the tub or in pots of soil; then fill the tub with lukewarm water. This needs changing in part once a fortnight or so. A few water snails will keep algae in check.

APOROCACTUS—*Rattail Cactus* (Aporocac'-tus). A small genus of the family Cactaceae. The chief member is Aporocactus flagelliformis, a native of Mexico and called the Rattail Cactus because of its curiously drooping and twisted, slender stems. These are clustered with small red-brown spines and bear crimson flowers which last for 3 or 4 days. It is a favorite window plant. A. Conzattii, also native of Mexico, has brown spines, red flowers and aerial roots. Aporocactus are easily increased by cuttings and are sometimes grafted on other Cacti. For cultivation, see Cacti.

APOSTLE PLANT. See Neomarica.

APPLE: POPULAR COOL-CLIMATE FRUIT
A Complete Guide to the Cultivation of This American Favorite

The Apple is the most important Temperate Zone fruit, being grown extensively wherever climatic conditions are suitable. It is one of the oldest of our cultivated fruits; several varieties were known hundreds of years before the time of Christ. The wild ancestors of the Apple are considered to have originated in the mountainous regions lying between the Black and Caspian seas, where there are large forests of Apple trees exhibiting great variation in fruit characteristics. The earliest settlers brought seeds to America, and by them, and the Indians, seedling Apple orchards were planted generally in the northern half of the United States from the Atlantic coast westward to the Mississippi Valley. From these seedling trees hundreds of varieties suited to many regions of the country have been selected, and some of them are now widely grown.

Temperature is the most important factor limiting the cultivation of Apples. The regions best suited to growing them are in Ontario, Canada, adjoining Lakes Ontario and Erie, and southward to Virginia and westward to the Mississippi Valley. British Columbia, Washington, Oregon and California are also important Apple-growing regions. In the Great Plains region and other cold areas a few very hardy varieties may be grown, but these are inferior to the varieties of the better regions. Southward a few varieties may be grown, but, as the Gulf Coast and southern California are approached, the lack of sufficient winter cold to chill the fruit buds is a limiting factor. Moisture is a limiting factor in the interior of the country, but irrigation, when available, makes Apple growing possible in dry regions.

Apples are subject to several diseases and insect pests which make it difficult to produce usable fruit unless careful spraying is practiced. Spraying, to be successful, must be thorough and timely. Small power sprayers suitable for garden use are available. Instructions as to materials and times of application must be followed carefully if diseases and insect pests are to be controlled. Unless these troubles are kept in check, Apple growing will be a failure. The small fruits are better suited to the home fruitgrower who is not prepared to do a thorough and intelligent job of spraying.

Apple trees are beautiful when in bloom; if given adequate care, they bear fruit bountifully.

The Site. The home fruitgrower has little choice in the matter of a site, but must use what is available. A knowledge of the characteristics of a suitable site should at least prevent the planting of Apple trees where there is little chance that they will succeed. Good air circulation favors rapid drying of the foliage after a rain, thus tending to reduce the opportunity for infection by diseases that depend on moisture on the leaves. Low spots, or frost pockets, where the cold air settles on still nights, are colder in winter and more subject to late spring frosts than higher elevations, and, thus, should be avoided as planting sites. In frost pockets many crops will be lost and the trees may be winter-injured. The best site is on sloping land raised above the general elevation of the area to provide good air drainage (see Drainage). The slope should be gentle because erosion may be serious on steep slopes. In small gardens the trees should be beyond the shade and roots of large shade trees.

The Soil. A well-drained soil where water does not stand after a rain is essential. Good drainage with the water table 6 feet below the surface of the soil encourages deep root penetration and gives the trees a large volume of soil to draw on for their moisture and nutrients. Trees in poorly drained soils make poor growth, suffer quickly from drought and are short-lived. Poor internal drainage is often indicated by a gray, rusty, mottled subsoil. The texture of the soil is not important if not extreme. In general, medium to heavy clay loams are suitable, but lighter and heavier textured soils may grow good Apple trees if well-drained and provided with an abundance of organic matter. Coarse sands and gravels or very compact clays should be avoided. The soil on a steep slope may be so badly eroded that only the subsoil is left; it is not suitable for Apple trees.

Soil Preparation. If a considerable number of trees are to be planted, as in an orchard, the whole area may be plowed and harrowed as a

Dwarf Apple trees are easy to spray, prune, and harvest crops from. They are especially well suited for home gardens.

vegetable garden is prepared. When ready to plant, the soil should be mellow and in good tilth. When only a few trees are to be planted, a row 4 ft. wide and as long as needed may be made ready. In the small garden, where the trees are to be set in sod, an area 4 or 5 ft. across may be mulched a year in advance with enough straw or hay to kill the sod. In the spring, before planting, the mulch is removed to permit the soil to dry out before the hole is dug. Soils that have long been cultivated without the regular addition of organic matter by plowing under stable manure or a green manure crop should be supplied with organic matter before the trees are set. Stable manure, if available, is excellent for improving the soil. This may be worked at the rate of 10-20 tons to the acre or 3-6 bushels to each 100 sq. ft.

If manure is not available, it will be necessary to grow a green manure crop for soil improvement and plow it under. For this purpose a grass sod that has grown 2 or 3 years and has been heavily fertilized to stimulate a vigorous growth is excellent. Clover or Alfalfa sods are also good soil improvement crops. Sweet Clover is very good, too.

If the drainage is not so good as it should be, tile drains may be installed, or the land may be ridged. The ridges should be at least 1 ft. in height with the base nearly as broad as the space to be occupied by the trees. It should slope so that the surface water runs off and is not dammed up by the ridge.

Intercrops. While the trees are growing up, the unused space between them may be used for other crops, vegetables, flowers, Strawberries and even Blackberries and Dewberries, if they are not allowed to compete with the trees. At all times the intercrops should be kept far enough from the Apples to prevent competition for soil moisture and nutrients. The space between the trees may also be used for growing mulching material for the trees.

Time of Planting. In milder regions Apple trees may be set in the autumn from the time the leaves begin to fall until the ground freezes. In the colder areas of the northern tier of states and in Canada, spring planting is safer, although in mild winter fall planting may be successful. Fall planting has the advantage that the trees are fresh out of the ground and have not spent the winter in a nursery cellar, and they are ready to grow as soon as the weather warms up in the spring. Trees to be planted in the spring may arrive late, and if the soil is heavy and dries out slowly, may be planted too late. Late spring planting followed by hot dry weather may result in poor growth, or the death of the tree. Spring planting should always be done as early as the ground can be prepared.

Purchasing Trees. Apple trees should be purchased from reliable nurseries that specialize in the production of fruit trees. The trees should be ordered by variety, size and age; these should not be left to the nurseryman's judgment. If the planter does not have this information, he should get it before ordering the trees. The order should be placed early during the fall or winter while the good varieties and sizes are still in stock. Late spring ordering is usually disappointing. Varieties and sizes wanted are then often out of stock; the trees may be dried out or already have started into growth; and, in the rush of shipping many trees in a short time, the latecomer's order is sure to be delayed. The larger grades of the 1- and 2-year-old trees are

A young Apple tree should have a well-developed root system. Before planting, cut off any broken or badly damaged roots.

bark should be smooth and shiny, not shriveled, and when cut into should be green. The trees, if not to be planted immediately, should be "heeled in." A trench wide enough to accommodate the roots and long enough to hold all the trees should be dug. The trees should be planted temporarily in this trench with the tops slanted to the south to prevent sunscald. The soil should be firmed around the roots.

Planting. The tree is prepared for planting by cutting off the ragged ends of damaged roots and broken roots. The hole for the tree is dug large enough to hold the roots without crowding them. When digging the hole, keep the topsoil, the darker top 6 in., in one pile and the subsoil in another. The topsoil may be mixed with half a bushel of wet peat moss or an equivalent amount of good compost, which is then shoveled into the hole around the roots. As the soil is filled into the hole, the tree is jiggled up and down to work the soil around the roots. It should be worked in under the roots with the

Left. Planting a young Apple tree. The stake is placed in position first. The roots should be spread full length and fine soil packed among them.

Center. To settle the soil among the roots, gently ease the tree up and down several times, then tread firm. As filling and firming proceed, break down the sides of the hole, and finish off with the soil slightly mounded to allow for settling.

Below. When planting young Apple trees, care should be taken not to bury the point of union between the rootstock and the variety grafted on it.

best. Larger sizes and the so-called bearing-age trees should be left for the nurseryman's brush pile.

Care of Trees on Arrival from Nursery. The bundle of trees on arrival from the nursery should be opened immediately and the contents examined and checked against the order to make sure that all of the items ordered have been received. If the trees are unduly dry the nursery should be notified immediately. The hands and at intervals should be packed down with the feet. When the job is finished the soil should be firmly packed around the roots, without any air spaces left. No fertilizer or manure should be used at planting time. During planting, the roots should not be allowed to dry out. The tree should stand 2 or 3 in. deeper than it did in the nursery. Care should be taken that the trunk is perpendicular and that several trees in a row are lined up carefully.

Trees on Dwarfing Rootstocks. Apple trees are propagated on several different rootstocks. Most are budded on seedling roots, or on the so-called French Crab, and these make the large-sized trees of the commercial orchards. For the very practical reasons of difficulties in spraying, harvesting, pruning and otherwise caring for these tall trees, the home fruitgrower would like a much smaller tree.

Small Apple trees are produced by budding the varieties on dwarfing rootstocks. These are known as Malling rootstocks because at the East Malling Research Station in England they were selected from older rootstocks in the nursery trade and made available under Malling numbers as clones (varieties reproduced vegetatively rather than from seeds) of known performance. Of the many numbers selected, two, Malling IX and Malling VII, are of interest to the Apple grower. Trees on Malling IX grow 5-6 ft. high, and start fruiting a year or two after planting. The apples are often larger, better colored and of better flavor than those of the same variety on seedling roots. The principal drawback to this rootstock is its brittle root system. Trees with a heavy crop blow over easily. To prevent this, a stout post treated with a preservative is set on the opposite side of the tree from the prevailing winds and the tree is tied to it. When the post becomes rotten and in danger of breaking off, it should be replaced.

There is also danger of roots developing from above the bud union, if it is in contact with moist soil, and establishing the tree on its own roots. It will then soon become a full-sized standard tree. To prevent this, the tree should be set with the union at least 4 in. above the surface of the ground. Once a year the tree should be examined to make sure that the union has not become covered with soil. Any roots that may de-

velop above the union should be removed. The restricted nature of the Malling IX root necessitates a good, fertile, well-drained soil. Trees on this root require garden care. They should be planted 12-15 ft. apart.

Apple trees on the Malling VII rootstock grow 8-10 ft. high or about as large as peach trees and come into bearing earlier than on the seedling rootstocks, but not as early as on Malling IX. The trees on Malling VII are better anchored and need no support. They should be planted 15-20 ft. apart. When trees on dwarfing rootstocks are wanted, the variety and rootstock should be specified, as, for example: Cortland on Malling IX.

Summer Care. During the first year, weed growth should be kept down around the young tree by cultivation or mulching. If a serious drought threatens, the trees should be watered, soaking the ground to a depth of 8 or 10 in. or more. In dry regions several waterings may be necessary. In succeeding years the grower may choose any one of several methods of soil management. Clean cultivation has often been practiced in the past, but it depletes the soil of organic matter and there is danger of erosion on slopes. Now many orchards are grown in grass sod which is mowed and left in the orchard. If desired, the grass cuttings may be piled around the trees as a mulching material.

Mulching is an excellent method of managing the soil. The mulch may be grown between the young trees by fertilizing the sod, or later, when the trees occupy most of the space, it must be hauled in from outside of the orchard, as the shade and root competition of the trees limit the growth of the sod. Various materials may be used. If grown on the farm or in the orchard, a heavily fertilized orchard grass sod is as good as anything. Sometimes rain-spoiled hay may be purchased cheaply, or had for the hauling from a nearby dairy farm. Wheat and other straws are good. Marsh hay is sometimes available. Bearing trees require about a bale of straw per year to maintain the mulch. Other materials that may be used are sawdust and peat moss, the latter being rather expensive for this purpose, but all right for small garden plantings. If a legume, or heavily fertilized grass hay, is used for several years, so much nitrogen may accumulate in the soil that fruit color is poor and the trees grow so vigorously that they become susceptible to winter injury. Under these conditions less mulch should be used and the grass should be allowed to grow a little.

Fertilizers. Nitrogen is the material most apt to be profitable in the Apple orchard. Phosphorus and potash are usually available in sufficient quantity for Apples in the average soil and certainly they will not be the limiting factor in a mulched orchard. The mulched orchard is not likely to need much supplementary nitrogen after the first two or three years. The rotting mulch supplies nutrients in abundance.

Nitrogen for the sod orchard may be had from ammonium nitrate, ammonium sulphate or nitrate of soda. Other carriers may be used to supply equivalent amounts of nitrogen as needed.

Ammonium nitrate at the rate of one fourth lb. for each year of tree age is suggested with mature trees receiving 5 lb. or more depending on tree vigor. This is applied early in the spring as soon as the buds begin to swell. Some judgment and experience will be needed to adjust the amount of nitrogen needed. Bearing trees in good vigor should be making 8 to 10 in. of terminal growth each year and have large, dark leaves. More or less growth will necessitate a downward or upward revision of the amount of nitrogen to be applied. Excessive vigor is undesirable, as the trees may experience winter injury from an unusually cold winter or a severe early freeze before the wood has matured for winter.

Pruning. One of the principal objectives of pruning is to build a tree that is structurally sound; to produce heavy crops of fruit for many years without the breaking of large limbs. As the trees become older, pruning removes the weaker wood, to prevent the center of the tree from becoming overcrowded and to reinvigorate the remaining wood to a certain extent. For this purpose, however, pruning is not a substitute for adequate nutrition and other conditions favoring vigorous growth.

Pruning tends to dwarf the tree and it also delays fruiting. For this reason only as much pruning as is needed to develop a structurally sound tree is advisable. Unpruned trees become so dense that spraying and harvesting are difficult

and many small, poorly colored Apples are produced.

Trees are pruned during the dormant season; in regions where severe winters may be expected, the less hardy varieties should be pruned

A young Apple tree, showing an ample number and distribution of branches from which scaffold (main framework) limbs are selected.

A young Apple tree after pruning, showing distribution of branches that are left to form scaffold limbs.

An Apple tree with a well-developed system of scaffold branches as a result of good pruning in early life.

Heavily cropped Apple trees should have their fruit thinned by reducing each cluster to 1 or 2 fruits, according to the size of clusters.

Apple blossoms, beautiful in spring, give promise of delicious fruit later.

ier pruning to remove the weak wood in the interior of the tree and to facilitate thorough spray coverage. A little pruning each year is much better than severe cutting at irregular intervals.

after the severe cold of winter is past. Summer pruning, except to rub out water sprouts, is not advisable.

At planting time, or before the tree begins its first season's growth, it is headed at about $3\frac{1}{2}$ ft., if it is an unbranched whip. If the tree is a 2-year old and well-branched, the strongest upward pointing branch is left as a leader. Two side limbs pointing in different directions and a foot apart should be left, the others being removed. Those branches which are left are the framework of the future tree, and their angle with the trunk should be as wide as possible. Narrow-angled limbs break easily at the crotch when heavily loaded with fruit.

For the next few years pruning should be very light and corrective only, designed to prevent the formation of weak crotches, which develop when two branches of equal size grow from the same point. When small, one is removed entirely, but as the tree becomes older one arm of the fork is cut back a little each year until it is either removed entirely, or becomes a lateral of the main branch. Until the tree comes into bearing this corrective pruning and a light thinning are all that is necessary. The novice should err on the side of too little, rather than too much pruning.

The bearing Apple tree needs somewhat heav-

Apple Varieties. Most Apple varieties are self-unfruitful and their flowers must be pollinated with pollen from another compatible variety if good crops of fruit are to be produced. Most varieties will pollinate each other, but a few important sorts, Baldwin, Rhode Island Greening, Gravenstein, Stayman Winesap, and others of lesser importance produce poor pollen and should not be used as pollinators for other sorts. It is important that varieties be planted together that have overlapping blooming periods.

There are many varieties of Apples, but relatively few are important, and the home gardener, unless he be a collector, will not need more than half a dozen to cover the season from early to late. If he lives in an Apple-growing region, he might better buy his fruit of the standard varieties of the region and grow some of the less easily obtainable, but choicer varieties. Lists of recommended varieties for the different regions may be had from State Agricultural Experiment Stations. Red bud sports of many sorts are now available and these have a solid red color as compared with the blushed or striped red of the parent variety. The quality of the fruit is the same, however.

Recommended varieties include:

Lodi, very early, yellow, larger and a few days later than Yellow Transparent, which it is replacing. Tree bears early and annually. Excellent for cooking.

Melba, very early, crimson striped, tender. Tree bears early and annually.

Early McIntosh, bright red McIntosh type, ripening in August in New York, bears biennially unless chemically thinned at blossoming time. Must be thinned to attain good size.

Gravenstein, striped red, medium-sized, good quality. Tree bears early and annually. Dessert and cooking.

Milton, bright pinkish-red, large, with tender flesh and high quality. Ripens a month before McIntosh. Tree bears early and annually.

Wealthy, bright red, medium-size, good. Tree bears early and biennially, is very hardy.

Twenty Ounce, red striped, very large, good cooking Apple. Tree bears early and annually.

McIntosh, very attractive red, large, excellent quality. Tree bears early, heavily and annually. Susceptible to scab and requires thorough spraying.

Cortland, bright red, large, McIntosh type and quality. Tree bears early and annually.

Macoun, a very high quality dark red McIntosh type requiring heavy thinning.

Jonathan, dark red, medium-size, very good quality. Tree bears early and annually. Grown south of New York and New England.

Monroe, red, medium-size, good quality. Tree bears annually, a promising new variety.

Delicious, striped red, or solid with the red spots, medium to large depending on region where grown, high quality. Tree may be a light bearer in some locations.

Sweet Delicious, an attractive dark, red, large, sweet Apple of good keeping quality. Tree an annual bearer.

Rhode Island Greening, greenish-yellow, large, standard cooking Apple. Tree bears early and biennially.

Rome Beauty, red, large, poor quality, but good for baking. Tree bears heavy crops early and annually.

Northern Spy, striped red, large, excellent quality. Tree bears late and biennially.

Golden Delicious, yellow, medium-size, of highest quality. Tree bears early and biennially.

Stayman Winesap, dull red, large, very good quality. Tree bears early and annually. Grown south of New York and New England.

Winesap, dark red, medium-size, good quality. Tree medium late in bearing and partially biennial. Grown south of New York and New England and on the West Coast.

York Imperial, light red, large, fair quality.

Because pruning has been neglected for several years this Apple tree has too many branches; as a result, the fruit is inferior in size and quality.

By proper pruning, the number of branches of this tree has been restricted. Leaves and fruit receive adequate light and air. Crops of highest quality are produced.

Tree comes into bearing medium-late and bears biennially.

Yellow Newtown, yellow, medium-size, high quality and a very good keeper. Tree bears late and biennially.

Crab Apples are grown principally for jelly and pickling. They are handsome ornamentals in flower and fruit. Standard varieties are Dolgo, Hyslop and Young America, the first being a handsome ornamental with its heavy load of deep red fruits.

Spraying. Apples must be sprayed or the crop will not be worth harvesting; often the tree as well as the fruit will be seriously injured by diseases or insects if not sprayed. Trees on Malling IX and VII rootstocks are much smaller than trees on seedling roots and are correspondingly easier to spray with home fruit-garden equipment. A small power sprayer that can be rolled about smooth ground by hand is suitable for the home orchard. Knapsack sprayers are of doubtful value for Apples as their pressure is too low for thorough coverage.

Spray programs for the different regions vary greatly, as climatic conditions in one area favor diseases that are unimportant elsewhere. Temperature and humidity influence the effects of different sprays on the tree, and some varieties are more susceptible to spray injury than others. Spray materials are changing rapidly now, as many new chemicals are being developed for insect and disease control. Some are very effective for a short time, and then tolerant races of insects appear and other materials must be substituted.

For these reasons the Apple grower should obtain the recommendations of his own State Agricultural Experiment Station. The County Farm Bureaus can usually supply these recommendations, adapted to local conditions.

Protection from Rodents. Mice can be very destructive to trees grown in sod or under a mulch. A space 3 ft. in diameter around the trunk should be kept free from anything that will harbor mice. A mound of gravel several inches high around the trunk provides good protection. Poison baits are much used by orchardists.

Rabbit injury to the trunk is prevented by encircling it with wire screen to a height of 15 to 20 in.

Physiological Troubles of Apples. Water core occurs in most Apple-growing regions but is most severe where temperatures and light intensities are high. The flesh has a water-soaked, glassy appearance near the core and is firmer. The cause of the trouble is not known. Fruits should be harvested before they are overripe and excessive thinning should not be practiced.

Bitter Pit or Stippen, of which characteristic symptoms are sunken, round, or angular spots on the surface of the Apple, with the flesh underneath brown, spongy, and bitter in taste, usually develops after picking, but was caused before harvest. Overgrown fruits such as occur on young trees, trees that are thinned excessively, or trees that are overpruned or fertilized heavily with nitrogen fertilizers, are most susceptible to Bitter Pit. Avoiding these conditions is about all that can be done to control this disorder.

Harvesting the Crop. Apples harvested at the right stage of maturity are superior in flavor and keeping quality to those that are picked before or after the optimum maturity. No hard and fast rule may be laid down for determining when all varieties are ripe. Probably the most reliable indicator of maturity is the change in color of the skin from leaf green in color to light greenish yellow. If the fruit releases readily when it is taken in the hand and turned up, it is ready to pick. Still, considerable judgment and experience are essential for determining the correct harvest date for all varieties.

Summer and early fall varieties ripen over a period of several weeks, and several pickings are necessary to get the fruit at its best condition. Early Apples should be picked promptly when still hard, as they go soft and may "water-core" very quickly if left too long on the tree. The fruits should be picked by hand, not shaken off or allowed to drop on the ground. Early varieties for home use may be allowed to drop on a thick straw mulch if they are to be used immediately. Every care should be taken to handle the fruit gently to prevent bruising.

Storing the Fruit. The small grower cannot afford mechanical refrigeration for his storage, but in the colder northern states common storage is useful. The storage is cooled by opening the ventilators on cool nights and closing them on warm days. The building should be well insulated and opened as little as possible when it is warm outside. The object should be to keep the storage temperature as near 32 degrees as possible. In a warm fall the storage temperature may be too high for too long, and the storage life of the apples will be shortened substantially.

APPLE, BALSAM. See Momordica Balsamina.

APPLE BELL. See Granadilla.

APPLE, CUSTARD. See Annona reticulata.

APPLE, KEI. See Dovyalis.

APPLE, MAY. See Podophyllum.

APPLE OF PERU. See Nicandra.

APPLE, ROSE. See Eugenia Jambos.

APPLE, THORN. See Datura.

APPROACH GRAFTING. The method of propagation sometimes called approach grafting or grafting by approach is also known as inarching. It is a procedure whereby a branch of one rooted plant is made to unite with the branch of another rooted plant. See Inarching.

APRICOT
A Handsome Tree That Bears Delicious Fruit

The Apricot is a native of western China, rather than Armenia, as its scientific name, Prunus armeniaca, might suggest. Forests of wild trees occur in Turkestan, and very hardy strains known as Russian Apricots have come from Siberia. Apricots reached England in the 13th century; they were grown in Virginia by 1720. In the United States, Apricots have become an important crop in California, where the fruit is dried, canned and sold on the fresh-fruit market. Some orchards are found in Utah, Idaho, Washington, and Colorado. Elsewhere the Apricot is only a dooryard tree in areas where late spring frosts are not a hazard.

The Apricot is a delicious and distinctive fruit that deserves more attention from eastern home fruit growers. It is the first tree fruit to bloom, coming before the Peaches, and the large, round-headed tree is very handsome. The trees are hardier than Peach trees, and in the case of the Russian varieties much hardier. The flower buds are hardier than those of Peaches, but they start to swell very easily during mild spells in the winter and are then killed by subsequent cold. The early-blooming habit with resulting frost injury and the susceptibility of the fruit to Curculio insect injury and Brown Rot disease have limited the culture in the East, but present-day spray programs and superior varieties make it worthy of consideration for the home fruit garden in favored areas where severe spring frosts do not occur after the trees are in bloom.

Site, Soil and Rootstocks. Northern and western exposures on elevated sites near large bodies of water are most suitable, as they tend to retard blossoming. In western New York dooryard trees of the Russian varieties frequently crop well. Apricots are not particular as to soils, but these should be well-drained and not extreme in texture. Sandy loams, such as are good for Peaches, are suitable for Apricots. The Apricot

Moorpark Apricot is a variety of highest quality well adapted for growing in California.

does well on both Peach and Apricot roots and is sometimes propagated on Myrobalan and Marianna Plum roots. In sandy soils, if nematode-infested, the Apricot root, or a special nematode-resistant Peach root, is better. The western Sand Cherry, Prunus Besseyi, is used as a dwarfing stock.

Soil Preparation, Planting, and Management. The Apricot has no special soil management problems. It may be grown like the Peaches. For preparation of the soil, planting, and mulching see Apple. What little experimental evidence is available indicates that phosphorus and potash are not likely to be limiting elements in tree growth and fruit production. The trees apparently get along on a somewhat lower nitrogen level than Peaches, and care should be taken not to make too heavy applications of nitrogenous materials. Trees in good vigor should make from 15 to 30 in. of growth each year.

Pruning. The Apricot tree becomes large with heavy branches and is similar to the Peach in fruiting habit. More spurs (short, stubby shoots that produce flowers) are produced with the Apricot than with the Peach, and most of the crop is borne on these spurs, although some is borne on one-year old wood. Regular pruning is necessary to renew these spurs, as they are usually not profitable after three years.

The modified leader tree is suitable, but the vase form is much used. The young tree, as received from the nursery, is much branched. As the laterals are not well spaced, they should be cut back to one or two buds. At the end of the first growing season three scaffold (main lateral) branches 6-8 in. apart and pointing in different directions are selected and headed (pruned) back to different lengths, the lateral that is to be the leader being left longer than the others.

At the end of the second growing season many laterals will have been produced. These are removed up to the point where the secondary scaffold branches are to be left. About five of these are left 4 or 5 ft. from the ground. These should be well spaced so they will not crowd later. The leader should always be longer than any of the scaffolds arising from it, these being cut back as necessary, to assure the dominance of the leader. Until the trees reach bearing age, pruning is mostly for maintaining a structurally strong tree. Excess branches and those interfering with the scaffolds are removed.

The bearing tree receives a moderate thinning and some heading (pruning) back to well-placed laterals. As the tree grows older and growth slows up, more severe pruning may be needed to stimulate vigorous growth and re-placement of the spurs, which are relatively short-lived.

Varieties. Royal and Blenheim, both very similar to each other and nearly identical, are the leading varieties in California, with Tilton third in importance. Royal is suitable for canning and drying, is large and of excellent quality. Tilton is not so good in quality and is less desirable for canning and drying, but its lateness makes it useful for extending the season. Moorpark is one of the highest quality varieties in California, but is not very good for drying or canning. Riland and Perfection are recent new varieties considered worthy of trial in California and in the state of Washington, where they originated. They require cross-pollination, whereas the other sorts are self-fruitful.

These varieties are usually unproductive in the East, owing to their early blooming and the susceptibility of the flowers to spring frosts. The Russian Apricots are somewhat more reliable, and many dooryard trees of this race produce good crops in the fruit-growing areas of western New York. The Russian Apricots were introduced into the United States as long ago as 1876 by Mennonites who settled in the Midwest. They were propagated from seeds.

Varieties which may be tried in the northern states where Peaches do well and where spring frosts are not too severe are Doty, a small-fruited Apricot of fairly good quality which originated near Geneva, New York, where it has fruited regularly. Another similar variety is Henderson, a dooryard seedling also in Geneva, where it has performed satisfactorily. Geneva, raised from seed of Italian origin, is a large, yellow Apricot of very good quality, worthy of trial for home use. The South Dakota Agricultural Experiment Station has introduced several varieties suitable for the Great Plains region.

APRICOT, JAPANESE. Prunus Mume, which see.

APTENIA (Apte'nia). A South African succulent plant that is popular in window gardens and greenhouses and that may be planted outdoors permanently in warm climates. It is separated only by technical botanical characteristics from Mesembryanthemum. It requires the same culture as Mesembryanthemum, which see. There is only one species, A. cordifolia, which is a spreading perennial; its variety named variegata has attractively variegated leaves.

AQUARIUM. A fresh-water aquarium which is well cared for is a constant source of interest and amusement. The secret of success is to have the plants and animals in well-balanced proportions. The tank must be stocked with suitable water plants to provide food for the fishes and to aerate the water. Submerged water plants, such as Anacharis, Myriophyllum and Utricularia, provide succulent morsels for the fish to nibble, and give off quantities of oxygen which help to aerate the water and keep it fresh.

A few water snails should be introduced as they assist in keeping the water clear by eating the green algae which quickly develop on the sides of the tank, and eventually foul the water.

How to Make an Aquarium. Various receptacles may be used for an aquarium. Well-constructed containers made of thick glass and metal framework can be purchased and are most satisfactory.

Preparing for the Plants. Place about 2 in. of soil in the bottom in which the roots of the plants are inserted. Cover the soil with 2 in. of sand which has been thoroughly washed in running water. The plants should also be washed before being inserted, to remove fungi, etc. Fill the tank with clear tap water, pouring it gently so as not to disturb the soil.

Before the fish are introduced the plants must be growing vigorously and there must be enough snails in the water to maintain an even balance of plant and animal life. Obtain the fish from a reliable source, as most failures are due to a fungus disease being on them when they are purchased. Do not overcrowd them.

Each large-sized fish should have about two gallons of water, but later, when the plants are growing more vigorously, it may be possible to introduce a few more. They should require little artificial feeding. A small quantity of dried fish meal, about as much as will go on a dime, and a few living or dried daphnia (water fleas), twice a week, are sufficient.

AQUATIC PLANTS are those which grow naturally in water; for instance, Water Lily (Nymphaea), Flowering Rush (Butomus), Cape Pondweed (Aponogeton), Arrowhead (Sagittaria), Bog Bean (Menyanthes). Garden pools or ponds made for the cultivation of Water Lilies and other aquatic plants have become very popular among amateurs. Full directions concerning them will be found under Water Garden.

AQUILEGIA or COLUMBINE
Favorite Hardy Flowers, Ideal for Cutting

(Aquile'gia). Hardy perennial plants which bear spurred, beautifully colored flowers from May to July. They grow wild in North America, Siberia and other North Temperate countries, and belong to the Buttercup family, Ranunculaceae. The word Aquilegia is derived from *aquila,* an eagle, an indication of the spurlike petals.

Planting and Suitable Soil. The Columbines or Aquilegias are delightful flowers of early summer; the plants, 6-24 in. high, last in bloom throughout many weeks and the flowers of the taller growers are ideal for cutting. They will thrive in ordinary garden soil but prefer rather moist, loamy ground which does not dry out quickly. Leaf mold, compost, or decayed manure should be added to light land. A sunny or partially shaded position suits them. Planting may be done in early fall or early spring.

When to Sow Seeds. In most gardens the Columbine will flourish for several years, but when the old plants begin to deteriorate it is wise to raise a fresh stock from seeds. It is a mistake to lift and separate the old plants. The seedlings will bloom in the year following that in which seeds are sown. As they grow rather slowly it is advisable to sow the seeds in a greenhouse in March, temperature 50-55 degrees. They may, however, be raised from seeds sown in a cold frame in April or directly outdoors in May.

How to Raise the Seedlings. The seeds are sown in pots or flats filled with a mixture of sifted loam and leaf mold with sand added. When the

Left. Blooms of a good strain of modern long-spurred Aquilegias.

Hybrid Aquilegias are graceful plants. They are useful in perennial borders and as cut flowers.

seedlings are large enough to handle, they are set 3 in. apart in flats filled with similar compost and are grown under cool conditions until they begin to crowd each other, when they should be planted 6 in. apart in rows in a nursery bed for permanent planting in early autumn or, preferably, where they are to remain, as they dislike being transplanted. If no greenhouse or frame is available, seeds may be sown in fine soil out of doors in May, the seedlings being set in their final positions 12 in. apart, in autumn or spring. A packet of mixed seeds of a good strain of long-spurred Aquilegias will provide beautiful flowers in a great variety of color.

Rock Garden Columbines. Several Columbines are charming rock garden plants. The favorite kinds are: Aquilegia alpina, from the European

The Siberian Columbine, Aquilegia glandulosa, is suitable for the rock garden. It grows 9-12 in. tall and bears blue flowers in April-May.

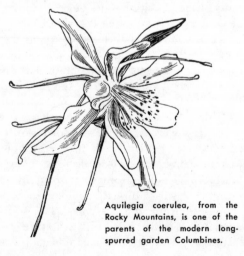

Aquilegia coerulea, from the Rocky Mountains, is one of the parents of the modern long-spurred garden Columbines.

mountains, blue and white flowers, of which Hensell Harebell is a fine form which comes true from seed; A. pyrenaica, from the Pyrenees, blue and white; A. glandulosa, from Siberia, blue; A. canadensis of North America, orange-red; A. canadensis flavescens, yellow; A. saximontana, blue and yellow, of Colorado and Utah; A. akitensis, from Japan, blue and yellow; A flabellata nana alba from Japan, white. They grow 9-12 in. high and thrive in deep soil of loam, leaf mold and sand in slight shade.

The blue long-spurred Columbine (A. coerulea), 2 ft., grows wild in the Rocky Mountains and has large blue and white, long-spurred flowers during May–June; this is one of the parents of the present-day race of garden Columbines; the other parent is the yellow Columbine (A. chrysantha), native of the Rocky Mountain region and Texas, with yellowish, long-spurred flowers. A. longissima, 2-3 ft., pale yellow, is another beautiful, long-spurred kind. The common European Columbine (A. vulgaris) is a woodland plant 1½-2 ft. high, having short-spurred purplish flowers during May–June.

ARABIS—*Rock Cress* (Ar'abis). Hardy perennial low-growing spring-flowering plants useful for the rock garden and wall garden or as an edging and groundwork for beds of spring flowers. They grow wild chiefly in the Mediterranean region, eastern Europe and Asia Minor and belong to the Mustard family, Cruciferae. The name Arabis is a Greek word meaning Arabian.

Planting and Suitable Soil. These plants thrive best in well-drained soil. On heavy land they are liable to die and become patchy in winter; such land, however, can be made suitable by digging and by adding sand, leaf mold, grit and decayed manure. The border kinds will, however, thrive in ordinary garden soil that is well cultivated. Planting is best done in early fall, though it may be carried out in early spring.

Summer Trimming. Plants of the vigorous kinds benefit if the shoots are cut well back as soon as the flowers have faded; this practice keeps the plants compact. If they are not pruned after flowering, the clumps become straggling and cover a great deal of ground.

When to Take Cuttings. Propagation is effected by inserting cuttings obtained as soon as possible after the flowers have faded. The cuttings, which should be about 3 in. long, are inserted in sand or sandy soil in a cold frame in partial shade. The cuttings will form roots in 4 or 5 weeks and may be transplanted to a nursery bed when they have a nice mass of roots 1-2 in. long. Space them 8 in. apart in rows 12 in. apart. In September the young plants are transplanted where they are to bloom.

Another method of propagation is to lift the plants in September, separate them into rooted pieces and replant. Seeds should be sown in a cold frame in early spring. When 1-2 in. high, the seedlings should be planted in a nursery bed in the same manner as recommended for rooted cuttings.

The Chief Kinds. Arabis albida, or Wall Cress, is a low-growing, free-blooming plant for the rock garden and wall garden; it becomes smothered in white flowers in early spring. The variety florepleno, which has spikes of large, double white flowers slightly later, is a favorite plant for spring flower beds, where it is used as an edging or as a groundwork for various bulbs. The plants should be set about 9 in. apart. The variety vari-

The double-flowered Arabis albida flore-pleno is a particularly good garden plant. Its flowers last considerably longer than the single kind.

egata has green leaves striped with pale yellow; Rosabella is a modern pink variety; A. Billardieri has gray-green leaves and pale rose-colored flowers. A. blepharophylla, a native of California, has fragrant rose-purple flowers; A. procurrens is a very fine, white-flowered, mat-forming species.

A. aubretioides has pale pink flowers in May (this plant is apt to die off unless planted in a rather dry, sunny position). A. alpina is similar to A. albida, but the white flowers are smaller. A. muralis, which grows 12 in. high, bears rose-purple flowers in April and May.

ARACHIS. See Peanut.

ARALIA. (Ara'lia). Hardy trees, shrubs and herbaceous plants, grown chiefly for the sake of their ornamental leaves. They are natives of Japan, China, Korea and North America, and belong to the family Araliaceae. The derivation of the word Aralia is not known.

Aralia cachemirica is a rare kind.

Shrubby Kinds. Three kinds that are leaf-losing, sparingly branched shrubs or trees are grown. These have large bipinnate green leaves 3 to 5 ft. long and 2 to 3 ft. wide, made up of numerous large leaflets, and bear small, whitish flowers in large panicles during late summer, followed by small black fruits.

Aralia spinosa, Hercules'-Club, or Devil's-Walking-Stick, is a spiny-stemmed tree of loose habit, up to 30 ft. high, native to the United States. It spreads rapidly by suckers and because of this may be troublesome unless it can be given plenty of space. A. elata, the Japanese Angelica

Tree, is a spiny-stemmed tree up to 40 ft. high, of which there are varieties variegata, white-margined leaves; aureo-variegata, yellow-variegated leaves; and pyramidalis, of more erect growth, with rather smaller leaves than the type. A. chinensis is similar to A. elata but is slightly less hardy.

All thrive in ordinary garden soil. They can be raised from seeds or by detaching sucker growths in March. The varieties can be grafted on sections of roots, or on young seedlings of their type, in a warm greenhouse in February or March. No regular pruning is required.

Herbaceous Kinds. Aralia hispida, Bristly Sarsaparilla, is an eastern American subshrub. A. californica is a stout, herbaceous perennial, a native of the Pacific Northwest, where it is known as Elk Clover. A. racemosa, American Spikenard, is a coarse herbaceous plant of eastern North America. A. nudicaulis, Wild Sarsaparilla, is a foot-tall eastern American herbaceous species. All the above have some value for planting in wild gardens in light shade in moist humus-rich soil. They may be increased by seeds or by division.

The greenhouse shrubs previously called Aralia Veitchii, A. reticulata, etc., are now referred to Dizygotheca, and the correct name of A. Sieboldii, a popular house plant, is Fatsia japonica, which see.

ARALIA, FALSE. See Dizygotheca.

ARAUCARIA—*Monkey Puzzle* (Araucar'ia). Evergreen trees, belonging to Pinaceae, a family of the cone-bearing group, Coniferae, natives of the southern part of South America, Australia, New Guinea, New Caledonia and Norfolk Island. The name Araucaria is from Araucanos, its Chilean name.

Planting, Taking Cuttings and Sowing Seeds. Planting should be done in spring. Araucaria is propagated by cuttings of erect shoots taken from trees which have been cut back; the cuttings are set in March–April in sand in a greenhouse or frame—minimum temperature 50 degrees.

Cuttings of the Monkey Puzzle tree will sometimes form roots if inserted in spring in sandy soil out of doors. Seeds may be sown in March in pots of sandy soil placed under glass in a temperature of 50 degrees.

The Monkey Puzzle Tree. Araucaria araucana (A. imbricata), the Chilean Pine or Monkey Puzzle tree, is a native of southern Chile and Tierra del Fuego; in the United States it is hardy in the far South and on the Pacific Coast; in Great Britain and in the milder parts of Europe it is fairly

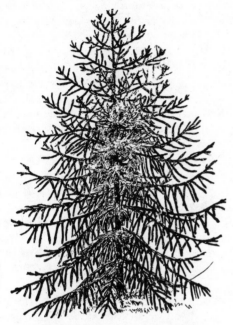

The Monkey Puzzle, Araucaria araucana, a conifer of bizarre appearance, is best planted as a specimen by itself.

commonly planted and forms a very distinctive feature in the landscape. It has dark green, leathery, sharp-pointed leaves which entirely surround the branches and persist for an indefinite period. Male and female cones are usually produced on different trees, occasionally on the same tree. When mature, the female cones are the size and shape of a large coconut.

This species gives the best results in rather damp climatic conditions, and in ground which is moist without being waterlogged. On dry, gravelly soils the lower branches die and trees soon lose their vigor.

A Favorite House Plant. Araucaria excelsa, the Norfolk Island Pine, is a good house and greenhouse plant; it is of neat, compact growth with regular tiers of flat, soft-leaved branches and in the house grows from 3-5 ft. high in pots. It thrives in a compost of loam two thirds, and leaf mold one third, with a free scattering of sand.

The plants should be repotted annually until they are placed in 7-in. or 8-in. pots; subsequently, no further repotting is necessary, though it is beneficial in spring to remove some of the surface soil and replace with fresh compost; a sprinkling of fertilizer every month from March to September will help to keep the plants healthy. This species is propagated by seeds and, preferably, by cuttings of terminal shoots that develop from specimens that have been cut back. It thrives best in a cool greenhouse or sunroom.

Another kind sometimes seen in climates that are frostfree, or nearly so, is the Bunya Bunya Pine of Queensland, A. Bidwillii. This has long, dark green, sharp-pointed leathery leaves and large cones.

Economic Uses. Several Araucarias produce very useful, easily worked lumber, more particularly A. araucana and A. angustifolia, from South America, and A. Cunninghamii (the Hoop Pine)

The Norfolk Island Pine, Araucaria excelsa, an attractive house plant.

and A. Bidwillii from New South Wales and Queensland. The wood is used for the same purposes as that of Pine. The seeds of A. araucana and A. Bidwillii are used for food in their native countries.

ARAUJIA SERICOFERA (Arau'jia). A South American climbing plant suitable for cultivation in a frostproof greenhouse, or out of doors in mild districts. In colder climates it is an excellent subject for planting outdoors for summer bloom, the plants being lifted and grown in a cool light greenhouse or sunroom over winter. It belongs to the family Asclepiadaceae. The plant is named for a Portuguese statesman, Antonio de Araujo de Acebedo.

This plant, which grows to a height of 20 ft., bears small white flowers in July. The most suitable soil for potted specimens is loam two thirds, and leaf mold one third, with the addition of sand. In February, the side shoots of the past summer's growth should be cut back to within three or four buds of the stem. Propagation is by cuttings of fresh shoots in March–April, in a propagating case in the greenhouse. Seeds germinate readily in a temperature of 60 degrees.

ARBOR. An arbor is a shaded retreat formed by interlacing the branches of vines or trees or, more often, by training vines over a supporting

A delightful arbor formed of espaliered Apple trees trained over an iron framework. In spring it is covered with lovely bloom, later with foliage and fruit.

structure of posts, rails and latticework. Usually, arbors are furnished with a seat or seats. They differ from summerhouses, gazebos, arches and similar garden embellishments in that their supporting structures are distinctly subordinate to the plants that cover them. Arbors should be neither architecturally elaborate nor prominent in the landscape.

The important point to consider when planning an arbor is that the supports should be durable and strong. Once they are covered with vines they are difficult to repair. Wood of a kind that does not decay readily when exposed to outdoor conditions is usually the most satisfactory material to use; Locust, Cypress and Redwood are excellent. The wood may be treated with a preservative such as Cuprinol, but creosote should not be used, because it is harmful to plants. It is advisable to use rustproof fastenings for joining together the wooden members of an arbor structure.

Non-rusting metals may also be used for constructing arbor supports, but usually the effect, because it is less rustic, is not as pleasing as when wood is used.

ARBORESCENS. A botanical term meaning of treelike growth, from *arbor,* a tree.

ARBORETUM. An area of land on which a collection of trees, and usually shrubs, is grown. On private estates such collections may be made to satisfy the tastes of the owner without any definite scientific intent, but in a botanical garden and similar institutions an arboretum is of very distinct scientific value, for in the space of a comparatively small area there are gathered together trees and shrubs from many countries where somewhat similar climatic conditions prevail. Thus it is possible to study the variations existing in living trees from distant countries, instead of relying altogether upon dried herbarium specimens; and to judge the possible usefulness of exotic kinds for cultivation in gardens and woodlands of the particular country where the arboretum has been established.

ARBORICULTURE. A term used especially in reference to the cultivation of trees and shrubs for aesthetic or scientific purposes, as distinct from that of trees planted under silvicultural conditions for the production of lumber, minor forest products, or for purposes of shelter. In its truest sense arboriculture includes all tree culture.

ARBORVITAE. See Thuja.

ARBORVITAE, FALSE. See Thujopsis.

ARBUTUS (Ar'butus). Hardy or tender evergreen trees or large shrubs, which belong to the Heath family, Ericaceae, and grow wild in North and South America, Asia Minor, southern Europe

The orange-red fruits of the Strawberry Tree, Arbutus Unedo.

and the Canary Islands. They bear attractive inflorescences of urn-shaped flowers during autumn or spring and some of them have showy fruits. Arbutus is an ancient Latin name, of which the origin is obscure.

Must be Planted When Small. Arbutus should be planted in a permanent place when very small for large plants are difficult to move with safety. Planting is best carried out in October or April. A little pruning may be necessary to keep the plants shapely; it should be done during summer.

Sowing Seeds and Layering. Propagation is best effected by means of seeds sown in pots of sandy peat in February; the pots are placed in a greenhouse—minimum temperature 50 degrees. The lower branches may also be layered during winter or early spring, the layers being left undisturbed until the following year, and special varieties are sometimes grafted in a heated greenhouse, in March, on stocks of their respective types.

Chief Kinds. Arbutus Unedo, the Strawberry Tree, grows wild in southern Europe and in Ireland, reaching 30 ft. or so in height. It grows well in California and parts of the South, and is often seen as a shapely bush to 15 ft. high. The clusters of small white or pinkish flowers are followed by round, warty fruits, which ripen to an orange-scarlet color a year later; they are very decorative, seen against the dark green foliage.

This Arbutus grows best in moist, peaty or loamy soils that are free from lime. The fruits are edible, though not flavorful except to birds. A. Menziesii, the Madroña, sometimes known as the Oregon Laurel, is a tall tree up to 100 ft.; it grows wild from British Columbia to California. It has showy panicles of creamy white flowers and orange-red fruits. The bark sheds annually to expose patches of terra-cotta coloring. The wood of Arbutus is sometimes used to make tobacco pipes and in cabinetwork. Among lesser-known species of Arbutus are A. Andrachne, a small tree from the Levant, which also sheds its bark; A. hybrida (andrachnoides), a vigorous natural hybrid of European origin; and A. canariensis, from the Canary Islands.

ARBUTUS, TRAILING. See Epigaea repens.

ARCH. Climbing shrubs and plants are desirable for the embellishment of every garden, and many of them are seen to advantage when trained over an arch. Arches are especially valuable in small flat gardens, for they give variety to the view and provide supports for those raised masses of bloom which do so much to relieve monotony.

Plans for two arches are given, one in rustic and one in squared wood. These can easily be made by anyone with the aid of saw and hammer; no elaborate tools are needed, for the joints are of the simplest nature.

Suitable Wood for Arches. Cypress, Redwood, and Oak are suitable, long-lasting woods. Although these may cost more than cheaper woods, the extra expenditure is economical in the end. For rustic work, generally speaking, the woods named, and Red Cedar, Locust, and other long-lasting woods are best; but even these are liable to decay at the ground level in a few years, and should be well tarred or creosoted from the bottom to 6 in. above the soil before being put in position. They will last indefinitely if set in concrete. When a post is set in the soil, not in concrete, it is a good plan to nail a piece of board firmly on the bottom; this keeps it upright. Thin posts should not be used, as they tend to warp and twist, and look flimsy and amateurish.

How to Make a Garden Arch. All dimensions are shown on the working drawings, which are more or less self-explanatory, so that a brief description of the method of assembly will suffice.

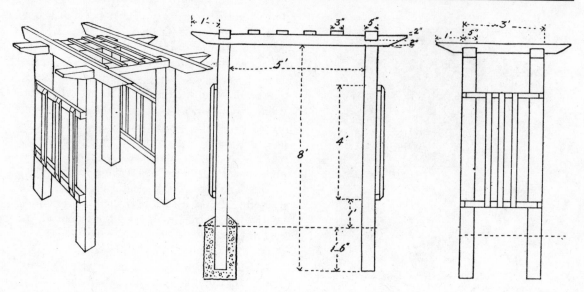

A garden arch of squared lumber, which could be constructed by any handyman. Working plans, showing front and side eleva- tions, with dimensions, are given at the right, and details of the method of construction are outlined in the text.

The four posts are first set firmly in the soil to a depth of 18 in., either in the earth or in concrete, as shown on the left-hand post in the front eleva- tion. The crossbars are then firmly nailed on the tops of the posts, which are 5 in. square, as are the long crossbars.

The side crossbars, 5 in. by 4 in., are next added, being sunk into the front bars to a depth of 2 in. and nailed down firmly. Both sets of bars project 1 ft. over the edge. The slats over the top are 3 in. by 2 in. and do not project. The upright bars on the sides are 2 in. by 1 in., and are nailed to cross pieces of the same size, the ends of all being cut off at a slant.

A Trellis Arch. A latticework arch forms an attractive feature in the garden when draped with suitable climbing plants. If made in the fol- lowing manner it can be constructed and erected in a few hours.

For the uprights, four strips of wood, 10 ft. by 2 in. by 2 in., are required and also two strips 4 ft. long of the same material for the sides of the top portion. In addition, 8 ft. of 2 in. by 2 in. will be required for the crosspieces.

Cut the side pieces about 2 in. less than the width of the latticework and slot them into the uprights. One piece is fixed 2 ft. from the bases of uprights, one halfway between this and the top, and the other across the top.

Cut the trellis to reach from the top to the low- est side support or crosspiece. This will leave two legs, 2 ft. long, which will be inserted in the soil. Nail the trellis on the framework, then construct the other side in the same manner. The top is made by nailing trellis to the two 4 ft. long strips, and this is then nailed on to the sides.

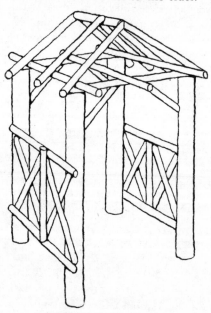

A rustic garden arch of very simple construction. The bark should be removed from the timber and the ends of the posts charred or treated with a wood preservative before they are sunk in the ground.

In June, this arch covered with climbing Roses is a blaze of colorful bloom.

While the arch is being carried to the site and erected, keep the lower ends in position by nailing two strips of wood across them. Fix them firmly but not too securely, as they will be removed after erection. Bore four holes in the ground in the required positions with an iron bar. Drop the legs into them and ram the soil firmly. The legs must be well coated with tar or a wood preservative to prevent rotting.

It is really well worth while making a permanent foundation for the bases of the legs, especially when they are set in heavy, clayey soil. They may be embedded in concrete or placed in drainpipes, the space between the wood and the pipe being filled with cement. They will then last indefinitely.

ARCHANGELICA. Another name for the herb Angelica, which see.

ARCHONTOPHOENIX—*King Palm* (Archontophoe'nix). Australian palms grown in southern Florida and in southern California out of doors, and elsewhere as pot or tub specimens indoors. They have single, smooth trunks and handsome crowns of gracefully curving, featherlike leaves. The name is derived from *archonte,* majestic, and *Phoenix,* a genus of palms. They belong to the family Palmaceae. Kinds grown are A. Alexandrae, its variety Beatriciae, and A. Cunninghamiana.

Outdoor Culture. Archontophoenix thrive in any ordinary soil but in hot, dry situations the leaves tend to be sunburned. A. Cunninghamiana withstands more cold than A. Alexandrae.

Indoor Culture. They grow best in a temperature of 60-70 degrees, with shade from bright sun and a fairly moist atmosphere. The receptacles in which they are planted should be well drained. A rich, porous, loamy soil suits them, and this should be packed firmly about the roots at potting time with a potting stick. Repotting should be done in spring, not every year but only when the plants are in obvious need of this attention, for, like most palms, these thrive best when their roots are rather crowded. Water freely from spring through fall, less liberally in winter. Feed well-rooted specimens with dilute liquid fertilizer weekly. Sponge the leaves occasionally to free them from dust and insects.

Propagation and Kinds. Seeds afford a ready means of propagation; they should be sown in a peaty, sandy soil in a temperature of 70-75 degrees at any time. Fresh seeds are much superior to seeds that have been stored for any length of time. When the seedlings have two strong young leaves, they should be potted individually in small pots in very sandy soil and kept in a close, moist atmosphere until their roots have made their way into the new soil.

ARCTOSTAPHYLOS—*Bearberry, Manzanita* (Arctostaph'ylos). Evergreen shrubs belonging to the Heath family, Ericaceae, which vary considerably in height, and bear clusters of pink or white flowers in spring and early summer. They grow wild in northern Europe and North America. The botanical name is derived from *arktos,* bear, and *staphyle,* a bunch of grapes.

These shrubs thrive best in peaty soil or in rather light loamy land which is free from lime. They should be planted in early fall or in spring. The trailing kinds, such as Arctostaphylos Uva-ursi, the Bearberry or Kinnikinnick, are useful for covering banks or for planting in the rock garden; the larger-growing kinds are useful shrubs for landscape work in California and in similar mild climates. They are good bee plants. No regular pruning is needed, but the trailing kinds may be cut back in spring when they have overgrown their positions. A. Uva-ursi is difficult to transplant from the wild; it is best to set out young nursery-propagated plants that are well established in small pots.

Taking Cuttings and Sowing Seeds. Trailing kinds are increased by cuttings placed in sandy peat in a frame in summer or in a greenhouse in October. They, and others too, can also be raised from seeds sown in spring or fall in well-drained pots filled with sandy peat. They must be grown in pots until large enough to plant out of doors and, when established, should not be disturbed.

The Chief Kinds. Arctostaphylos Manzanita is a Californian bush, 8 ft. high, with thick, leathery leaves and pink or white flowers in terminal clusters from February to April. A. tomentosa, native to California, has hairy shoots and leaves, and spring flowers which may be white or pink. A. Uva-ursi is a trailing plant bearing pink flowers in spring which are followed by red berries. Its attractive green foliage assumes handsome tones of bronze in the fall. It is a native of eastern North America.

ARCTOTIS (Arcto'tis). Annuals and tender perennials, 1 to 2½ ft. high, generally with woolly leaves, from which the single-stemmed flowers—white, orange, or rose—open during summer. All are natives of South Africa and belong to the Daisy family, Compositae. Arctotis is derived from *arktos,* a bear, and *otos,* an ear, alluding to the hairy scales of the flower head.

When to Sow Seeds. The annual kinds are most popular. They are raised from seeds sown in a greenhouse in spring, temperature 50-55 degrees, in fine, sandy, loamy soil. When the seedlings are an inch or so high, they are set 3 in. apart in flats filled with a porous soil. They are watered well and are then grown in a cold frame until danger from frost is passed and are then planted out of doors 12 in. apart. Flowering will commence in June and, in favorable climates, continue until September where nights are fairly cool, provided faded blooms are removed. The plants fail with the coming of really hot summer nights.

These plants are also useful for the decoration of the greenhouse during the late winter and spring months. The seeds are sown in September and the young plants are potted singly in 3-in. pots and later are repotted in 5-in. pots and kept under glass. Care must be taken not to overwater. They need full sunshine and a night temperature of 45-50 degrees.

A favorite kind is Arctotis stoechadifolia

Arctotis stoechadifolia grandis, a beautiful white-flowered half-hardy annual from South Africa.

grandis, with large, pearly white, marguerite-like flowers on stems 2 ft. high. The short-stalked A. breviscapa, 12 in. high, bears orange-yellow flowers, each with a black center, during late summer.

ARDISIA (Ardis'ia). A large genus of tender evergreen shrubs and trees of the Myrsine family, Myrsinaceae. The word Ardisia is derived from *ardis,* a point, and refers to the pointed corolla lobes.

Ardisia crispa (A. crenata, A. crenulata), has scarlet fruits, is suitable for cultivation in a greenhouse having a minimum temperature of 50 degrees, as a house plant, and outdoors in the far South. It has small, glossy, evergreen leaves and in time will form a bush about 4 ft. high. Small plants in pots are useful and are very attractive when laden with scarlet fruits in autumn. The

Arctotis breviscapa bears orange-yellow, black-centered flowers in late summer.

small white flowers, which open in spring, last a long time; the berries remain in good condition for several months, so that it is a common sight to have flowers and green and ripe berries on the plants at the same time.

have flowers and green and ripe berries on the plants at the same time. These shrubs belong to the family Myrsinaceae. The word Ardisia as from *ardis,* a point, and refers to the pointed corolla lobes.

Ardisias bear clusters of small flowers which are followed by long-lasting berries. This is A. humilis.

Potting and Pruning. Repotting should be done in February and March, a little of the old soil being removed and the plants set in slightly larger pots. Peat, loam and leaf mold in equal parts form the best compost. The soil is kept moderately moist in winter and is watered freely from spring through fall. Established specimens benefit from weekly applications of dilute liquid fertilizer. Very little pruning is required as it is best to grow pot specimens with one central stem. When growing them outdoors, prune to shape.

Cuttings Produce the Best Plants. Small side shoots are removed with a heel or piece of the old branch in spring and are planted in sand, sand and peat moss, or vermiculite in a propagating case or under a bell jar in a warm greenhouse. Air layering is a sure way of obtaining good specimens quickly. Seeds may also be sown in summer or in spring in a similar compost. It takes 18 months from seeds to fruiting plants.

A. paniculata, the Marlberry, a native of southern Florida and the West Indies, is sometimes planted in the south. It is a shrub or small tree with small white flowers and glossy black berries. A. humilis also has black berries.

ARECA (Are'ca). Feather-leaved Palms, native to Madagascar and other tropical regions. They belong to the family Palmaceae. Areca is derived from the local name, *Areec.* Areca Cathecu yields the well-known Betel Nut of commerce so much in demand in Eastern countries for chewing. The plant previously grown as Areca lutescens is now called Chrysalidocarpus, which see.

Indoors, Arecas form attractive pot plants when young. They need a minimum temperature of 60 degrees and the same general cultivation as Howea, which see. They are suitable for outdoor culture in southern Florida and other subtropical and tropical regions.

The kinds most commonly cultivated are A. Cathecu, the Betel Palm, probably a native of Malaya, a slender kind with a trunk up to 100 ft. tall; A. glandiformis, also tall and slender, a native of the Moluccas; and A. triandra, from India and Malaya, which has several 5- to 10-ft.-tall stems and is very attractive. A. Cathecu is often misspelled A. Catechu.

ARECASTRUM—*Queen Palm* (Arecas'trum). One variable kind of feather-leaved palm, family Palmaceae, that is a native of Brazil and is commonly planted outdoors in southern Florida and southern California and in less favorable climates is cultivated indoors in pots and tubs. Its name is derived from *Areca,* a genus of palms and *as-*

An Arecastrum Palm in the Huntington Botanical Garden, San Marino, California.

trum, like, and refers to the similarity in appearance of Areca and Arecastrum.

Culture. Arecastrums thrive best in a deep, fertile loam but will grow in a variety of soils. Situations not subject to high winds should be chosen for them; otherwise their leafstalks kink or bend and detract from the beauty of the head of leaves. They are handsome when used as street trees but are not particularly long-lived. William Hertrich, Curator Emeritus of the Huntington Botanical Garden at San Marino, California, observes that in that locality they deteriorate in appearance after they are about forty years of age. When grown indoors, these palms require the same treatment as Archontophoenix, which see.

Kinds. A. Romanzoffianum, 30-50 ft., is often grown under the name Cocos plumosa; its variety australe, as known in cultivation, is a smaller but not less graceful grower; its variety botryophorum is a more robust kind that under favorable conditions develops into a magnificent specimen.

AREGELIA (Arege'lia). Tropical plants, belonging to the Pineapple family, Bromeliaceae, that are natives of South America. They are epiphytes and have prickly margined leaves arranged in basal rosettes, and dense clusters of white, violet or blue flowers. The name commemorates the 19th-century botanist E. A. von Regel. These plants are also named Neoregelia.

Culture. Pot in well-drained pots in osmunda fiber or in a mixture of osmunda fiber and half-decayed leaves with charcoal added. Pot firmly, in spring. Water freely from spring through fall, moderately in winter. Grow in sunny position (with light shade from strongest sun) in temperature 60-70 degrees. Apply dilute liquid fertilizers to well-rooted specimens.

Propagation. Remove suckers or side shoots and pot them separately in March. Seeds sown in sandy peat in spring germinate readily.

The chief kinds are A. marmorata, pale violet flowers; and A. spectabilis, white and pale blue.

ARENARIA—*Sandwort* (Arenar'ia). Hardy low-growing or creeping rock garden plants which belong to the Pink family, Caryophyllaceae, and bloom during spring and summer. They grow wild in various parts of Europe and North America. The word Arenaria denotes sand-loving and is derived from *arena,* sand.

Planting and Taking Cuttings. The Arenarias should be planted in early fall or spring; most of them thrive in well-drained soil of loam, leaf mold and sand in a sunny place in the rock garden. They are propagated by lifting, separating and replanting in September; by inserting cuttings in sandy soil in July in a frame kept close, and by sowing seeds in similar soil in a frame in March–April.

Arenaria montana, a beautiful white-flowered trailing plant for rock garden or rock wall.

The commonest kind is Arenaria montana from Spain; it forms a dense mass of creeping stems and bears rather large white flowers in May and June. It likes a sunny place in sandy, loamy soil. A. balearica, which is found wild in the Balearic Islands, is a charming little plant which will cover the shady side of a rock with a delicate tracery of tiny green leaves, and bears minute white flowers in May; it should be planted in a compost of loam, leaf mold and sand in

Arenaria verna caespitosa is a mosslike plant that bears white star-shaped flowers for a short period in spring. It is ideal for planting in crevices between paving stones in sunny locations.

shade at the foot of a rock or stone. It is not quite hardy in the vicinity of New York City.

Other notable sorts are A. purpurascens, a Pyrenean plant with rose-purple flowers; A. laricifolia, from the Swiss mountains, with small white flowers; A. grandiflora, from the Tyrol, which bears large white flowers; and A. tetraquetra, from the Pyrenees, which has small white blooms. All these flower in May. Arenaria verna caespitosa furnishes a compact leafy carpet of mosslike greenery, studded with small white flowers in May; the variety aurea has yellow leaves.

ARENGA (Aren'ga). Feather palms belonging to the Palm family, Palmaceae. They are natives of tropical Asia and Malaya. The name is derived from the Malayan name *Areng*. In Arenga the sexes are on different plants and in some cases the trees die after fruiting. Arengas are planted outdoors only in the warmest parts of the United States. They are propagated by seeds. Their culture is the same as that for Archontophoenix, which see.

The kinds most likely to be cultivated are A. Engleri, a low-growing kind that does not usually exceed 10 ft.; and A. pinnata, the Sugar Palm, a magnificent species that grows to a height of 40 ft., and bears an immense head of leaves, the largest of which may exceed 20 ft. in length. The Sugar Palm dies when it has ripened its fruit. It is cultivated in India for the sugar made from the sap, Palm sugar, and for Palm wine. A variety of sago is made from the pith.

AREOLE. As applied to Cacti this term refers to the small specialized areas on the stems from which tufts of spines or hairs arise.

ARETHUSA BULBOSA (Arethu'sa). An attractive terrestrial Orchid of eastern North America sometimes cultivated in gardens. It likes a sheltered position and a cool, moist, acid soil. It bears large, bright rose-purple, fragrant flowers, usually singly on 10-in. stems, in May. Arethusa belongs to the family Orchidaceae and is named after Diana's nymph, who was changed into a fountain.

ARGEMONE—*Prickly Poppy* (Argemo'ne). Tender plants from North and South America, which grow about 2 ft. high, have bristly leaves and bear poppy-like flowers in summer. They belong to the Poppy family, Papaveraceae. The origin of the name is due to the supposed medicinal value of the plant, from *argema,* cataract of the eye.

Sowing the Seeds. They may be treated as hardy annuals. Sow the seed in early spring where the plants are to flower, and thin the seedlings to

The white-flowered Prickly Poppy, Argemone grandiflora.

about 9 in. apart. They like full exposure to sun, and light, well-drained soil. For early summer flowering, seed may be sown early in small pots, a few in each; the seedlings are singled to the strongest and grown in a greenhouse or frame for planting out in May.

The chief kinds are: Argemone grandiflora, 2½ ft., with grayish, white-veined leaves and white flowers; A. mexicana, 2 ft., with light yellow flowers, and A. platyceras, 3 ft., flowers white or rose-purple.

ARGENTEUS. A term meaning silvery, usually in reference to the leaves and shoots, as in Achillea argentea, the Silvery Yarrow.

ARGUTUS. Distinctly notched or toothed, as for instance the leaves of Spiraea arguta.

ARGYREIA (Argyre'ia). Tropical Asiatic vines related to the Morning Glories and belonging to the same family, the Convolvulaceae. They are suitable for outdoor cultivation in southern California and in the warmer parts of Florida. The name is derived from *argyreios,* silvery, and refers to the appearance of the foliage.

Argyreias are propagated by division in spring, by cuttings inserted in a greenhouse, and by seeds. They grow readily in any ordinary garden soil and need a sunny position.

The commonest kind is A. splendens, silvery Morning Glory, a tall climber with rose-colored flowers. A. speciosa is a handsome vine with silvery undersides to its leaves.

ARGYRODERMA (Argyroderm'a). Succulents from South Africa which, together with Lithops and other related kinds, are called Stone Plants because they so closely resemble pebbles. They are excellent examples of plant mimicry. At one time they were called Mesembryanthemums; they belong in the family Aizoaceae. The name is derived from *argyros,* silver, and *derma,* skin, and refers to the color of the leaves.

Culture. These plants grow best in extremely gritty soil that is perfectly drained. They may be potted in pans and grown in a cool greenhouse or window where they receive full sun, except in the hottest summer months, when a little light shade is beneficial. Watering must always be done with caution; from May to September they should be kept almost or quite dry, but not allowed to shrivel seriously; at other times they should be kept moist but on the dryish side. Repotting is needed only at intervals of three or four years; it should be done in September.

The plants may be propagated by seeds sown in early fall and by division at that same season. The most commonly cultivated kinds are A. octophyllum (A. Lesliei), flowers yellow; and A. testiculare, flowers white. Both are about 1 in. tall.

ARIDARIA (Arida'ria). South African succulents allied to Mesembryanthemum and requiring the same culture. (See Mesembryanthemum.) Kinds cultivated are: A. pentagona, flowers orange to golden-brown; A. radicans, flowers white to pale yellow; A. splendens, flowers white.

ARIKURYROBA—*Arikury Palm* (Arikuryro'-ba.) One Brazilian Palm allied to Cocos. It grows 2-8 ft. tall, is feather-leaved and belongs to the Palm family, Palmaceae. Its name is a variant of its native name. A. schizophylla requires the same culture as Arecastrum, which see.

ARIOCARPUS (Ariocar'pus). Spineless or nearly spineless cacti from Mexico. The name is from Aria, the White Beam Tree, and *carpos,* fruit, and refers to the aria-like fruit. For culture see Cacti.

Kinds cultivated are: A. retusus, Seven Stars, flowers white to pink; A. scapharostrus, flowers purple-red; A. trigonus, flowers pale yellow.

ARISAEMA (Arisae'ma). Tuberous-rooted plants which resemble the Arum Lily and belong to the family Araceae; they are chiefly natives of the Far East and of North America. The word Arisaema indicates the resemblance of this plant to the Arum—*aris,* Arum, and *haima,* blood, some of the species having leaves with red blotches.

The Jack-in-the-Pulpit, Arisaema triphyllum, a native of eastern North America, is an interesting spring-flowering plant for woodland gardens.

The tender kinds are grown in a greenhouse in which a minimum winter temperature of 50 degrees is maintained, or out of doors in the South. They thrive in a compost of equal parts of loam and leaf mold, with the addition of coarse sand. The tubers should be potted in early spring; the best time to repot old plants is just when fresh growth begins in spring. During the summer, water is required in abundance; but from October until March, when the plants have died down, the tuberous roots must be kept quite dry.

Propagation is effected by separating and potting the tuberous roots in spring as soon as fresh growth is seen, and by sowing seeds, as soon as ripe, in woodsy soil. Tender kinds include Arisaema speciosum, 18 in., which bears white flower spathes in March; and A. concinnum, 12 in., with white flower spathes in June.

Hardy North American kinds, which will thrive in semishady, moist situations in rich, woodsy soil, are Arisaema triphyllum, Indian Turnip or Jack-in-the-Pulpit, 1-3 ft. tall, with purple-green spathes; and A. Dracontium, the Dragon Root, to 4 ft., with handsome leaves and greenish spathes. Both are useful for the woodland garden. They may be propagated by seeds and division. Both have attractive red or orange-red fruits.

ARISARUM (Arisar'um). Curious, rather than beautiful, tuberous-rooted dwarf herbs from the Mediterranean region, belonging to the Arum family, Araceae. The name is that given by Dioscorides.

These curious flowers are of Arisarum pro-boscideum, an interesting little plant for the woodland garden.

The most interesting kind is Arisarum proboscideum, 6 in., which may be grown in open woodland, or in a shady place in the rock garden, in humus-rich soil, and is easily increased by division in early spring. Its spathes, produced among the leaves in spring, are whitish and olive-green, narrowing into tapering tails 4 or 5 in. long. It is hardy at least as far north as the vicinity of New York City.

ARISTEA (Aris'tea). Evergreen perennials from South Africa that have firm-textured grass-like leaves and flowers, usually blue, in early summer. The name is from *arista*, a point or beard, and refers to the stiff tips of the leaves. These plants belong to the Iris family, Iridaceae.

Culture. Aristeas are suitable for cultivating in the outdoor garden in California and in similar mild, dryish climates; they thrive without special care in any fairly good, well-drained soil.

Where winters are colder they may be grown in pots in a sunny, cool (winter temperature at night 45-50 degrees) greenhouse or sunroom. They are easily propagated by seeds sown in sandy soil in early fall or spring or by division in spring. Pot plants need moderate supplies of water at all times and benefit from weekly applications of dilute liquid fertilizer, from spring through fall.

Chief Kinds. A. capitata, 4 ft.; A. compressa, 18 in., flowers green, white, and brown; A. Ecklonii, 18 in.

ARISTOLOCHIA—*Dutchman's-Pipe* (Aristoloch'ia). Hardy and greenhouse climbing plants and a few erect herbaceous kinds, which bear flowers of extraordinary shape, while those of some kinds emit a most unpleasant odor which serves the purpose of attracting the insects required to ensure pollination and fertilization.

The Dutchman's-Pipe, Aristolochia durior, is grown for the decorative effect of its large leaves.

The favorite hardy kinds grow wild in California and the southern United States; those suitable only for a greenhouse are from Brazil, Guatemala, West Africa and other tropical countries. They belong to the family Aristolochiaceae. The botanical word indicates the medicinal virtues which the plant was thought to possess; from *aristos,* best, and *locheia,* birth.

Planting and Propagating. The climbing hardy Aristolochias are rampant plants with large, heart-shaped leaves and rather small, pipe-shaped flowers. They flourish in ordinary soil, and may be planted in early fall or spring. Cuttings will form roots if set in sandy soil in a cold frame in August. In March the branches may be cut back if the plant is covering too large an area.

Aristolochia argyroneura is a tropical species with green leaves veined with white.

The favorite hardy kind is the Dutchman's-Pipe, Aristolochia durior (A. Sipho), which may be set at the base of a pergola or arch, or near a large tree so that its shoots can climb among the branches for support; it bears small brownish-yellow flowers in June and grows to a height of 30 ft. Another hardy kind is A. tomentosa, yellow and purple flowers in July. Aristolochia Clematitis is a hardy herbaceous plant, 2 ft. high, suitable for planting in a shady border; it bears small yellow flowers in summer. A. Serpentaria, the Virginia Snakeroot, erect, 3 ft., a native of the eastern United States, is sometimes planted in wild gardens.

The greenhouse kinds thrive best when planted in a bed of prepared soil or in tubs in a greenhouse having a minimum winter temperature of 55 to 60 degrees. Good drainage must be provided. The best compost consists of one part turfy loam, one part leaf mold and one part well-decayed manure, to which sand must be added.

Planting or potting can be done in February or March. Wires must be fixed to the roof as supports for the twining stems. The plants need an abundance of water during the summer, when growth is vigorous, but little from October to March, when the plants are resting, though the soil must be moistened occasionally.

Pruning, which is done in March, consists of thinning out superfluous shoots to prevent overcrowding, and cutting off straggling ones.

A Remarkable Plant. The most remarkable kind is Aristolochia grandiflora Sturtevantii, the Pelican Flower. The purplish-white flowers are 18 in. in diameter, and have a tail 3 ft. in length. A. elegans, Calico Flower, bears purple and yellow flowers 3 in. wide. Its blooms are scentless. It is a good vine for planting outdoors in frostproof or nearly frostproof regions. A. californica, with greenish-purple flowers, needs similar conditions. A. argyroneura is an attractive tropical foliage plant with green leaves veined with white.

ARISTOTELIA (Aristote'lia). Evergreen trees and shrubs mostly native of Australasia and South America, and sometimes planted in gardens in southern California. The name commemorates Aristotle, the Greek philosopher. They belong in the botanical family Elaeocarpaceae. They are propagated by cuttings of ripe wood inserted in a propagating bed in a close atmosphere. Kinds grown are: A. fruticosa, 8 ft., New Zealand; A. Macqui, 7 ft., flowers greenish, Chili; A. racemosa (New Zealand Wineberry), 25 ft., flowers pink. The berries of these plants are edible.

ARIZONA, GARDENING IN. See Regional Gardening.

ARKANSAS, GARDENING IN. See Regional Gardening.

ARMATUS. A botanical term meaning armed, usually with thorns or spines; for example, the spiny-leaved Osmanthus armatus.

ARMERIA—*Thrift, Sea Pink* (Armer'ia). Hardy evergreen plants of low, tufted growth, some of which are commonly used for edging flower beds and borders; others are charming rock garden plants. They are natives chiefly of Spain, Portugal and southern France; the common Thrift, Armeria maritima, grows wild in maritime districts in Europe, Greenland and Iceland. Armeria belongs to the family Plumbaginaceae. The word is derived from the Latin name for one of the wild Pinks.

Planting and Suitable Soil. The Thrifts are happiest in well-drained, rather light or sandy soil where they soon spread into large tufts and bear a profusion of small, rounded heads of bloom in summer. Heavy soil can be made suitable by adding sand, grit and leaf mold. They should be planted in early fall or spring in a

Armeria maritima Laucheana has bright pink flowers and blooms freely in May. It is an excellent plant for sunny locations in rock gardens and flower borders.

sunny place. The common Thrift and its varieties make an admirable evergreen edging.

Propagation. If an increased stock of plants is wanted, the old clumps should be taken up in September and separated into rooted pieces for replanting. Thrift can be raised from seeds sown in sandy soil in a cold frame in September or March, but the seedlings are slow growing. When large enough to be transplanted, they should be set in a nursery border in well-drained, light soil.

The Best Kinds. There are several varieties of the common Thrift, Armeria maritima, which have flowers of richer coloring than the typical plant and they are grown in gardens in preference to the latter. Two of the best are Laucheana, rose, and Vindictive, crimson; the variety alba has white flowers. All these are of low growth and are suitable for edging plants.

Several Thrifts are taller, more vigorous plants with flower stems 12-24 in. high. Among them are A. pseudoarmeria, 12 in., rose-lilac, and its variety splendens, 12 in., bright rose. The kind known in gardens as A. gigantea grows 2 ft. high and bears rose-colored blooms, and the one called Ruby, the best of all the tall Thrifts, has deep rose-pink flowers on stems 2 ft. high.

For the Rock Garden. The most beautiful rock garden Thrift is Armeria juniperifolia (A. caespitosa), a compact plant, 1-2 in. high, white or rose-colored flowers; it must be planted in a sunny place, in well-drained, very gritty or stony soil, or in the moraine. A. juncea, 3-8 in., with lilac-rose flowers, needs similar conditions.

ARMORACIA (Armora'cia). The botanical name of the genus of plants to which the horse-radish, A. rusticana, belongs. See Horse-radish.

ARMYWORM. See Pests and Diseases.

ARNEBIA ECHIOIDES—*Prophet Flower* (Arne'bia). A hardy herbaceous perennial plant from Russia, 12-18 in. high, which bears primrose-yellow flowers in May; five purple spots appear on each blossom after it has opened, and subsequently disappear. This curious characteristic has given rise to the popular name of Prophet Flower, for, according to legend, the flowers represent the fingermarks of Mahomet. This plant belongs to the Borage family, Boraginaceae. Arnebia is from the plant's Arabic name.

The white-flowered Armeria maritima alba is a fine plant for a sunny location and well-drained soil.

Planting and Taking Root Cuttings. It should be planted in early fall or in spring in well-drained, loamy soil, in the rock garden or in a sunny, dry wall. The best method of propagation is by root cuttings in September; pieces of the root, 2 or 3 in. long, are placed in sandy soil, the part which was nearest the stem being uppermost, and the tips covered with half an inch or so of soil. If placed in a cold frame for the winter, the soil being kept moderately moist, they will form roots and may be planted out of doors in spring. Another name for this plant is Macrotomia echioides.

A. cornuta, the Arabian Primrose, is an annual species that may be raised from seeds sown outdoors in spring. It grows 2 ft. tall and has yellow flowers with black spots that change to maroon and finally disappear.

ARNICA (Arn'ica). Hardy perennial herbs, native of northern temperate regions extending into the Arctic region, belonging to the Daisy family, Compositae. The name is from *arnakis*, lambskin, in reference to the leaves. The chief kind, Arnica montana, from the mountains of central and southern Europe, is a good plant for the large rock garden, in peaty loam soil. Up to 2 ft. tall, with heads of yellow flowers in July, it is increased by division in spring. The medicinal product known as Arnica is obtained from this plant. A tincture produced from its roots is used for the external treatment of sprains, bruises and chilblains. Several native Arnicas are sometimes brought into cultivation in wild gardens and rock gardens. They all respond to the culture that suits A. montana.

AROID. All plants that belong in the botanical family Araceae, the Arum family, are aroids. Most are tropical or subtropical, although some, such as the Jack-in-the-Pulpit and the Skunk Cabbage, are natives of the temperate regions. Well-known Aroids include: Anthurium, Arum, Caladium, Calla, Dieffenbachia, Monstera, Hydrosme, Philodendron, and Zantedeschia.

AROMATIC PLANTS. Many plants are renowned for the aromatic properties of their leaves or wood. The aromatic character is almost always due to an essential oil contained in the particular part of the plant in question. Man has taken advantage of these peculiarities, for he sometimes forms special gardens of aromatic herbs, but more frequently turns the oily secretions to profitable account, for by means of steam distillation, solvents, or absorption, he extracts the essential oils and uses them for perfumery. Some aromatic woods are distasteful to insects; therefore they are used for the insides of cabinets and for drawers in which clothing and household linen are stored, as a protection against moths. Cedarwood and Camphorwood are examples.

This aromatic character is sometimes found in the fruits of plants, such as pepper, which also has been brought into daily use by man. The nutmeg is another instance, while in ginger we have

a case of the aromatic property being developed in the underground stem. A rather similar instance is in that of Iris florentina and I. germanica; the rhizomes or rootstocks possess a violet-like odor which forms a base for many of the so-called violet perfumes. The clove is an example of an aromatic substance contained in the flower buds.

In coffee the aromatic character of the seeds is only brought out after the seeds have been roasted.

Resins produced by some plants have aromatic properties, notably those produced by shrubs in the Myrrh family, Burseraceae, Myrrh and Frankincense being instances.

Plants with Fragrant Leaves. Most conspicuous among hardy aromatic plants are those belonging to the Mint family, Labiatae, for in it are the Thymes, Sages, Mints, Nepetas, Lavender, Rosemary, Marjoram, Horehound, and many others. In the Daisy family, Compositae, are other aromatic plants, notably the Wormwood or Artemisia. A well-known and popular aromatic-leaved shrub is the Scented Verbena, Lippia citriodora, while the aromatic flowers of the Sweet Shrub, Calycanthus, are favorites. Among well-known aromatic woods are various kinds of Cedar and Juniper.

ARONIA—*Chokeberry* (Aro'nia). A small genus of hardy, leaf-losing shrubs, belonging to the family Rosaceae. The name is derived from Aria, a subgenus of Sorbus. They are natives of North America, attractive in flower and autumn foliage, and thrive in any average soil. They are propagated by seed, suckers, division, and cuttings of ripened shoots in autumn.

Aronia arbutifolia, the Red Chokeberry, is a bush 6 to 9 ft. high, with clusters of white or pinkish flowers in April–May, followed by red fruits. A. prunifolia (atropurpurea), the Purple Chokeberry, grows up to 12 ft. high and has glossy purple-black fruits, and A. melanocarpa, 4 ft., has black fruits.

ARPÓPHYLLUM (Arpophyl'lum). Summer-flowering orchids, from Colombia and other parts of Central America, which must be grown in a greenhouse with a minimum winter temperature of 55 degrees. They belong to the family Orchidaceae. The botanical name means a scimitar-like leaf, from *arpe,* a scimitar, and *phyllon,* a leaf. The inflorescence, produced from the junction of the pseudobulbs and leaf, consists of many small but brightly colored flowers in cylindrical spikes.

Summer and Winter Management. In winter these orchids should be watered sparingly. In summer, water may be given freely particularly when, in sunny weather, the temperature reaches tropical heat. Light shading only is necessary. Repotting is done in early spring, just as growth commences; the pots must be well drained. As a potting medium either osmunda fiber cut or pulled into small pieces or Fir bark may be used.

The chief kinds are: A. cardinale, bright rose-red flowers; A. giganteum, the largest, with rose-purple flowers; and A. spicatum, which resembles A. cardinale, but has paler flowers.

ARRANGEMENT OF PLANTS. A garden may contain a first-rate collection of trees, shrubs and plants and yet be lacking in charm if the arrangement is faulty. The commonest mistake is to set solitary plants of the same kind at in-tervals instead of grouping them. This fault is particularly noticeable in the herbaceous or hardy flower border, which offers splendid opportunities for grouping. The effect is especially unpleasant if plants bearing highly colored or white flowers are scattered indiscriminately along the border. Even a small flower border will present a far more attractive appearance if the plants are grouped than if they are set here and there without method. They should be in groups of three, five, seven, or more, according to the size of the border; they will then be seen to the fullest advantage when in bloom.

How to Group Plants. Most of the tall plants must be placed at or towards the back of the border, but here and there a few of them may be brought slightly forward to add variety of contour to the display. In a small flower border it is, of course, impossible to group masses of plants of one kind or variety; that would make it difficult to provide for a succession of bloom throughout the summer and early autumn

Perennial plants grouped attractively at both sides of them lend importance and dignity to these steps.

months, but smaller groups ought certainly to be planted.

The groups should be as dissimilar in shape as possible; some of them may follow the line of the border, others should run from back to front. The more irregular they are in outline the more natural will be the appearance of the border. Planting in a straight line is to be avoided.

A Common Mistake. It is just as important to group trees and shrubs. If they are scattered without method the garden will lack that sense of repose which is so essential for its full enjoyment. A common mistake is to plant trees and shrubs, and to set flower beds, over the greater part of the lawn: as a result the lawn itself is so cut up as to be spoiled and the trees, shrubs and flowering plants are not seen to advantage. A lawn sets off the grace and beauty of trees, shrubs and flower beds perfectly, providing it is an expanse of turf unbroken save near the margin, where the trees, shrubs and plants should be set.

As with the plants, so with the main features of the garden itself; they should be grouped. The lawn should remain a lawn, an unspoiled stretch of green turf, for it is beautiful in itself, restful to the eye, gives a sense of spaciousness and is in vivid contrast to the brightly colored flowers which it sets off to advantage.

Roses should be grouped in a garden or in a border where nothing else is planted. Hardy flowers should be gathered together to form the herbaceous border and rock plants should be set in the rock garden. Only by following this method will the trees, shrubs and plants be displayed perfectly and in such a way that they add to rather than detract from the sense of restfulness which marks the well-planned garden.

ARROWHEAD. See Sagittaria.

ARROWROOT. A starchy food product obtained from the underground stems of a tropical American and West Indian plant, Maranta arundinacea. The fully matured underground stems are dug up, washed to remove soil and the scaly covering, then ground or grated to a pulp and washed to separate the starch. This starch is then very carefully washed and dried. The plant is grown in many tropical countries, for the starch, or arrowroot, is a very important,

easily digested food substance much used for invalids in the form of puddings, blancmanges, etc.

ARROWROOT, EAST INDIAN. See Tacca pinnatifida.

ARROWROOT, SOUTH SEA. See Tacca pinnatifida.

ARROWROOT PLANT. See Maranta.

ARROWWOOD. See Viburnum dentatum.

ARTABOTRYS—*Tail Grape* (Arta'botrys). Tropical, evergreen climbers that are planted in the open in the far South and occasionally in greenhouses elsewhere. They belong to the Custard Apple family, Annonaceae. The name is from *artao,* to support, and *botrys,* grapes.

They thrive in rich soil and are propagated by seeds sown as promptly after they are ripe as possible, and by cuttings of ripe shoots inserted in a close, warm propagating case in spring. Kinds grown are A. odoratissimus, Climbing Ylang-Ylang, flowers greenish or yellowish, fragrant; A. uncinatus, flowers reddish-brown, fragrant.

A well arranged perennial border. The plants are set in attractive groups.